SUBTERRANEAN SAPPERS

SUBTERRANEAN SAPPERS

A HISTORY OF 177 TUNNELLING COMPANY RE
FROM 1915 TO 1919

IAIN M^cHENRY

UNIFORM
PRESS

Uniform Press Ltd
66 Charlotte Street
London W1T 4QE

A catalogue record for this book is available from
the British Library

5 4 3 2 1

ISBN 978-1-910500-10-1

Cover design Vivian@Bookscribe
Typeset by Vivian@Bookscribe

Printed and bound in Great Britain

CONTENTS

ACKNOWLEDGEMENTS

Peter Barton, Jeremy Banning, Simon Jones, Johan Vandewalle and Kristoff Jacobs, all five of them published authors on tunnelling related books and material, for their kind and generous support.

Rebecca Nash, Lori Jones and Amy Adams at the Royal Engineers Library and Museum for their time and patience in looking after me on my research trips.

Hugh Alexander and the staff at The National Archives for their permission to reproduce many of the pictures in this book.

Garry Woollaston, a grandson of a 177 man, whose stalwart support and assistance in the research leading to this book has been unfailing.

Johan Regheere, a sincere Belgian friend, for his excellent local knowledge and passion related to World War One, who became an excellent travel companion in research trips both to the UK and on the ground over and under which 177 Tunnelling Company worked and fought.

Jonathon Porter for his drawing on my listening.

Arthur Stockwin and Parapress publishers for their kind permission allowing me to reproduce both excerpts and complete letters from their Book *30 Odd Feet Below Belgium*.

Philippe Oosterlinck for the kind permission to reproduce photographs in his collection from an album once belonging to Oberjager Helmbrecht, 1st Company, 25th Reserve Jager Battalion who served opposite Railway Wood in July and August 1915.

WO1 Phillip 'Moff' Moffitt and Ellie Moffitt for the countless night's hospitality when visiting the Royal School of Military Engineering at Chatham. Fernand Robaeys, Ypres Tourist Office and the deputy mayor of Ypres, Frans Lignel, for their help and patience in helping and allowing me to gain access to the Ramparts dugout.

Val Hutchings for the information regarding her grandfather's brave action which high-lighted the circumstances behind the deaths of Sappers Cadman, Creegan and Hull.

The late Walther Huyghebaert, the farmer who for many years worked the land under which the Railway Wood sector tunnels now lie silent, for his kind permission in allowing me access to his land on many occasions.

Corinne Dalgas, granddaughter of Captain Agner Emil Dalgas MC, 177 Tunnelling Company for the photographs and infor-mation relating to her late grandfather.

Guy Smith and Jerry Whitehead for their kind permission to reproduce Linesman trench maps.

Members of The Great War Forum for their advice: Ian Riley for his expert knowledge on the 55th Division and Jon Cooksey for his expert knowledge on the 14th Division.

Paul Reed and other fellow guides and historians at Leger holidays whose ever growing joint knowledge of the battlefields is exemplary and whose support has been greatly appreciated.

Jayne Cheslin for the information on her grandfather, Alfred Parton who served in 177.

Richard Pinkett, Ian Newby, the grandchildren of Oscar Earnshaw, Ralph Whitehead, Theresa Murphy, Colin Taylor, Kate Collins, Anthony Byledbal, Janet Willey, Philip Rowe, Niek and Ilse Benoot-Watteyne with baby Louis, Richard Van Emden and Richard Porter whose friendships, help and support for the book have been a firm rock.

John, Roz and Elisabeth Wilkinson, for the information behind the death of their uncle Major Maurice Wilkinson MC RE.

My friend Kate Collins whose friendship and support has been much appreciated.

Helen French, Great Grandaughter of Alice Gordon who was in the forefront of the campaign to erect a permanent memorial to 177 Tunnelling Company, for the information and photographs.

Finally to Donna, Tara and my Mum and Dad without whose support and encouragement this book would still be on the backburner.

PREFACE

Whilst I was serving in the British Army, I was posted to SHAPE (Supreme Headquarters Allied Powers Europe), a large multinational NATO base just outside the Belgian town of Mons. I had more than a passing interest in World War One at the time but my two years at SHAPE would be an almost nonstop continuous study of the battlefields. The famous town of Ypres was a seventy-mile drive away and the battlefields of the Somme just over eighty miles away and both were very accessible to me during my free time and leave periods. In fact, the history began right on my doorstep. Just a few hundred yards away from the Berlin Gate that serves as the main entrance to SHAPE, is the location where, on the 22nd August 1914 at about 7am, Cpl Edward Thomas of the 4th Royal Irish Dragoon Guards fired the first shot in anger for the British Expeditionary Force in World War One.

As my knowledge grew with visits to the battlefields and my perpetual reading on the subject, I became more than aware of a war fought within a war; a war fought deep underground. My interest in this subterranean struggle grew rapidly and I became frustrated with just how little there was remaining to see today apart from the remains of various mine craters that dot the old front line and the very few tunnels open to the public that are now heavily sanitised. I was also disappointed with how few books were available on the subject, although those available at the time were very good indeed.

It was in the autumn of 2007 that I had a chance meeting with author and historian Peter Barton. I had seen Peter's UK Channel 4 documentary on the underground war and I also had a copy of his recent book *Beneath Flanders Fields*. Peter was in the early stages of planning an archaeological project with ABAC (Association of Battlefield Archaeology and Conservation). Together with co-author and tunnelling specialist Johan Vandewalle, and directed by tunnelling author and historian Kristof Jacobs, the project was to focus on the excavation and study of the Vampir dugout, located near Borry Farm alongside the old Ypres to Zonnebeke road. Peter kindly invited me to become a volunteer on the project that would eventually see me spend more than twenty days underground in the dugout. I can only describe the experience of working on the project as a life-changing moment.

Every day in the dugout I discovered something new about these special breed of men who served and fought underground. I was amazed at their engineering masterpiece, at how they had improvised in places and how they had used their knowledge of mining to provide a haven from hell for the soldier on the surface.

No one had been in the dugout for ninety years. It was filled with water which had acted as a great preservative, so when we stepped into it we were seeing it as the tunnellers had almost a century before. At the time of its construction by 171 Tunnelling Company, Royal Engineers, the surface surrounding its location resembled a lunar landscape of water-filled shell holes, so this small dugout, built for just fifty men, would certainly have provided much needed accommodation if it had ever been used. Vampir was discovered to be unfinished, abandoned in the straightening of the British lines due to the early successes that was part of the second phase of the final German offensive of the war in April 1918.

At the end of the project over 400 people had visited the dig site and descended the shaft into the dugout. It was clear to see that all were amazed, with many of the locals, not normally interested in the Great War, surprised that their landscape was dotted with over 400 dugouts of various sizes built during the war to accommodate troops; all now water-filled and silent.

With the project over I wanted to do something for these men, to give something back to the battlefields, and came up with the idea of writing a book on the history of a specific Royal Engineer Tunnelling Company. I was advised that the war diary of 177 Tunnelling Company was full of information and plans and it seemed an obvious candidate to choose. So began a project to write the history of 177 Tunnelling Company and a focus on the many officers and men who served in it.

With many visits to the home of the Royal Engineers at Chatham, The National Archives and smaller centres of study and research, here is the result of that work. It is not intended as a dull historical statement of fact, rather an attempt to put flesh on dates and times by using official documentation and personal memoirs belonging to those who served in its ranks.

Throughout this journey of research and writing about the life of 177 Tunnelling Company I have been lucky to meet many people related to the men who served within its ranks. As with anyone who writes on a band of men for a period of time you get to feel like you have come to know some of the characters in the book even though they are now all long gone.

Even though I was not badged Royal Engineers during my own military service I can say that the fine modern men and women of the Corps of Royal Engineers can be rightly proud of their forefathers many of whom served as tunnellers. The tunnellers' work remained so secret during the war it ranked second only to the espionage war. The fruits of their labours and information regarding their work remained an official secret until 1962.

I have not started this book with a long account of how the war began or the early days of the fighting on the Western Front before the formation of the Brigade Mining Sections and Tunnelling Companies. There are plenty of books available that describe in great detail the early fighting. This book focuses on the history of 177 Tunnelling Company, so I have used the introduction to briefly cover the time period leading up to the formation of the tunnelling companies and, in particular, 177. In the narrative I have used First World War British map references where possible. These references may be confusing to some readers but are put in for those battlefield visitors who may wish to follow in the footsteps of 177 Tunnelling Company. A full description on how to refer and understand a British trench map reference is available on the Website of McMaster University: http://library.mcmaster. ca/maps/ww1/MapRefNo.htm.

I have also used imperial measurements as per the war diary of 177 Tunnelling Company. For reference one yard is equivalent to 0.91 metres and one inch, 2.54 centimetres.

Colour plans for the many underground workings are also included and are important to refer to in order to follow the growing evolution of tunnel and dugout construction.

I alone am responsible for the contents of this book. I am also responsible for any errors and/or omissions. I have made every reasonable effort to trace copyright holders of material reproduced in this book, if any have been inadvertently overlooked I will be glad to hear from them.

Here is the story of the officers and men of 177 Tunnelling Company during the Great War. I do hope you find it of interest.

IAIN MCHENRY

INTRODUCTION

Mine warfare is ancient and has been used by armies for many thousands of years, falling under the tactic of siege warfare. Although used by the British Army in wars past and with research into mine warfare being exercised by the Royal Engineers in the years leading up to the Great War, mine warfare was not a subject given much thought by an army equipped for mobile war. Why would one think of an age old tactic like this? Especially since the war the British are entering will be fast, and hopefully, over by Christmas.

The early stages of the Great War were mobile and moved fast. With the deployment of the British Expeditionary Force in August 1914, the cavalry element, meant for fast mobile warfare, engaged the Germans for the first time just a few miles outside the Belgian city of Mons on 22nd August 1914. The Battle of Mons and the famous retreat that followed, in the face of an overwhelming superior enemy, was also mobile and rapid. The men of the Royal Engineers played a vitally important role in the early days of the fighting, the third VC of the War being won by an RE officer, Captain Theodore Wright RE.

Following the retreat from Mons, the battles of the Marne and the Aisne and the race to the sea, the British Army held the line from the Belgium town of Ypres running south. The BEF had been joined by a Corps of the Indian Army which would be tried and tested over the next few months. In October and November 1914 the BEF fought what became known as the First Battle of Ypres; it was a battle to hold the high ground around Ypres, a series of small ridges. Following this battle both sides lost momentum as they slowed down in the face of the approaching winter. With the BEF licking its wounds, many of its soldiers now seriously doubted the fact that the war would be over by Christmas. The German army, on the offensive since the beginning of the war, also needed to rest and resupply. Although no war-winning offensive would be launched over the winter of 1914, both sides now static, dug into the ground to hold their lines, never letting the other side forget that they were there. It was also during the first battle of Ypres that the Messines Ridge was taken by the Germans. The ridge would play a vital role to the Germans allowing them good observation over Allied lines to the south of the Salient that was formed around Ypres. The retaking of the ridge by the British in June 1917 was vital and it was here that the men of the tunnelling companies would have 'Their finest hour'.

With the lines of the protagonists established opposite each other and the spectre of static warfare raising its head, it made the perfect opportunity to use the age old tactic of mine warfare. The Germans are given the credit of the first use of it. With their tactical doctrine stating that should the front lines fall within a hundred metres of each other, their Pioneer companies would actively seek to use mine warfare, if the geology allowed. It is important to remember that the German army was the occupier and had a siege mentality about it when compared to the Allied opposition.

Holding the line about 30 miles south of Ypres, opposite the two small French villages of Festubert and Givenchy, were the men of the Indian Corps. In between these two villages was a small hamlet, Le Plantin, eastwards of which was the British Line, running north to south and held by the men of the Sirhind Brigade. On 20th December. ten German mines were fired under the trenches held by the Sirhind Brigade. This opening strike preceded a German infantry attack supported by artillery and trench mortar bombardments. The Sirhind Brigade was taken by surprise and in the face of the German attack fell back to their reserve lines some 500 yards to their rear. The ten mines fired by the Germans at the opening of this attack was the first recorded use of mine warfare against the British in WWI. Although the charges were small it is important to realise the moral and physical effect these mines had on the British. As well as facing death and destruction from surface warfare, they now faced it from below. What's more there seemed to be little protection against it.

Prior to the German attack on the 20th December, there had been a number of official moves from the British side on the subject of military mining. General Sir Henry Rawlinson, Commander of IV Corps at the time, suggested to GHQ the formation of a special battalion of sappers and miners to undertake work relevant to mining. This was met by approval and then shelved! The second approach, in the form of a letter to the War office on 15th December 1914 came from a British Cavalry officer, John Norton Griffiths, Member of Parliament,

engineering contractor and keen imperialist, he had recently raised the 2nd King Edward's Horse. In peacetime he was the head of a firm of engineering contractors which had carried out numerous engineering tasks around the Empire, tasks that included tunnelling. Norton Griffiths, or 'Empire Jack' as he was commonly known, was remarkable for his energy and enthusiasm. With a fiery temperament his active spirit had so far been curbed by the boredom of training troops at home. He was very eager to find other ways to unleash his pent-up energies. His letter to the War Office stated that he had access to men with expertise in driving tunnels under London, Manchester and other cities.

These men, he explained, were expert 'clay kickers' or 'workers on the cross' meaning that their expertise lay in the fact that they could work speedily and noiselessly in a very limited space. Norton Griffiths informed the War Office that sapping would be of the utmost importance on the front and requested permission to gather a group of specialists and take them to the front where they could demonstrate their expertise. Norton Griffiths' letter was subsequently received by the War Office and forwarded to GHQ in France for consideration. Norton Griffiths' idea of utilising 'clay kickers' along the British Front was not received with much gusto by GHQ. They argued that military mining and civilian mining differed considerably in that civil mining would not work on the Western Front. One of the main issues raised by GHQ was the discipline of the miner and their belief that he would be unable to work under the pressures of being close to and under the enemy lines, with the ever-present threat of entombment.

11

The German mines of the 20th December seriously forced GHQ to reverse their prior rebuttal of Norton Griffiths' War Office letter. Orders were issued for the British Army to proceed with sapping and mining; with the divisional field companies of the Royal Engineers already overworked, this order cannot have been received with much jubilation. Winter was upon the BEF and the weather changing for the worst, siege warfare had begun and British troops needed a safe, workable infrastructure in order to survive on the Western Front. On the surface, trenches were dug that would stretch from the Belgian coastline to the border with Switzerland. The British sector of those trenches did not initially allow for underground workings. More to the point the Royal Engineers lacked the experience needed to start an underground war. There were miners and men with vast experience in mining already serving in the army. Britain's army was a professional army and upon mobilisation in 1914 the BEF was made up of many soldiers who had finished their contract with the army and had gone on to civilian life. But there was a clause that if you remained fit and healthy enough and if your country needed you, then they could call upon and mobilise you. Britain's regular army just before the war consisted of about 274,000 regular soldiers, small in comparison to their European counterparts. Considering the huge size of the British Empire at this time the army was very much employed as an imperial police force, scattered far and wide across the Empire. Once the BEF was mobilised in August 1914 to move to continental Europe it was made up initially of regulars and the many reserve soldiers who were called up. Many of those men mobilised went to their local regiments, including many men recruited from the mining areas of the UK and who in civilian guise would have been miners themselves.

It was now a race to find those with mining experience and form them into units that could combat the German mining threat. There was one man for this job, John Norton Griffiths!

The army itself was not slack during this period and to help out the field companies of Royal Engineers, special Brigade Mining Sections were formed usually consisting of an officer and about fifty men. These Brigade Mining Sections went to work immediately, in some places assisted by RE field companies, fortress companies, divisional engineers and field squadrons.

Shallow mine shafts were sunk and galleries driven out for listening purposes. Although it looked like the army was responding to the threat, the work was done with too great a haste with not much strategic thought about the siting of the various underground workings. The British Army lacked those at top level with mining, counter-mining experience and the knowledge of building this massive infrastructure. The last time a British Army had actively mined was in the Crimean War, sixty years before the First World War. With German workings being driven much deeper than British defensive mining works, and German charges wrecking both British trenches and shallow mining systems, it seemed as if the British were losing the mining battle with haste.

As 1914 moved into 1915 it became apparent that the Germans were mining on a well thought out and planned system. On 20th January 1915, the call went out from the War Office for the raising of specialist mining units. The scheme worked by the War Office was advised by none other than John Norton Griffiths who, with his fiery temperament and lusting for getting the job done properly, set to work straight away. He in turn was under the command of the Engineer in Chief at GHQ, Major General Sir George Henry Fowke.

Then the Germans struck again. At 07.30 am on 25th January 1915 there was a single large explosion south of the La Bassée Canal to the south of the village of Givenchy followed shortly afterwards by a series of violent explosions, twenty or more in number along the British front line trench. On the back of the falling debris and the subsequent confusion caused by the mines, the German attacked and, meeting little opposition, soon overran British front and support trenches, finally being brought to a standstill at a strongpoint to the rear known as 'The Keep'. The ground was held by the Guards Brigade at the time and, although counter attacks were carried out, the ground was not recovered from the enemy. This was the second blow to the British within a month that resulted in considerable casualties. Something had to be done and it had to be done quickly.

Norton Griffiths arrived on the Western Front on 13th February accompanied by two of his civilian employees from his contracting company – an assistant engineer named Leeming and a foreman named Miles. They met with army commanders and visited the ground in front of Givenchy. It was here that Norton Griffiths Foreman ran the Givenchy soil through his fingers.

"It's ideal isn't it, Miles?" asked Norton Griffiths.

Miles nodded, smiled and looked at Norton Griffiths, "It makes my mouth water," he said!

Norton Griffiths left three days later with a letter for the War Office that highlighted the serious situation that faced the BEF from German mining. By 18th February Norton Griffiths had been given the nod to go ahead and start recruiting. He asked for an interview at the War Office with Lord Kitchener and was shown to his office. Kitchener, an ex-Royal Engineer, listened attentively to Norton Griffiths: "The position is so serious for the poor devils in the trenches. You can't expect them to be shot at from the surface, booted at from above and blown to hell from below…" Kitchener agreed.

As he left Kitchener's office he heard from his assistant that twenty recently laid off clay kickers were on their way from Manchester to London. They arrived the next day to be medically inspected by the army, eighteen passed and were spoken to by Norton Griffiths as to what their duties and jobs in France would be. They were then sent later that day to the home of the Royal Engineers at Chatham. Here they were kitted out and given the most rudimentary of training. A professional soldier of the day would probably have had a shock on looking at this motley crew, seemingly unfit for the parade square, but relied on heavily for the work that awaited them. The same applied to civilian miners and mining engineers that were thrown quickly into the army's rigid and disciplined system. Although Chatham is the hallowed home of the Royal Engineers, of which they are rightfully proud, it did not always bode well with the newly recruited miners and mining

13

engineers. Passing through Chatham in 1929 on his way back to the Western Front on a British Legion pilgrimage, Capt B D Plumer MC, late of 185 Tunnelling Company wrote:

Chatham, as RE Headquarters in my memory represents all that was worst in the British military system. It may have served its purpose in inculcating in one an overpowering desire to get overseas. To me it seemed to epitomise all that was snobbish in the British Army. Its theory seemed to be that the King's Commission most emphatically did not entitle the temporary officer to consider himself or to be considered a temporary gentleman and I remember that I was very glad to get away from the place and the sight of it as our train passed through brought back unpleasant memories of what it was a decade and a half ago. Time softens one's feelings. however, and I was soon to learn that regular RE officers were jolly good fellows as individuals though the army system made them somewhat overpowering in the mass.[1]

Just three days later this group, still at odds as to which end of a rifle the bullets come out from, arrived in France. Here they were joined by twelve miners that had been drawn from 8th South Wales Borders, 11th Welsh Regiment and the 8th South Staffs. The drafting for the new tunnelling companies had begun. Both GHQ and the War Office were suspicious of these civilian men in uniform and viewed them as ill disciplined, free thinking men who were at odds with the discipline shown by the army. Some miners arrived in France with preconceived ideas that they were going to be mining behind the front or would be taken to their place of work every day by motor car! Some refused point blank to do drill, insisting that they were here to mine only. Using his experience gained from his campaigning days as a politician in exciting a crowd's enthusiasm, Norton Griffiths was using every trick in the book recruiting men for the tunnelling companies.

Questions regarding the miners' pay raised its head from time to time, a much publicised happening in London involved a group of qualified miners who refused to work for 'Two and Two' per day. As each of the group of twelve went in front of Norton Griffiths to be interviewed, each one of them refused point blank the rate of pay awarded them. All seemed grim when Norton Griffiths ordered the Sergeant Major who had escorted them to London, to take them back. The party had gone but a few paces when the order came from Norton Griffiths to bring them back. Stiffling his anger, the realisation that the army badly needed these men was of more importance. The men were signed up for six shillings a day. This jump in pay though did create some confusion once the tunnelling companies were formed. Trained clay kickers were the ones meant to be awarded the six shilling rate, whilst others, tunnellers' mates, received only two and two per day. This pay scale led to feelings of discontent.

With both the civilian mining drafts arriving in France and the miners now being actively sought from the ranks of the army, the men beefed up the numbers of Brigade Mining Sections.

Norton Griffiths was now using his wife's Rolls Royce, which the army had bought off him for £750 and had it moved to the Western Front. He drove up and down behind the lines using every possible unorthodox method involving cajoling and bribery to recruit his miners. Hampers of kippers and bottles of whisky regularly changed hands!

As the recruiting continued, so did the mining war. On the 16 February 1915 four sections of miners were dispatched from their temporary base at Rouen and sent to the four RE Field Companies of the 1st and 2nd Divisions with their purpose to carry out offensive and defensive mining against the Germans. These four sections formed the nucleus of 170 Tunnelling Company, Royal Engineers.

On 17th February, engineers of the British 28th Division fired the first British mine at Hill 60, two miles south of Ypres. Later that same morning German miners blew a mine in the vicinity of Hill 60 but their troops were driven out by the 2nd KOYLIs. On 21st February the Germans struck again in the Ypres sector. A mine was blown under the 16th Lancers' holding trenches at Shrewsbury Forest a few miles to the southeast of Ypres.

Throughout February to June 1915 in the midst of mining and countermining operations being undertaken, seven more tunnelling companies were formed under the badge of the Royal Engineers, 170 to 177 Tunnelling Companies. These tunnelling companies were unique to the rest that followed in that their first OCs were regular engineer officers with little to no mining experience. The army had initially requested the formation of eight tunnelling companies. Their make up would be fairly similar to each other. A company's strength would be about six officers and 227 men. Company

Headquarters, under which operated four Sections, each commanded by a junior officer with a mining engineer background, holding temporary commissions in the RE or other Regiments / Corps. In the case of those that came from outside the Royal Engineers, they were first seconded to the RE for their work. SNCOs were found from various RE field and fortress companies along with miners who had experience in management. Junior NCOs and Sappers were either drafted from the mines at home via Chatham or were experienced miners already serving in other army units. Each of the four sections would contain three reliefs and be capable of driving twelve headings. Clay kickers were not solely used for mining in the clay, soon the tunnelling companies were filled with miners from all types of geological backgrounds. It became apparent as the mining war progressed and got bigger, that more than eight tunnelling companies would be needed. By July 1916, on the formation of the last tunnelling company, 256 Tunnelling Company, 32 such companies existed in the British Army, 25 British, 3 Canadian, 3 Australian and 1 New Zealand. In addition to the tunnelling companies a support unit known as the Australian Electrical and Mechanical Mining and Boring Company (AEMMBC or Alphabet Company as it was known) was formed to provide all kinds of support to the tunnelling companies including powering and lighting of the mine and dugout systems and drilling test bores to check suitability for future underground workings.

177 Tunnelling Company of the Royal Engineers was formed on 8th May 1915 at the headquarters of the British Second Army, under the Command of General Sir Herbert

Charles Onslow Plumer. The Second Army HQ at that time was located at Château de Jardins in the small village of Oxelaëre about one mile south of the French town of Cassel. 177's location was moved to Terdeghem where, for the remainder of May, the unit received drafts of officers, men, supplies and stores. Those young officers that were selected for 177 were already receiving instruction in their new jobs as they were detached to other units. Throughout May 1915 they arrived at Terdeghem and joined 177. The OC, Captain Philip Wheeler Bliss was a regular RE officer. Earlier in the war he had served as a subaltern with 42 Fortress Company RE and had joined the Army in 1908. He arrived ready to take over 177 on 15th May 1915. From 25th May 1915 the structure of the company formed as it received its allocation of Motor Transport – four 3-ton lorries, horses with four limbered GS Wagons. On 26th May, twelve NCOs and men of the RE join the company shortly followed by ten men from the infantry to act as officers' servants. From the 1st to the 7th of June the unit continued to collect its stores, in preparation for its movement to the front. On the 8th June they moved to a new location, St Sylvestre Cappel where they were joined by eighty-four more NCOs and men. They continued increasing their stores and training the new arrivals. Another draft of sixty-two NCOs and men arrived on the 14th June and the final draft arrived in the form of seventy NCOs and men on the 16 June 1915. 177 Tunnelling Company was now ready for the front.

Supplying a tunnelling company upon its formation was no easy task. The army simply did not have the up-to-date specialist mining equipment. Unfortunately little reference survives today to tell us the trials and tribulations faced by 177 as they were getting their act together. There is, however, a little information on the equipping of other tunnelling companies. Lack of suitable equipment often brought Norton Griffiths close to despair. Much of the equipment that was supplied to the new tunnelling companies was outdated or was so useless it had to be abandoned. Twenty-one-year-old Lieutenant Edmund Pryor of 178 Tunnelling Company who went through months of exhaustive and desperate fighting underground early in his tunnelling career, had urgently ordered special ventilating equipment from the UK for his tunnelling company. He was reduced to tears when the truck arrived carrying the equipment as when opened he found it consisted of four immense deep sea diving bells! Even earlier than the diving bell incident the first draft for 173 Tunnelling Company was dumped on a railway platform at Estairs, fifteen miles south of Ypres, dumped next to them was their company equipment. One of their men, Sapper Harry Mosley, a Yorkshire man with some ten years' mining experience was shocked to discover that he could hardly recognise the digging and ventilation equipment that sat on the platform. Most of the equipment was leftovers from the Crimean War and had sat in RE stores since 1854 gathering dust. The army had neither the time nor experience to learn from exercising in mine warfare in peacetime and therefore the equipment just did not exist at RE or any other army stores. It was going to be a tough road ahead for all the companies, with equipment designed, trialled and tested on the spot and the results communicated to other companies.

There were still those who doubted the reliability and effective use of the tunnelling companies. After all this was a new type of warfare and used a vast amount of men who would have seemed untrained in the eyes of a regular soldier. What the army needed was an officer savvy of mining to represent them at major HQ levels such as Division, Corps, Army and GHQ. As 1915 progressed, in the Ypres Salient, things were certainly not rosy.

The Germans on 22nd April had launched the Second Battle of Ypres and started by defying the peacetime treaties which banned the use of poisonous weapons in war. They discharged chlorine gas onto two French divisions holding the line to the northeast of Ypres. The Second Battle of Ypres raged from 22nd April to 24th May 1915.

The German military machine forced back the BEF from its positions and shrank the Salient so by its end the Germans held vitally important ridges and high points. Hill 60, the Frezenberg Ridge, Bellewaerde Ridge were all now held by the Germans who could overlook Ypres from their points of advantage. The British were in no position at all to retake these positions anytime soon. Casualties sustained during the battle had vastly weakened the British. Vital artillery shells needed to support both defensive positions and troops in attack were in horribly short supply. This 'shell scandal' made its way into the public domain back home. All was not lost for the British though. The Germans had succeeded in pushing back the Allied lines around Ypres, but they had not broken through; the Allies defended what lines they had.

The Territorial Force had been mobilised in October 1914 and had sent TF Divisions to beef up the BEF; these divisions were really cutting their teeth during Second Ypres. The rest of the British Empire did not sit idle, forces were being raised all over, notably the Australians and the New Zealanders had formed ANZAC, the Canadians the CEF. Its 1st Division held the far left of the British line, bordering the French at the opening of Second Ypres, many of its men falling casualty to the German gas. Just as it was going to take time to raise a British Force on the Western Front capable of pushing back the Germans, the line that the Allies did hold needed to be defended, from both above and below.

---

1 Tunnelling Old Comrades Association Bulletin

CHAPTER ONE

JUNE 1915

On 18th June 1915, 177 Tunnelling Company, 243 officers and men strong, set up headquarters about half a mile west of Château Couvie which sits on the Poperinge to Proven Road about fifteen miles behind the front. The company NCOs and men were made up of miners who were already serving in other units in the BEF and also of miners that had joined the Royal Engineers during John Norton Griffiths' recruiting drive through the mining areas of the UK. There were men like 45-year-old Henry Bailey, a tunneller's mate from Staffordshire, 43-year-old John Bradley, a miner from Bishop Auckland, Durham and joining the company on the day it set up its HQ at Proven 49-year-old George Campbell, a miner from Southmoor Durham. These men represented a microcosm of the total makeup of 177, but it can clearly be seen that their ages were far in excess of many of the men to be found in other infantry units.

That same day the call arrived for the OC, Capt Bliss, to attend a meeting at VI Corps HQ where he would meet the CRE of the Corps. VI Corps held what was the left side of the British Front lines around Ypres. The Corps was made up of the British 4th and 6th Divisions and it was later that day that Captain Bliss, accompanied by 2nd Lt MacFarlane, made their way to the HQ of the 11th Infantry Brigade of the 4th Division. The Brigade HQ was located in the ruins of Fly Farm and it was here they were shown around the 11 Brigades' front trenches where commanders on the ground told

Bliss of their suspicions that the Germans were both mining and fortifying their trench lines. Bliss and MacFarlane drew up plans on the spot to mine the enemy under his trenches at two points.

Two shafts would be sunk and designated the names 'Windsor Castle' and 'Buckingham Palace'. The shafts were located at map references C.7.d.1.4 and C.7.c.4.6 on sheet 28NW that covers the Ypres area. Once these shafts were at the required depth, a gallery would break away from the bottom of the shaft which would make its way under the British lines out under No Man's Land until both galleries were under the German trenches at map reference C.7.d.2.6 and C.7.c.4.6.

That night the 9th Field Squadron RE set about and made two shaft covers to protect the tunnellers whilst they worked to sink their mineshafts. The next day, one officer and eleven men from 177 arrived at each shaft location and started work, each shift being relieved nightly. As the days wore on the number of men working on these shafts increased. The section of German trench that both sets of tunnellers were aiming for was very close to the British front line with about 120 feet separating the two trench lines. By 28th June the shaft of the Buckingham Palace mine had been sunk to 35 feet and the team were ready to break out a gallery.

Things, however, were different at the Windsor Castle mine shaft. On 26th June, whilst 20 feet deep, the shaft suffered a small cave-in. By 29th June the shaft was down to 26 feet but at 2am on 30th June

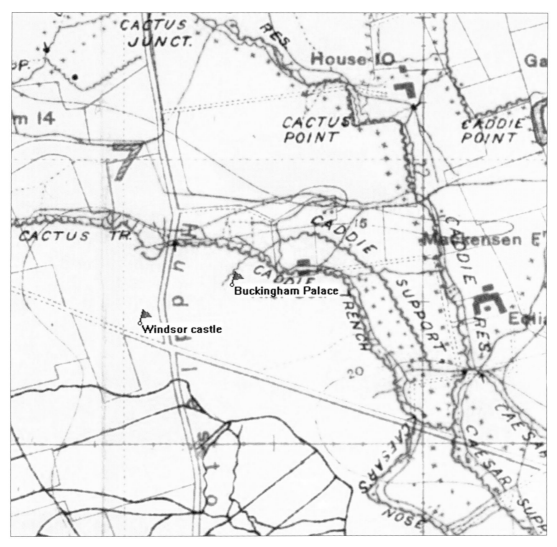

Windsor and Buckingham workings, 177's first underground workings following their formation as a tunnelling company. (Courtesy Great War Digital)

2nd Lt MacFarlane, the supervising officer, was wounded. Due to lack of supervision the shaft was later lost that day to a cave-in caused by bad ground, with the damage irreparable. Not to be outdone a second shaft was ordered.

JULY 1915

On 1st July the digging of a second shaft was begun, still carrying the name Windsor Castle, but also known as number 3.

Work still continued on the Buckingham Palace system, known officially as working number 1. Leaving a 2-foot sump in the bottom of the shaft, at 33 feet deep, a gallery was broken away and started on 3rd July. This working became known as 1A and by the end of the day had been pushed forward 7 feet. On 4th July, due to a gas attack on the surface, the heavier gas fell into the mine hampering the tunnellers' efforts to push forward gallery 1A. By the end of 5th July the gallery was 13 feet long but the tunnellers had to be removed due to the weight of German shellfire hitting the vicinity of their workings.

On 2nd July, at 21 feet down the shaft, a second tunnel was also started. This was not going to be driven all the way to the German lines. This gallery known as 1B was to be a defensive working that would serve listeners, alert for any sounds of German mining. By 5th July this gallery was driven out 16 feet. Happenings on the surface moved quicker than those below ground and a short time later the infantry attacked on the surface taking their objectives, including the targets of the ongoing mining. As a result, work ceased on Buckingham Palace. The replacement shaft at Windsor Castle continued and by 20th July the shaft was 39 feet deep.

Here work had not been easy. There had been a suspension of work due to tactical reasons from 5th July to 15th July; on returning to their shaft the tunnellers found the last 10 feet of it full of water. Their work was far from easy as they sank the last 17 feet of shaft. Between the 22nd and 31st July work continued to strengthen the shaft, sink a sump and break away a gallery. By 26th July, the gallery, now 45 feet long, suffered a bad cave-in which slowed up work. By 31st July, and many cave-ins later, the gallery was 56 feet long.

As work continued through the month of July, 177 was ordered to carry out more works. On 9th July work began to drive a subway under the Yser Canal, near bridge 6d within map square B13a. On each side of the bank both an inclined drive and vertical shaft would be constructed. On the east

bank the inclined work was known as A, with the vertical shaft as B. On the western bank the shaft was known as C with the incline as D.

Incline A, located at Prowse Corner, was sunk on a 1 in 4 slope with dimensions of 6 feet by 3 feet. By 14th July the incline was 35 feet long. There had been cave-ins due to shelling and heavy rain. A lot of water had gathered at the face of the incline and it was decided to suspend work and finish it from the bottom of shaft B when it had reached the required depth. As shaft B was sunk the tunnellers struck soft ground with a consistency of running sand. Attempts to drive in sheet piling met with failure so the tunnellers switched to a wooden caisson 4 feet by 4 feet and proceeded to sink the shaft. At a depth of 15 feet the miners found the pressure required to drive down the caisson was splitting the shaft planks.

Meanwhile, on the west bank the miners were having the same problems as those on the opposite bank. Shaft C, with a proposed depth of 46 feet, had been sunk to 15 feet by 13th July. A caisson was prepared but on 15th July, whilst attempting to sink it, the bottom set cracked open. The west bank incline D, located 125 yards south of bridge 6d, was driven on a slope of 1 in 4.7, using the same dimensions as its east bank counterpart. Exactly the same problems faced by those on the east bank arose and on 15th July after 48 feet of the incline had been driven, work was suspended. It wasn't just the bad ground that hampered the canal tunnel works, heavy German shelling played its part. Rather than completely abandon the plan of making a canal tunnel, on 28th July a new site on the west bank of the canal near bridge 6c, was chosen. This shaft, known as E, was sunk and by the end of July the shaft and a small dugout had been constructed.

The final task given to 177 in July 1915 was at Railway Wood, a spur of high ground protruding westwards from the Bellewaerde Ridge just a couple of miles to the east of Ypres. This was a vital part of the British trenches that formed the Salient around Ypres. Following the end of the Second Battle of Ypres, the Germans had taken a large portion of the important high ground surrounding the British trenches. But here, at Railway Wood or *Eier Waldchen* to the Germans, the British had a slight height advantage where they could overlook the German trenches running to the north towards the Frezenberg Ridge. The Germans, aware that the British had this advantage, were going to try and take it from their enemy by any means possible, including mining. The arrival of 177 in the Railway Wood sector heralded the start of a relationship the tunnellers would build with both infantryman and the ground that would last until September 1917. This is where 177 and its miners would really cut their teeth. They would be providing the vital defence against German mining for the many infantry divisions that would hold the trenches in this sector. The ability to provide this defence for the troops was vital to their morale. They would be facing the normal 'hate' thrown at them by the Germans on a daily basis in the form of sniping, shellfire and trench raids. They would also face the elements as the year grew older. The rain would play havoc with the trenches, filling them with water, rendering many impassable. Morale and health would suffer.

As mentioned before, the average age of a miner in the company was far higher than that found in other army units and therefore health problems inherent with the men's ages and the conditions they were serving in were commonplace. All this coupled with the threat of death from below would just highlight the importance of the task that the tunnellers had before them to try and ease the lot of the infantryman above. They were just a tiny cog in the giant wheel that rotated in order for the army to operate, but they were an important part of it. They were to provide the underground defence for the very apex of the Ypres Salient.

Prior to looking at 177's time in the line at Railway Wood it is important to look at how the use of military mining changed as the war progressed. Although the tunnellers chain of command enabled them to jump over the heads of their resident brigade and division, it was vital that they formed a relationship with whoever was the resident brigade in the line. The General Officer Commanding of that brigade would rely heavily on the tunnellers for providing the necessary subterranean defence and mine warfare support for his troops during localised attacks and offensives. Although infantry brigades in the early days of underground warfare on the Western Front had mining support from the hastily thrown together Brigade Mining Sections, these sections lacked the vital link at the higher level of the chain of command which would help with time to provide a mining strategy on the Western Front. Even with the arrival of the first tunnelling companies at the front there still seemed to be an element of confusion as to who they were responsible to, and it was not uncommon to see brigade and divisional commanders misusing tunnellers. As time went on and they learnt from their mistakes, it became very apparent that if one unit was to remain on the front for a protracted period of time it would be a tunnelling company. Military mining was a job that could not be rushed. Planned schemes took many months and in some cases years to develop. As 1915 progressed it became clear that in spite of many localised mining successes, the mining situation in general was far from satisfactory. There was no proper plan and little control over mining operations and more importantly it lacked strategic concept.

Twenty tunnelling companies had been formed, up to 1,000 men served in each company including RE, attached infantry and other troops used as labour. The progress of war weighed heavily on the tunnelling companies. There was little to show for it. There were promising mine schemes under construction but many lacked strategic forethought. Towards the end of 1915, the War Office sent GHQ a letter suggesting that an officer of high rank be appointed 'Inspector of Mines' and given general control of the tunnelling companies to coordinate efforts. GHQ approached General Fowke, Engineer in Chief and voiced their request. Fowke, although supportive to the tunnelling companies, remained doubtful that they were making the grade. GHQ was asking for the post of 'Inspector of Mines' to be formed with the posts of 'Controller of Mines' subordinate to him at Army Headquarters. Fowke agreed and put the wheels in motion in setting up this command chain. At GHQ Fowkes' main assistant was Colonel Robert Napier Harvey RE, a man who fully understood the need for this new tunnelling chain of command. As Harvey drew up the jobs specification for the new role he took the opportunity to provide the Inspector of Mines with the necessary amount of power and, most importantly, freedom of movement outside the Army's traditional restrictive control over movement. Harvey stated: "I drew up a charter which would enable the Inspector of Mines to visit any mine, anywhere, and at anytime, without any reference to the headquarters of the formation."

There was only one other officer in the BEF that could move like this, the Commander in Chief himself. Harvey, though doubtful his proposals would be agreed, was delighted when he heard that they had been accepted. The question still stood as to who was going to fulfil this post. Initially Fowke looked at Brigadier-General H. Thuillier to take the post, but because tunnelling was new to the army and also, since the beginning of the Second Battle of Ypres, was the use of gas as a weapon and Thuillier was hoping for the new appointment as Director General Gas Services he consequently turned down the appointment of Inspector of Mines. Harvey stepped forward and asked to be put forward for nomination. Fowke agreed and Harvey got the post, newly promoted to Brigadier General! He officially became the British Army's Chief Tunneller on 1 January 1916 at the age of 47.

When 177 took over the Railway Wood sector, on 25th July, the men of the 42nd Brigade of the 14th (Light) Division were in the process of relieving their sister 43rd Brigade. This sector was known as 'H' sector and the trench numbers here were all prefixed with the same letter. The relief was completed by 1.30am on 27th July. The new working taken over by 177 Tunnelling Company, at the eastern tip of the Railway Wood was started by Lieutenants Firebrace

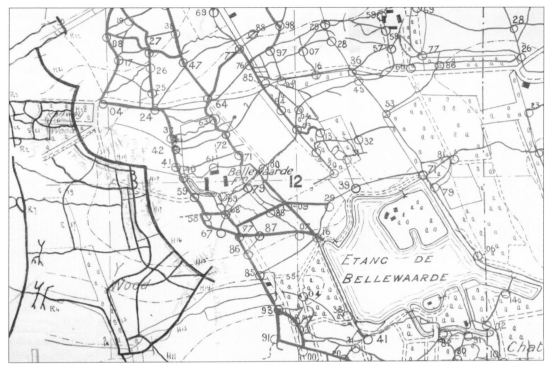

Trench map from 16th Brigade war diary showing the "H" numbered sections across the British front line trenches in the Railway Wood sector. (TNA. WO95/1864)

and McKelvie of 175 Tunnelling Company on 30th June. They were pulled out of the Railway Wood sector on 23rd July after handing over to 177 as their company was going to take over the tunnels at the ominous Hill 60 a couple of miles south of Ypres. 177's new mine working was to be an offensive mine and was known as working number 4. Started in June off trench H21 at map reference I.11.b 9.4, it was located 250 feet from its objective, an enemy redoubt. At the time the working was taken over by 177, the shaft, 24 feet deep, had been completed and a gallery had been driven out towards the enemy line that by the end of July was 38 feet long. Work here was not only hampered by shellfire as elsewhere but also by the lack of carrying parties bringing up wood, itself in short supply, to be used in the construction of the gallery.

AUGUST 1915

Tunnelling work continued in August; the mine working at Windsor Castle suffered a number of setbacks. The ground mashed up and softened by continual shelling and water from the ground poured into the shaft through every crack in the wooden shaft lining. The shaft was finally abandoned on 6th August. Aside from the usual problems of cave-ins, water that was pumped from the mine was now flooding surface trenches and could not be properly disposed of. This was alienating the tunneller from his infantry counterparts, a problem faced throughout the underground war.

On 9th August the 14th Division supported the 6th Division as they counter-attacked to retake trenches lost at the end of July. The trenches in 'H' sector were badly shelled by the Germans.

23

Lack of manpower and materials continued to plague the tunnellers at working 4 under the Railway Wood sector, flooding also being a major problem, although by 27th August a system was in place to drain the water. Working 4 was now 86 feet long and a small chamber 8 feet and 6 inches square was constructed on the left of the gallery at its end. On 15th August, sharp-eyed observers in the British line detected possible signs of enemy mining 'owing to the colour of the sandbags appearing on the enemy parapets'.[1] Listening arrangements were put in place with five men per hour on duty, but no sounds were detected. On 25th August at 66 feet out from the shaft at working 4, at 90 degrees to the left, a defensive gallery was started; by 28th August this was 41 feet long and known as 4A.

On 14th August the Headquarters of 177 moved to a location on the Poperinge to Proven road, opposite the entrance to Château Couthove. It was in this locality that in late 1915 the Second Army mine school would be set up instructing in the various arts of military mining, to be discussed in a forthcoming chapter.

It was also during the month of August 1915 that a start was made by 177 of constructing tunnel dugouts within the medieval ramparts at Ypres south of the Menin Gate.

SEPTEMBER 1915

Joining the company in September was Lt Basil Sawers, a Canadian who found himself uprooted from his job in a field company of Canadian Engineers, commissioned, and posted to 177 Tunnelling Company.

An aerial photograph of the Railway Wood sector taken just before the Loos diversionary attack and the blowing of 177's first mine of the War. (IWM aerial BB451, Box 9, 1915)

Men stood outside the Ramparts' dugouts just north of the Menin Gate, Ypres. The dugout was constructed by 177 in late 1915. (Photo courtesy of Peter Barton)

"I was a mining Engineer in British Columbia. When war broke out 15 of us enlisted in the 1st Field Company. We knew nothing about the army and all went into the ranks......" [2]

Corporal Basil Sawers and his company saw their first action during the Second Battle of Ypres where he witnessed the first gas attack. After two weeks in the Salient his unit moved down to the Givenchy area in France. It was here that he would meet John Norton Griffiths and be picked up for his mining experience.

"At this time we heard that Norton Griffiths had been given carte blanche to start a tunnelling company. Two of our men got away somehow and joined him, in 177 Company. About August

when we were in front of the Messines Ridge, he came to see me. Somebody must have told him that I was a mining engineer. Suddenly one evening a fellow came rushing into my tent saying: 'There's a bloody General out there looking for you.' I went out and saw a great limousine, may have been a Rolls Royce, and a Colonel with red tabs and a red hat. He seemed rather surprised I'd never been underground before, but seemed satisfied. I had actually worked in about 12 different mines and was studying at McGill. He said, 'You will hear in a day or two.' He never went near the officers, always came direct to the men. He told me what he wanted."

Cpl Sawers didn't have long to wait. Three days later a signal arrived stating: "2nd Lt

Sawers to report to RTO Steenwerck for transportation to 177 Company."

"I believe there was a big row amongst Canadian high command about this order. No, by your leave or anything! They held it up about six days before they let me know. Then I got my commission, went to the RTO and they gave me a chit to go to Poperinge to 177 Company. Bliss met me there at the station showed me around and said, 'You'd better have 3 days leave to get fitted up.' I was still in Corporals uniform. Went to London and within half an hour was on the street in brand new outfit as a Second Lieutenant. Rejoined my unit and started work. That was about the 8th September, 1915. I was now in the British Army, Royal Engineers, as a tunnelling officer."

The war diary of 177 records Basil Sawers as joining the company on 13th September 1915. Upon his joining the company he was sent up to Railway Wood to supervise the tunnelling operations taking place there. He described the sight that befell him:

"The half company that was in Railway Wood was there all the time. Our dump was called Hell's fire Corner (sic). It was at the junction between the Roulais (sic) railway and the Menen Road. Just after the railway crossed the road it went into a cutting and to the right was a bit of a bump – this was Railway Wood. It was one of the few high spots we held in the line, and had a look over the Boche line. We could look half left over Wilchy (probably meaning *Wieltje* – Author)

and St Julien. High command decided we must keep the hill. When I got there, there was no green in the wood at all; just a few battered stumps. Just before, a mine had been blown on the Menen road at Hooge, so we were moved into Railway Wood to keep the Germans from blowing it. It was the worst part of the Western Front for our work – had to pump as soon as we got down to 2 feet. It was a clayey loam full of water."

Work on the number 4 working took on a new edge when on the night of the 31st August to 1st September reports from the infantry holding trench H21 about 150 yards north of the shaft reported the noise of enemy mining. Immediate counter measures were taken by 177 and a camouflet charge of 65 pounds of guncotton was placed in the chamber of working 4 and then tamped. With haste, gallery 4A was pushed out to 55 feet. Whilst working on this system on 2nd September, Sapper Robert Onions[3], a 26-year-old miner from Great Barr, Staffordshire, was killed in action on the surface. He was one of many civilian miners to join, enlisting initially as a tunnellers mate. On 3rd September, 27 feet along gallery 4A another gallery was driven out to the right. Labelled as 4B, this gallery was 9 feet long by 4th September, when a camouflet charge of 35 pounds of guncotton was placed at the end of the gallery. After careful listening from trench H21 it was deemed that the sounds heard were not conclusive and that they were at some distance off to the left of the current working. The chamber at the end of 4 was reopened and the charge removed. Work recommenced here on 6th September when a shaft was sunk into the floor of the chamber, this becoming known as 4C. This shaft started out as 5 feet by 5 feet reducing as it went down to 3 feet by 3 feet.

By 10th September the shaft was down to 13 feet and a gallery pushed out from it. The total depth of shafts 4 and 4C was now 37 feet. As the gallery was pushed out the miners were relieved to find less of an issue with water at this depth.

The Germans continued their harassment of the British lines in the Railway Wood sector throughout the month. The wood always drew the attention of the German gunners and was pounded incessantly. An anonymous officer is quoted in the 43rd Brigades HQ war diary, for September, as describing the wood as "...a positive menace to life."[4] On 19th September British

retaliatory shellfire dropped short hitting trenches in the wood killing a few of their own men. Disaster almost struck 177 when a similar situation arose again just two days later with a 'friendly' shell just missing the shaft of the number 4 working.

On 22nd September, 102429 Sapper Henry Newby and 102713 Sapper Arthur Thomas were killed in action by German shellfire. Henry Newby was a 36-year-old miner from Esh Winning, Durham and Arthur Thomas from Tow Law, Durham was a transferee from the 26th Northumberland Fusiliers, The Tyneside Irish[5].

By 23rd September, gallery 4C had been driven 149 feet and was now estimated to be under the enemy redoubt at map reference I.12.a 0.4. At noon, charging commenced and 2,500 pounds of black

German soldiers amongst the ruins of Bellewaerde Farm July/August 1915. (Photo courtesy of Phillipe Oosterlkinck)

powder was packed into the tunnel end. One instantaneous and three electrical fuses were placed into the charge. Everything was ready to go by 2pm on the 24th.

The mine was placed to support an attack due to be made by the men of the 42nd Brigade, who held the trenches above. The mine had been ordered by their Brigade Commander, Brigadier General F A Dudgeon. Along with troops from the 3rd Division to the right of the 14th Division and supported by heavy rifle and machine gunfire from the men of the 6th Division to the left of the 14th Division, the 42nd Brigade was to advance in a line stretching from about 150 yards north of the railway to about 300 yards south east of Railway Wood and straighten their line in order to join trench H22 up with H21. It was also to capture the enemy's trenches in the vicinity of Bellewaerde Farm. If this attack was successful the Brigade Commander would then push forward his left of line until it reached the railway barrier at trench H22.

The attack was to commence at 4.20am on 25th September. By 1.00am the three attacking battalions were lined up and ready in their trenches. These were men of the 9th Rifle Brigade, 5th Oxfordshire and Buckinghamshire Light Infantry and the 5th Kings Shropshire Light Infantry. All three of these battalions suffered casualties due to enemy shellfire, and sadly, friendly fire when a 6-inch howitzer of No 4 Siege Battery, dropped a number of its shells short of the German lines, into British lines.[6]

At 4.19am that morning, 177 Tunnelling Company fired its first offensive mine of the war. The crater that resulted from the blow was not measured but believed to be about 110 feet long, 85 feet wide and 25 feet deep. The enemy redoubt was destroyed and with it two machine guns and an estimated 80 to 100 men. Unfortunately the mine caused a few casualties to the men of the 5th Ox and Bucks, blowing them over and dazing

German annotated photograph showing their consolidation work in the crater fired by 177 on 25th September 1915. (Photo courtesy Niek Benoot)

them. At 4.20am, under cloudy skies and in poor light, the assault took place. By 5am most of the German first and second lines had been taken by attacking troops although there was a wedge driven between the 5th Ox and Bucks and the 9th Rifle Brigade. By 7am the Shropshires and the Ox and Bucks were trying to consolidate their gains when the 9th RB fell back exposing the flank of the Ox and Bucks. It was along the front of the two battalions and the flank of the Ox and Bucks that a German counterattack developed which pushed both battalions back to their starting trenches by 8.15 am. By 8.30am all attacking troops were back in their trenches. The 42nd Brigade suffered heavy casualties as a result of the attack, 40 officers and 1,500 other ranks. To their right the attack by the 3rd Division also failed. This attack was in fact a diversionary attack in order to try and divert the Germans' attention away from the largest offensive yet launched by the BEF.

The battle of Loos started on 25th September about 40 miles south of Ypres and was fought by the British First Army in conjunction with French Forces further south. It would rage on for a month with little gain and high cost, with casualties numbering 50,380 killed and wounded. Following the diversionary attack at Bellewaerde, the galleries of the Number 4 system then filled with water and were left.

Along the section of line being held by British troops in the Railway Wood sector there were a few shallow dugouts some built by the 14th Division's Brigade Mining Section and others by the divisions RE field companies. These were utilised by the tunnellers as listening posts. One such post, located approximately 40 feet east of a barricade that had been placed on the Ypres to Roulers railway line, was 11 feet deep and pushed 30 feet forward of the British line when, between 14th and 24th September it was extended a further 158 feet. Known as working 5, on 24th October, three bore holes, 17 feet in length, were started at 9pm. This was a mine that had been ordered by the Brigade Commander holding the line, but due to tactical reasons it was not fired; the tunnel, now disused, was allowed to fill with water.

OCTOBER 1915
As 1915 progressed the British Army had grown bigger and bigger. Kitchener Divisions, full of men who had rushed to their countries call in 1914, had begun to arrive on the Western Front, the first of these divisions being involved in the battle of Loos. A second Canadian Division had joined their first on the Western Front. The second Canadian Division now held the line on the front opposite Wytschaete village. The village sits on the rise of ground, known as the Messines Ridge. Lost to the Germans during the First Battle of Ypres in 1914, the German soldiers had a clear view over the British lines and had begun to mine on the Messines sector. On 10th October 177 received the orders to assist the 2nd Canadian Division on the Wytschaete/Messines front and half of the company deployed to this front, setting up their headquarters at the crossroads in La Clytte. The half of the company assisting the Canadians was known as the right half, the remaining left half of the company remained in the Railway Wood sector.

The right half of the company took over a rabbit warren of workings adding more galleries to them. Working 26 was a shallow incline 8 feet deep that by 24th October was 65 feet long and being used as a defensive tunnel for listening. From looking at the war diary of 177 it can be seen that some of the workings they took over required a lot of clearing out and retimbering. On the 25th October, close to working 26, at grid N.30.a.3.7, at trench G1, working number 29 was begun. It was also an incline and was driven to 16 feet deep. The reason for its construction was that working 26 had begun filling with quicksand. The incline was in timber 4 feet high and 4 feet wide.

In the same trench yards away at map reference N.30.a.2.7 was another shallow incline taken over by 177 on 10th October. This incline ran to 8 feet 6 inches deep and the subsequent defensive gallery that ran from the bottom of the incline was 140 feet long by the end of the month. There was also an offensive working, known as 28, being

started by the end of October in trench G1 at the same map reference as working 29.

Just south of trench G1 was trench E1 (Left) and on 10 October at map reference N.30.c.3.2, a defensive working was taken over consisting of an incline driven to 9 feet deep with a gallery of 175 feet length pushed out from it, in which listening was taking place.

At trench E1, map reference N.30.c.4.2, a defensive incline and gallery known as 32, had been pushed out at 10 feet deep and 60 feet long. At the end of 32 a left and right branch was started. The left branch, 32A was pushed out 45 feet; the right branch 32B was pushed out to 115 feet. At 65 feet it connected with working 31.

Just a few yards away from 32 was working 33, similar to 32 in that it was an incline 10 feet deep with a gallery driven to 60 feet long. A half left branch was begun 25 feet along 33 and became known as

Map showing numbered workings opposite Wytschaete. A detachment from 177 developed these workings in October and November 1915. (Courtesy Great War Digital)

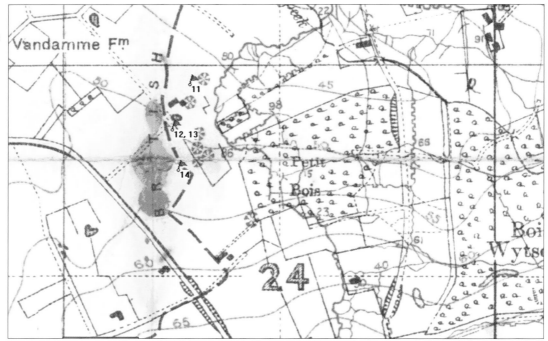

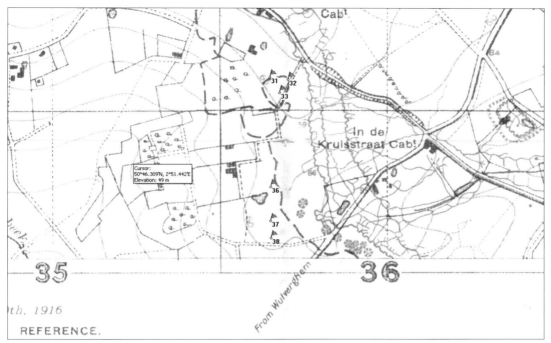

British workings opposite the Kruisstraat worked on by a detachment of 177 in October and November 1915. (Courtesy Great War Digital)

33A which, when 65 feet long, connected with working 32B. A half right branch 33B, opposite 33A was also started, which was 125 feet long by the end of the month and also used for listening purposes.

A couple of hundred yards further south, at map reference N.36.a.3.5 opposite the Kruisstraat in trench 15, lay working number 36. It was another incline, 15 feet deep, taken over by 177 on 10th October. Marked as a defensive working, the main gallery was 70 feet long. At the end both a left and right branch was constructed. The left branch, 36A was a 105 feet long by the month's end, with the right branch, 36B, being pushed out to 80 feet by 24th October. This working, defensive in nature, was used as a listening post.

Working 37 was started on 19th October at map reference N36a 3.3, along trench 14. This incline and gallery was 15 feet deep and 45 feet long by the end of the month and was also utilised for listening purposes.

Careful study of the plans after taking over the sector, led to the discovery on 25th October of yet another working, designated number 38. An incline driven to 13 feet deep, with a gallery 65 feet long, there was a branch to the right, at the end of 38, which was 120 feet long and designated 38A. A left branch at the end of 38, designated 38B, was 65 feet long. At 35 feet along gallery 38A there was a left branch, the gallery designated 38C was 20 feet long.

Meanwhile, during October the left half of 177 continued its work further north in the Ypres Salient at the Railway Wood sector. Another project took the form of machine gun positions constructed on the west bank of the Yser Canal at the bend at map reference B.25.b.9.1. Work also continued on the dugout in the Ramparts of Ypres between the Menin Gate and the sally port (*see page 32*).

31

The Ramparts dugouts just north of the Menin Gate, Ypres. (TNA)

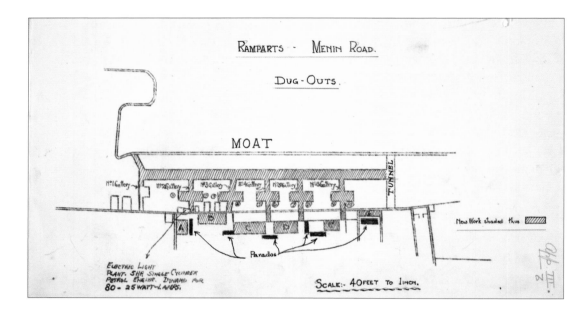

Up at Railway Wood at 5.20am on the 17th October the Germans blew a mine at the east end of the wood under the junction of trenches H20 and H21. The debris from the explosion damaged trench H20 considerably and buried twenty to thirty men from the 5th Ox and Bucks Light Infantry. The resultant crater was described as being about 40 yards in diameter and 30 to 40 feet deep. The 5th Ox and Bucks set about immediately to rescue their buried comrades and succeeded in digging many of them out even though they were severely hampered by German sniping during the rescue work. They lost two officers and 13 men killed with 22 others wounded as a result of the enemy blow. There was no attempt by the Germans to follow up in an attempt to capture the crater after the explosion of the mine, although about an hour after the blow the British front trenches were hit by German bombers throwing grenades. It was believed by 43rd Brigade that the German blow was taken as a defensive measure.

The 5th Ox and Bucks then worked tirelessly that night to repair the trenches around the crater. Many of the men in the battalion had just arrived on the Western Front, this being their tour of the trenches. They handled the situation splendidly and were praised for their work by the Brigade Commander.[7]

At working 5 in trench H22, 177 Tunnelling Company and its opposing German Pioneers finally came face to face, albeit briefly. No major work had been done in working 5 in October apart from the replacing of the sandbags at the end of the working which had been put in place by 14th Division's Brigade Mining Section. This was done so the charge which lay in place could be replaced. Problems with water showed no signs of easing off and the company was having a problem finding waterproof containers in which to place the charge. On 28th October at 12.30pm, German Pioneers broke into working 5, a single German being seen. A shootout commenced in the gallery, buying time until a charge of 120 lbs of guncotton was placed into the shaft and fired by Lt Campbell. That night Lts Campbell and Davies fired two charges of 90 and 150 lbs of guncotton. On the night of the 29th a final third charge of 270 lbs was fired by Lt Campbell. These last three charges were placed into surface shell holes or depressions outside the parapet of our trench and destroyed at least 50 to 60 feet of the gallery of working 5.

On 31st October at trench H22 a shaft was sunk about 50 feet north of the abandoned number 5 working. This was to be a defensive working to compensate for the loss of working 5 and was designated working 11.

On 18th October working 4 was taken over again. The shaft was wrecked and although gallery 8A ran into it, the system was found to be flattened and no exploration was possible. Where 8A led away from working 4 it turned half left and by 31st October it was 75 feet long. From this point another gallery commenced leading off to the half right, designated working 8C.

On 20th October at trench H20 a shaft to a defensive system was begun, at map reference I.11.b.8.3, designated working 6A. It was about 130 feet south of working 8 and just over a week later was 27 feet deep when a gallery was driven off the shaft through water-laden soil and clay, which by 31st October was 54 feet long.

Throughout October, 177 took over more workings from the 14th Division's Brigade Mining Section as they were slowly absorbed into the company. 150 feet south of working 6 on 18th October a defensive, designated working 7, was taken over. At 12 feet deep it consisted of a gallery 40 feet long at the end of which were branches to the left and right of two galleries running 15 and 25 feet respectively. This working was used at the time for listening purposes only.

The night of the 21st and into the early hours of 22nd October saw the men of Brigadier General Nicholson's 16th Infantry Brigade, 6th Division come forward to take over the 'H' sector trenches and relieve the weary 42nd Infantry Brigade. With the weather worsening the 2nd Yorks and Lancs took over the ground from the Ypres to Roulers Railway across to and including Railway Wood, which came in for some heavy shelling in the first few days of their holding the position. To their right side were the men of the 1st Buffs. They found the trenches in a bad condition, damaged by recent heavy rain and frequent German bombardments. It quickly became apparent to the newcomers that the Germans were carrying out a lot of work on their trenches in preparation for the onset of winter, including improving methods for draining their trenches.

NOVEMBER 1915

As 177 continued work into November 1915, work on the Menin Gate dugouts progressed. The galleries of this dugout were timbered with 2-inch lagging between frames of 5 feet by 5 feet set 4 feet apart.

On 5th November, where trench H22 crossed the Ypres to Roulers Railway, the 2nd Yorks and Lancs holding the trench, withdrew due to the poor state of their trench. This was made worse by the deteriorating weather conditions. Taking over from them were the 1st Buffs, who had one of their companies cut off from the remainder of the Battalion due to the state of the trenches. Their war diary stated: "Some trenches were full of water up to the lips."[8] Work was continuous day and night to recover and repair the trenches. With no defence above them, the tunnellers in number 11 had no option but to abandon their work.

At the number 6 workings under trench H20, its eastward running gallery, 6A was 125 feet long by the 8 November when listeners heard sounds suspected to be that of enemy mining. A charge of 230 lbs of guncotton was readied and fired in gallery 6A at 2 am on 9th November. The blow didn't damage too much of 6A and left 100 feet of the gallery still usable. Some men were injured by gas left in the gallery following the blow and there was an afterdamp explosion as a result of methane produced by the camouflet, but no men were injured.

On 16th November at 11am further sounds were heard from 6A and, after a period of careful listening, a camouflet of 100 lbs of guncotton and 80 lbs of blastine was fired at 1.45 pm. The blow wrecked 6A back to the 80 feet mark and wrecked gallery 6C, a right branch off 6A, completely.

On 6th November another gallery was started 70 feet along 6A to the left and would connect the number 6 workings with the number 8 workings. By the middle of the month this gallery, 6B, was 50 feet long. A right branch at 20 feet off 6B, labelled 6D was 15 feet long by the 22nd of the month. 6E was a gallery located on the right at 50 feet along 6B. It was wrecked on 24th November by a camouflet fired from the number 8 workings. A right branch at 78 feet along 6A was 10 feet long by 22nd November. A camouflet charge of 100 lbs of blastine was placed in the gallery and then

the gallery tamped in readiness, but the charge was not fired. At 58 feet along 6A off to the right, gallery 6G was driven to 95 feet by the 29th of the month.

On 10th November the 51st Brigade, 17th (Northern) Division relieved the 6th Division as they went back to the rear for a period of rest. The 16th Infantry Brigade had been very impressed with the defensive work carried out by 177 Tunnelling Company during their tour of the front. This was noted in the Brigade war diary for November 1915:

> "The mining operations, thanks to the ability and energy of Lt Campbell, 177 Tunnelling Coy RE resulted in the positions being practically covered by protective galleries, and a German gallery was successfully camouflet."[9]

The 51st Brigade took over the network of trenches and set about digging themselves in. With the worsening of the weather the trenches were literally collapsing in places due to water damage

The number 7 workings along trench H19 at map reference I.ll.b.9.2, which had been taken over on 18th October, were not worked on during the month and were used for listening only. The Germans fired a mine on 19th November at 9.30pm in the vicinity of the old number 5 workings alongside the Ypres to Roulers Railway at trench H22. The trench was unoccupied at the time so no casualties resulted from the blow. A crater 30 feet across marked the spot of the mine and by daylight the next day the British had the crater wired into their positions with artillery ready to bring down fire just in case the Germans attempted to rush forward and capture the crater.

On 20th November an interesting young officer joined 177 Tunnelling Company. 2nd Lieutenant Agner Emil Dalgas would make his mark on 177 Tunnelling Company and play a major part in its perpetual remembrance after the war. At 28, he was Danish by birth and had held a commission in the Danish Army before taking a three-year leave of absence to travel to Canada. On his arrival in Canada he took employment as a civil engineer's assistant in Victoria, BC. His leave of absence was almost up when war was declared. He then resigned his commission in the Danish Army and joined the Canadian Expeditionary Force's 7th Battalion rapidly rising to Sergeant. He stepped forward when the call went out for miners and was interviewed by John Norton Griffiths who then recommended he be commissioned and transferred into the Royal Engineers.

Meanwhile, under trench H20, gallery 8A was pushed out further and by the middle of the month was 153 feet long. On 15th November at 83 and 103 feet along 8A, two galleries were begun off to the left. Designated 8C and 8F, by 29th November 8C was 33 feet long. On 22nd November a small chamber was made at the end of 8F in the face of which a 6-inch push tube containing 170 lbs of ammonal was inserted. The chamber was packed with 200 lbs of blastine and at 3am on 24th November, both charges were fired from a depth of 25 feet. The resultant crater was 60 feet in diameter and 15 feet deep. The blast wrecked gallery 8F back to the 15 feet mark and also gallery 6E to 17 feet.

At the bottom of shaft 8 at the beginning of November a northward driven gallery, labelled 8B, had begun. By 15th November

Lt Agner Dalgas after receiving his MC. (Photo courtesy of Corinne Dalgas)

it was 88 feet long and at the end of it to the left and right ran two branches, 8D and 8E which by 29th November were 25 feet and 62 feet long respectively.

The mine crater blown on 25th September by 177 came in for plenty of trench mortar and heavier battery shoots. Intelligence started to ascertain that the Germans may have a mine shaft or ventilation shaft in the crater. The 51st Brigade felt that the Germans held the upper hand in the mining war in this sector, with 177 always being on the defensive. This feeling went a long way to affect the relationship between Capt Bliss and John Norton-Griffiths.

On 23rd November a trench raid was to take place in which infantry, accompanied by Lt Campbell and a small group of men from 177 equipped with mobile charges, would

Map showing numbered workings astride the Wytschaete to Kemmel road. A detachment from 117 developed these workings in October and November 1915. (Courtesy Great War Digital)

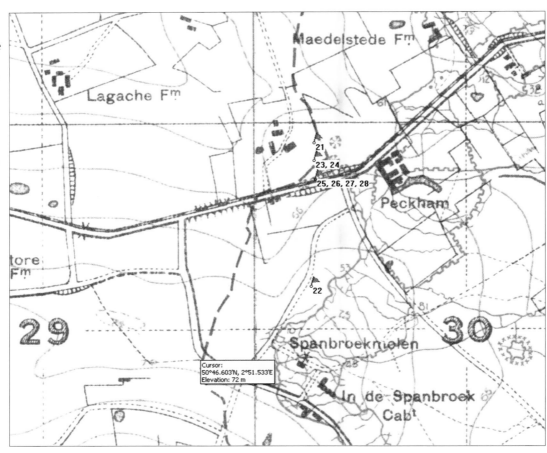

move forwards, reconnoiter and destroy any enemy mine workings they discovered. trench mortars would hit the German wire and cut it prior to the men launching the raid. Unfortunately the enterprise had to be cancelled when the enemy artillery replied in force to the trench mortars of the 51st Brigade which also failed to cut the Germans barbed wire around their positions.

Working number 10, started towards the end of the previous month was continued. By the 15th of the month the shaft was down to 27 feet deep and an east running gallery, 10A, was begun. By the month's end it was 78 feet long. At 73 feet to the left along 10A, both left and right branching galleries were started. Galleries 10B and 10C were 29 and 11 feet long by the end of November.

DECEMBER 1915

On 1st December, observers in the British front line were confident that one of the German shaft heads in the mine crater located on his front line took a direct hit from a 9.2inch howitzer firing in support of the troops at Railway Wood.

177 Tunnelling Company was tasked to support the 49th Division in the north of the Salient as it prepared for an offensive.

A number of shallow dugouts were constructed in support of the division. Work also commenced on a tunnel dugout just north of the Menin Gate.

At Railway Wood an attempt was made to sink the main shaft of the number 6 working, deeper. They managed to get the shaft down to 42 feet deep but then the sides of the shaft caved and slipped and the shaft was filled back up to 27 feet. 6F, a right branch along 6A at 78 feet was driven out to 33 feet. On 7th December the last 11 feet of the gallery was widened to 6 feet. A push tube, containing 80 lbs of ammonal was inserted into the face and was driven down 39 feet where the tip broke, possibly against the wood of a German gallery. At 5.30pm that day the tube was fired, the resultant explosion wrecking 6F back to the 10 feet mark. Elsewhere in the number 6 workings, 6G, a right branch at 58 feet along 6A was 129 feet long just before the middle of the month. A left branch at 51 feet along 6A, designated 6H, was 20 feet long by the 10th of the month and connected to 6B. 6J a left branch at 85 feet along 6G was 28 feet long by the month's end. Another left branch along 6G at 106 feet, known as 6K was begun and by the 20th was 5 feet long. 6M a right branch at 22 feet along 6A was 47 feet long by the 22nd and connected with 6G. At 58 feet along 6G a right branch, 6N, was started which was a stepped incline to the surface to come up inside the parapet of trench H20. On 7th December, along 6A, 35 feet from the centre of the shaft a 12 feet long, 6 feet wide chamber was constructed, in which a second shaft, known as a winze, was sunk. By 20th December this winze was 23 feet deep. The total depth of the number 6 workings was now 50 feet and a new deeper

second level was about to be built. Attempts were made to break away both east and south from the winze, but failed due to treacherous ground. Eventually a gallery running north, from the foot of the winze was started. It was known as 6WA and by the end of December was 37 feet long.

Tension was also high in the adjoining 27 feet deep number 8 workings in December. On the 9th, the Germans were heard at the end of 8C, a left branch at 83 feet along 8A. Noises were made to see if there was any reaction from the Germans but nothing was forthcoming. This worried the men underground as it was highly possible that the enemy were in the final stages of charging a mine and not wanting to be disturbed. A charge of 200 lbs of blastine and 150 lbs of ammonal was placed in 8C. Two sections of 18 feet of solid tamping separated by 12 feet of air were made ready and the charge was fired at 5pm. Initially only the detonators fired. The tamping was removed and a new detonator was inserted into a stick of blastine. The charge finally fired successfully at 8.15pm. A small crater about 15 feet long formed on the surface. The resultant blow wrecked the whole of 8C and 40 feet of 8A. Gallery 8G, a right branch at 106 feet along 8A was utilised during the month as a magazine to store explosives. 8H a right branch at 106 feet along 8A was 48 feet on 20th December and connected into 8G replacing the damaged part of 8A. 8B, a northward driven gallery, was pushed out to 117 feet long by the end of the month.

At 7.45pm on 14th December, the Germans fired a large mine centred about 50 feet north of galleries 8D and 8E. The estimated depth of their workings was 25 feet and the resultant mine explosion formed an oval crater 90 feet long and 70 feet wide. Sapper George Chatt, a 41-year-old miner from Crook, County Durham, was on listening duty in gallery 8D or 8E and was killed and buried.[10] An infantryman on duty in a bombing post was killed by the shockwave on the surface. The Germans sent over eleven bombers to try and hold the crater but they were seen off by men of the 7th Borders who had the crater in their possession by 10.45pm and began to wire it into their defences.

2nd Lt Dalgas, newly arrived at 177 the month before, took up his first stint in the front on 5th December when he was detailed as officer in charge of number 10 defensive working located 27 feet deep under trench H18. Dalgas was no stranger to the front line having come over from the Canadian infantry, but even he was shocked at the state of the ground at Railway Wood sector. His personal diary described the trenches:

"… I thought I came from bad ones, but no. Things here are in an awful mess. My first job is officer i/c the night shift at mine number 10."[11]

Dalgas went on to compare his new surroundings from where he had been previously:

"The difference between this place and Plugstreet is that here we are shelled all the time! The Ypres Salient is the most absurd thing on God's green earth."

Consisting of only three galleries, the working was hampered throughout the month by bad weather, heavy shelling and a lack of manpower. Dalgas described the working in his diary entry for the 8th December:

"I am doing my uttermost. No 10 shaft is without doubt the front line trench of Hell."

German shelling of the sector was merciless and continuous. Dalgas mentions that German *Minenwerfers* fell all around the number 10 workings, destroying the trench leading to the workings and cutting off the sappers from the rest of the sector. With the few sappers he had working underground on the number 10 workings he commenced to dig out a new communication trench replacing the shelled in trench.

Dalgas' diary entries for this period also interestingly observe personality clashes and disagreements at the front between officers in the company. In particular Lts Campbell and North who took turns at the front in overseeing the work being done by 177. Dalgas' diary entry mentions:

"Lieut Campbell relieved Lieut North. These two officers are in charge up here, taking a week at the time, but unfortunately, they don't agree. What the one is doing, the other is undoing, but Campbell stands alone. North has everybody behind him. However, Campbell doesn't approve of my new trench so I guess it won't go any further. Too bad."

At 4.40am on 19th December the Germans began a heavy bombardment. This is the day that Phosgene gas was used in the Salient for the first time. At 3pm Number 10 shaft suffered three direct hits by German shelling. The third shell is believed to have exploded at the bottom of the shaft where it left a 15 foot deep crater. Six Infanteers of the unit holding the surface trenches were sheltering from the shelling in the number 10 workings and were buried and cut off. Sadly all attempts to pick up these workings again failed. A German attack was heavily expected and materialised on 20th December although it failed. Dalgas' diary further mentions on 21st December that the gas still hung around and that 1,500 casualties had been reported due to the recent shelling and attack.

It was a sad end to 1915 and to the company's first six months in the line.

---

1 War diary HQ 43rd Infantry Brigade, 12th August 1915. WO95/1903

2 Interview with Alexander Barrie and Basil Sawers in preparation for the book War Underground. Barrie papers – RE Library Chatham.

3 102951 Sapper Robert Onions is commemorated on Panel 9 of the Menin Gate, Ypres.

4 War diary for 43rd Infantry Brigade HQ. September 1915 WO95/1903

5 Sappers Henry Newby and Arthur Thomas are both buried side by side in Bedford House Cemetery, Enclosure 2, Plot 6, Row A, Graves 75 and 76.

6 Information taken from 14th Div HQ and 42nd Brigade War Diaries and appendices September 1915. WO95/1897

7 War diary for 42nd Infantry Brigade HQ, October 1915 WO95/1897and 5th Ox and Bucks war diary for 17th October 1915, WO95/1900. Strangely there is no mention of this enemy mine explosion in the war diary of 177 Tunnelling Company.

8 War diary of 1st Buffs 9th November 1915. WO95/1608

9 War diary of 16th Infantry Brigade for November 1915. WO95/1605.

10 102449 Sapper George Auty Chatt is commemorated on the RE Grave memorial to 177 Tunnelling Company and its attached infantry.

11 Private unpublished diary of Agner Dalgas.

CHAPTER TWO

JANUARY 1916

As 1916 dawned, the strength of the company had grown and was recorded as being 17 officers and 322 other ranks strong. At the Railway Wood sector on the 5th January the 17th (Northern) Division was relieved in the line by the men of the 17th Brigade which was attached to the 24th Division. The weather over the winter period depressed the men and played havoc with their work both above and below the ground. Lt Basil Sawers experienced the conditions at first hand:

"Conditions that first winter of 1915/16 were very uncomfortable. I don't suppose any troops anywhere else had the discomfort we had in the Ypres Salient. In the infantry no individual would stay more than two days. We had no reliefs. We were there all the time in the wet and the mud. The thing that held us together was the rum. No one knew what we were up against, so we could get anything we liked from stores. We managed to get an issue of rum every day. When the rum ration was being dished out, I would hold out my mug and look away so that he went on pouring! Don't know why we didn't get sciatica and lumbago, but we didn't. We lived in gum boots. Had a little Tamboule that winter in which the two officers had to live; 2 feet of water on the floor, blankets were sopping wet. One fellow claimed he had 35 days at a stretch up there. We only got back to back camp once in a while for a bath and clean underwear. The rest of the time we were plastered in mud. Gum boots were the only special clothing we had for the job – we wore an ordinary uniform."

A series of Dugouts was begun along Cambridge Road which ran just West of Railway Wood. This would eventually evolve into a huge system with multiple inclined entrances well capable of accommodating many hundreds of men underground, and would be linked to the ever growing system of workings being developed by the 177 under the Railway Wood sector. 2nd Lt Agner Dalgas' diary for January 1916 describes just how the company came about to start this dugout construction. It makes for some interesting reading:

During this month a dugout system had been started at Cambridge Road. The honour of introducing underground dugouts falls to Lieut Campbell. The casualties in Cambridge Road support line were rising by a fright and one day Campbell met the General commanding the Brigade holding that part of the front and said, "It is simply murder for no purpose General, you must do something." "But what am I to do?" asked he. "I will make you shell proof D/O system right here if you will give me the men for the labour." Thus was the first underground dugout started in Flanders.

The company was also involved in preparations for a possible offensive to have taken place in the Boesinghe sector. Originally held by the 49th (West Riding) Division, the front lines were taken over by the 14th (Light) Division, old friends of 177 who had recently moved from the Railway Wood sector. 177 were involved here in making ten shallow dugouts and laying Decauville narrow gauge railway from Bridge 6 on the Yser canal to Lancashire Farm.

Defensive workings number 6 and 8, situated side by side, located just inside the eastern tip of Railway Wood, progressed during the month with galleries being driven further under the ridge forming the protective network for the troops holding trenches on the surface. Working 8, at 27 feet deep, stretched out from under trench H20 was further developed. 8M, a left branch at 38 feet along 8A was driven out to 53 feet during the month and connected 8A to 8B.

At 7.30am on the 8th January listeners on duty in galleries 8F and 6D picked up suspicious noises suspected to be that of enemy mining. 17th Brigade HQ was alerted and informed of 177 Tunnelling Company's planned action. A camouflet was planned and 150 lbs of blastine was placed at the end of gallery 6E, a right branch at 50 feet along 6B. 20 feet of solid tamping was placed into 6E and 6B with the charge being fired at 7.30pm. The resultant explosion wrecked galleries 6B, 6E, 6D and wrecked 20 feet of 6WA. The damage in 6B was particularly bad in the part of the gallery that connected 6D to 8F. 6P, a left branch started at 10 feet into gallery 6H, connected with 8G and replaced gallery 6B. Miners at work repairing damage in gallery 8L, a left branch at 16 feet along 8F, were using a bore when they struck and released a pocket of gas. The gas must have formed a pocket as a result of the camouflet fired the evening before. The resultant release of gas then exploded but miraculously caused no casualties or did any damage.

The phenomena of these secondary explosions as a result of gas were reported periodically by tunnelling companies. The danger of carrying a naked light into a mine in which gas was known to be present in small quantities was not always appreciated. The gases formed as a result of the detonation of high explosives vary in their quantity and composition according to the types of explosive used. The gases generally formed are carbon monoxide, hydrogen and methane, sometimes known as Firedamp. All of these gases are combustible and if present in the proper proportion, explosive. Large quantities of these gases normally form where there has been an imperfect detonation. Methane is never formed at the time of explosion but results from the action of hydrogen on the oxides of Carbon when the gas rapidly cools in the galleries. In some of the secondary explosions investigated by tunnelling companies there was so little Carbon Monoxide present that canaries exposed to the atmosphere were unaffected. It was very common when these explosive gases were ignited, that they exploded some considerable distance away from the source of the primary detonation. In places where the gases are present in non-explosive percentages there were sometimes flashes of flames. There were reported cases of tunnellers suffering from burns and injuries as a result of secondary explosions underground. Generally the

41

effects of these gas explosions were limited to small areas as there was not sufficient gas to feed the flames to cause extensive explosions found elsewhere in coal mines where gas was being continuously formed by the distillation of coal dust.[1]

Gallery 6L, a left branch at 83 feet along 6A was pushed out to 85 feet and connected into 8L. 6G was worked on and pushed forward when the necessary manpower was available. By the end of the month it was 135 feet long. 6J, a left branch at 85 feet along 6G, was lengthened to 65 feet where a further left branch was started and labelled as 6R. 6N was a stepped incline to the surface located at 92 feet along 6G and broke the surface in a trench just south of the sunken road that ran up the side of Railway Wood. At the 50 feet deep, second level, of the number 6 workings, gallery 6WA had been wrecked back to the 72 feet

mark by the camouflet of the 8th January. This camouflet came in for some criticism from Lt Dalgas who was dubious as to whether sounds of German mining had been detected. His diary entry about this camouflet states:

> "...we blew a camouflet between 6 and 8 shafts. The blow was directed against supposed enemy mining. Personally I think it was wind. This was my first experience in the camouflet line."

Left and right branches were started at the 72 feet mark known as 6WC and 6WB respectively. 6WC was 20 feet long and 6WB was 62 feet long by the 23rd of January. Also begun at the end of 6WA was a stepped incline which went up into a chamber located along gallery 8G, in the number 8 workings at 27 feet deep. Another

Number 2 Crater today, located just a few metres north of the RE Grave Memorial. (Author's collection)

right branch along 6WA, at 13 feet, was started and pushed out to 59 feet by the 30th January. Known as 6WD, this gallery also had a right branch, at 59 feet, known as 6WP which was a stepped incline into 6G of the number 6 workings. The two levels of the number 6 workings were now connected by winze and stepped incline, with an incline from the deeper level connecting the number 8 workings.

Work also continued on the dugout just north of the Menin Gate. The dugout was located in the ramparts of Ypres. The ramparts, a design of the famous French military engineer, Vauban, surrounded a part of the town together with a moat. When they were constructed they contained a number of subway tunnels linking the town side of the ramparts to the moat side. These subways survive today and it was from within one that the main entrance of the Ramparts North dugout was started. Once the tunnellers had broken through the brick walls they drove a north running gallery about 240 feet in length. Off this gallery, facing west ran six other galleries and midway along each of these galleries a chamber was constructed. There was also a short gallery that ran north east and exited the dugout into the moat. The dugout was powered by a petrol driven single cylinder five horsepower generator which lit the dugout with eighty 25 watt light bulbs. The dugout was completed by the end of the month and was used to great extent by 177 T Coy as accommodation for the men whenever they finished their shifts at the front and also as a Brigade Headquarters. Even though the last tunneller left this dugout over ninety years ago, the main entrance is still visible today, located two

thirds of the way along the subway carved out of the brick.

Getting the men from the relative safety of their billets to the front was a learning curve for the company in its early days. Until the dugout under Railway Wood was finished there was no accommodation for the men at the front. At the end of their eight hour shifts they would make their way back towards Ypres to the Ramparts North dugout, which could accommodate 180 of the tunnellers. Lt Basil Sawers describes the situation:

"To the right of the Menin Gate there are a lot of dugouts which we built. Eventually Brigade HQ had one patch and we kept our men in the other patch. At that time there was no living accommodation up in the line. Our men had to live in the ramparts at Ypres, and walk up at dusk and come back at dawn. Those were the two shifts. Eventually when we got organised we had dugouts in the support line where the men lived…That first winter there was nothing like that, we had to work, with the men in Ypres. Then we had trouble on the roads, people getting knocked off. We worked out a system that saved a lot of casualties. Each man knew which face he had to be at and when, and so long as he was there at the right time we didn't mind when or how he got up. So they used to travel up and down in little packs of two or three… just to prove that I wasn't frightened every second night when I was in charge of Railway Wood, I used to walk up through Ypres, up Menin Road to Railway Wood, look around and have a drink or two and then go back before dawn."

Life in the Ramparts dugout, sharing with a Brigade HQ, was far from comfortable. The tunnellers were a far different breed of man compared with the pre-war regular or his TF counterpart. At times Brigade HQ was at odds with the lack of discipline and respect shown by the tunnellers. Lt Sawers continues:

"Some of the Generals, old timers, nearly had heart failure at the lack of discipline. They would drive past men living in the ramparts at Ypres and who used to spend the day sitting in the road in front of the dugouts. When the parade of generals went past on its way to Brigade HQ, which was on the same road, not one of the men would move or salute. There were reports back, but we were General HQ troops and could tell any Brigadier or Divisional Commander to go to hell and get away with it! I remember one particular case. Some enthusiastic Brigadier came in for the first time and insisted that I should bring in the maps of our tunnelling business. We had an unwritten law that the maps should never leave the back camp. So I explained gently that we never let the maps go as far afield as Brigade HQ. He went up in the air and insisted that I bring them in. So I told the boss and he got straight through to General Headquarters and the General got rapped over the knuckles. We could always get through first to GHQ with our story before any complaint sifted through Brigade and Divisional HQ."

The lack of respect shown by the tunnellers may have seemed at odds to those who realised the need for a disciplined force due to the nature and conditions the men were working in. But to many in the tunnelling companies, they had no time for parade squares or marching around. They were here to get underground and destroy the enemy. Basil Sawers continues:

"Our men had never done any time on the square and nobody bothered about training them up. All we cared about was their performance at the face. At the back camps so long as they kept out of the hands of the Military Police no one cared what they did?"

January also saw the establishment of a forward HQ for 177 up at the front line, utilising both a surface dugout and the first dugout chamber to be completed of the new system off Cambridge Road. Lt Dalgas diary continues:

At the same period we moved our HQ up to the front line (within 20 feet) in a surface D/O. There was also one D/O completed at Cambridge Road. Before the first D/O could be a gallery, two incline staircases to the surface had to be constructed. We used this first dugout ourselves as sleeping quarters.

January also saw the death of 86953 LCpl John Hayward, 47 years old and from Middlesex, who died at home of wounds received earlier at the front.[2]

FEBRUARY 1916

February 1916 saw the company's pace of

work increase. Preparations continued for a planned offensive to the north east of the Salient, in the Boesinghe sector, and the month saw 177 supporting both the 14th and the 20th (Light) Divisions. The Decauville light railway track started the month before was completed and now ran as far as Lancashire Farm. 130 feet of 7 feet deep revetted trench was constructed in the area and test bores carried out in the vicinity to test ground for future use. However, the strength of the company was not invincible, in fact at the beginning of February it was 19 officers and 305 men strong, and work in the Boesinghe sector was stopped by 177 to allow them to carry on with their ever-increasing scheme of tunnels under the Railway Wood sector. The war diary for the month shows a return, for the first time, of the amount of infantry attached to 177 for labouring and other tasks. As mentioned before there were still plenty of men who had mining experience in the ranks of the infantry. Units, when not in the line, could be used for a variety of tasks, including being attached to tunnelling companies as labour. The many tons of soil and clay dug out by tunnellers and placed in sandbags needed removing from the galleries. In some cases the bags were used to beef up defensive positions on the surface. Sometimes, due to the secret nature of tunnelling work, the spoil was taken some distance away before being disposed of, normally under the cover of darkness. At the beginning of February, 177 had 6 officers and 352 other ranks attached to it from other units. As divisions holding the trenches on the surface relieved each other and took their places in the front and went back for periods of rest, so too did the units that were attached to 177 for labouring tasks.

German miners were also active under Railway Wood sector supporting their surface troops. On 14th February, the British trenches from H13 to H19 were very heavily shelled from 12.45pm. 73rd Infantry Brigade was holding the line at the time and the whole brigade 'stood to' expecting the bombardment to be followed up with infantry attacks. At 6.30pm that evening the Germans blew two mines in front of trenches H16 and H18. The men of B and D Companies of the 9th Royal Sussex immediately went forwards and captured both craters. The Germans later made a failed attempt to capture both craters. The CO of the 9th Sussex, Lt Col J Langdon DSO showed remarkable gallantry and coolness that night, even giving three cheers to the retreating German attackers! Lt Eric MacNair, a platoon commander with the 9th Royal Sussex, was awarded a VC for his actions that night[3]. That night the 103rd Field Company, Royal Engineers came forward and consolidated the crater with the 9th Royal Sussex linking the crater with trenches back to H16. A bombing post was established in the crater opposite trench H18. Overall, the 9th Royal Sussex sustained fifty casualties, with one platoon of D Company being buried alive as a result of the enemy mine blows; the remainder were sustained during the capturing of the craters.[4]

On 25th February the 6th Division returned to the Railway Wood sector when the 16th Infantry Brigade of the Division took over from 73rd Infantry Brigade of the 24th Division. The Brigade were not slack in adapting back to their old haunt and had patrols out in No Man's Land almost immediately gathering intelligence on the Germans. One such patrol carried out by 2nd

Lieutenant Gordon of B Company, 1st Buffs, left trench H20 at 12.30am, and patrolled No Man's Land to report on the strength of the German barbed wire defences. As they carried out a listening watch in the vicinity of the German lines, it became apparent that the Germans had utilised the crater blown under them by 177 on the 25th September 1915, turning it into an advanced listening post.

A section of the company was also employed just to the south of Railway Wood, at Hooge, where on 19th July 1915, Lt Cassels of 175 Tunnelling Company, had blown the well-documented Hooge mine forming 'Cassels Crater'. 177 had been trying to sink a shaft from the cellar of a house ruin and were severely hampered when shellfire had filled their shaft with brickwork from the ruin. Another cellar was chosen, but this time the shaft was wrecked, again by shellfire, when just 4 feet deep. It was in the course of this shaft sinking that Sjt H Byles of the company rescued a number of men from the wrecked shafts whilst under heavy shellfire. This action, coupled with a successful attempt not long after to bring up rations to the front whilst under heavy shellfire, would get Sjt Byles the DCM[5]. Third time lucky, another cellar was chosen, just off Grafton Street trench at map reference I.18.b.2.6. Some time was taken to reinforce and strengthen their position here and on 21st February sinking of the shaft commenced. This working became known as working number 21 and was 16½ feet deep by the end of the month. The dugout scheme under Railway Wood continued to be worked on. It now consisted of a number of subterranean passages about 6 feet high and 3 feet wide off which were constructed rooms, the whole system, like

their offensive/defensive workings, being lined with wood. By February, the dugout had at least four inclined stairways and a shaft serving it from Cambridge Road and a further two stepped inclines that served it off West Lane communication trench that ran up through the wood connecting to the front line.

The defensive, double layered, number 6 working saw a flurry of activity during the month. On the first level, at 27 feet deep, saw 6G, the right branch at 58 feet along 6A pushed out to 170 feet. Most of the work, however, took place at the lower level, 50 feet deep. Within the first week of the month 6WB, a right branch at 72 feet on 6WA, was out to 80 feet. Off 6WB, at the 80 feet mark, gallery 6WF, a left branch was out to 15 feet long. 6WG, a right branch off 6WB at 80 feet, was 44 feet long towards the end of the month. It also connected to gallery 6WH. 6WE, a left branch at 72 feet on 6WA was 87 feet long towards the end of the month. 6WD a right branch at 13 feet on 6WA, was out 88 feet. 6WH, a left branch at 88 feet along 6WD, was driven out to 84 feet and as stated above connected to 6WG. 6WJ, a right branch at 42 feet along 6WE, was out to 34 feet just before the middle of the month. Interestingly, 6WZ, a left branch at 70 feet along 6WD, was 7 feet long, when a chamber 6 feet high, 5 feet wide and 10 feet 6 inches was constructed. In this chamber another winze, known as 6Z, was sunk. This internal shaft was constructed out of steel caissons, sections of steel about 18 inches high, bolted together to make a circular shaft, three pieces making up a circular section. The internal diameter of the shaft was 5 feet 4 inches. More caissons were bolted onto one another as the shaft was sunk. By 20th February, 6Z was down 35½ feet. A gallery was driven away on a north easterly heading of 76 degrees and by the 27th of the month, 6ZA as it was known, had been driven out 43 feet.

A new working was also started by the company during February under the sector. In the vicinity of trench H16, a dugout completed by one of the RE Field Companies of the 6th Division, was hit by shellfire and destroyed on the 23rd of the month. A new site was chosen by 177, 300 feet west of H16 and 30 feet north of Muddy Lane communication trench and on the 28th sinking of the shaft commenced.

MARCH 1916

March 1916 sees a slight change to the war diary held by 177. A new form, the Weekly Mine Report, brainchild of Major Henry Hudspeth RE, 171 Tunnelling Company, was implemented by Inspector of Mines at GHQ for all tunnelling companies to use. It allowed for the war diary to contain both information relevant to the running of the company, written onto the war diary, Army Form C2118 and also the information relevant to the progress of the construction of workings and dugouts, written onto Army Form W3404. The new form also required a greater amount of technical information regarding the workings to be included[6]. The company also sadly reported the death of one of its Canadian officers on 6th March when Lt Robert MacFarlane, a mining engineer graduate of McGill University, died of wounds received earlier in the day. He was returning to Ypres from the Railway Wood sector when he took a chance crossing open ground and was hit by German machine gun fire. Robert MacFarlane had arrived on

the Western Front in February 1915 and had previously served as a Sergeant with the 1st Canadian Division Cycling Company before transferring over to the Royal Engineers.[7]

The Railway Wood dugout scheme was continued with some slight alteration to the plan in hand. A few extra dugouts were added to the plan and the total footage removed here during March was 400 feet. By the end of March over 200 men could be accommodated in this unfinished dugout system. Gallery 6G, at the 27 feet deep layer of the number 6 workings, was worked on for sixteen days during March. This 4 feet 6 inch high, 2 feet 3 inch wide gallery (size of the inside timbers) was driven out to 409 feet by the 19th of the month. At this footage mark at map reference Sheet 28 NW I.12.a.1.0 the continuation of the gallery became known as 11G. The number

The grave of 2nd Lt Robert MacFarlane at Lijssenthoek Military Cemetery. (Author's collection)

47

11 workings were born 20 feet under trench H18. Not to be confused with the old number 11 workings at map reference I.11.b. 8.9, abandoned since November 1915. In the deeper 50 feet level of the number 6 working, gallery 6WK, a right branch at 94 feet along 6WE was pushed out to 30 feet by the 26th of the month. It was only worked at odd times during the month and when pushed out the work was done cautiously by those on listening duty within the gallery.

The 16th Infantry Brigade still held the front lines around Railway Wood. Continuous patrols gathering intelligence on the Germans and general harassment paid off on the nights of 6th and 7th March when Lt Davies of the 1st Buffs, noticed an interesting point of observation:

"The enemy crater is strongly wired on either flank, but in the centre – at the point nearest to us – there appears to be little or none, though it may be concealed under the lip of the crater. The ground everywhere is muddy, especially on the left of the crater, but not so bad on the right between the shell holes. A point of interest is that steam can be seen rising from the enemy shafts on a frosty night, in the light of star shells. While out, I imagined this to be smoke, but on my return I noticed the same phenomenon, over our saps, and then I realised this excellent method of locating mine shafts."

His report also stated:

"Shortly before midnight on 6th March, a 'Presnail' rifle grenade (Mills grenade) was fired into the crater in the German lines opposite H20. This burst like shrapnel and caused a good deal of confusion and crying out in the crater. The Germans retaliated by throwing bombs, which did not reach much further than their own wire, and were silenced by rifle fire from our trenches. Later on another 'Presnail' grenade was fired with similar effect. This led to a grenade duel between our bombers and those of the Germans. The German grenades, as before, did not range much beyond their own wire – while ours went right into the crater. At the end of half an hour the Germans gave up the contest. We had no casualties. Judging from the noise they made, the enemy probably had many." [8]

Via the light of exploding bombs, a patrol was later able to get a visual picture of the inside of the crater. With little to no wire defences around the crater itself they observed what looked like a covered gallery protruding from the south side of the crater. This was suspected to be the cover for either the entrance to an underground gallery or a shaft head to a mining system. [9] The useful information gleaned by these British patrols would be passed back to Brigade HQ who, in turn, would request for harassing artillery fire to seek out and destroy these German workings. The success of this intelligence gathering enterprise also went a long way to raise the morale of troops holding the line. As far as they were concerned, No Man's Land was 'ours' and that they were more than capable of interfering with any work the enemy did in it or near it. One of these barrages onto the suspected enemy workings fell on 12th March. 16th Infantry Brigade was almost certain that the barrage

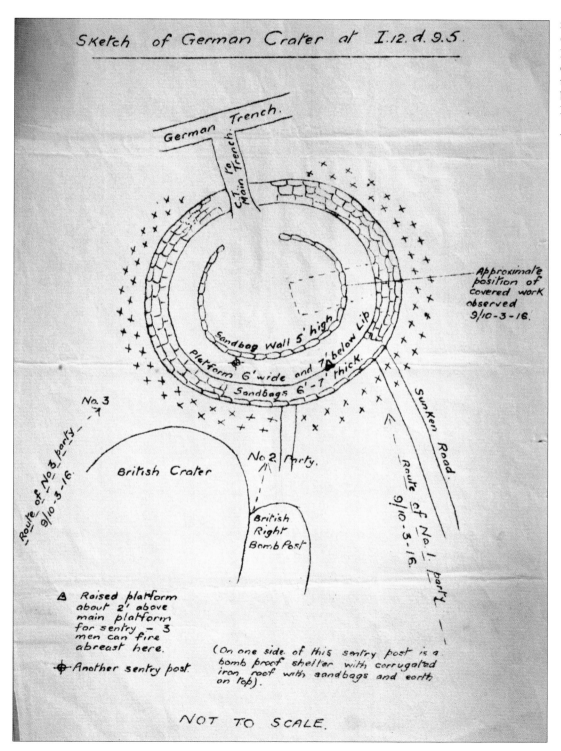

Sketch of the German-held British mine crater following the trench raid by the 1st East Kents in March 1916. (TNA. WO95/1608)

Railway Wood
No 6 workings
joining No
11 workings,
March
1916. (TNA.
WO95/404)

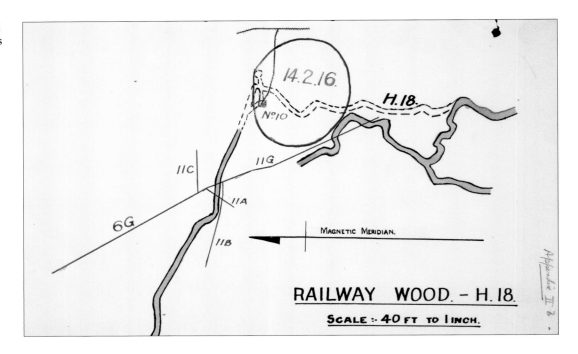

had done some damage as the Germans retaliated by shelling the British front line trenches around Railway Wood with an estimated 1500 shells. Miraculously, casualties were few.[10]

Underground, the new gallery 11G, now serving the number 11 workings was worked on for 12½ days and by the end of the month was 150 feet long. At the point where 6G became 11G a right branch known as 11A was begun. This gallery was 5 feet 6 inches high and 2 feet wide and was an inclined stairway that led to the surface. Gallery 11B which was located 16 feet to the right along 11G, 4 feet 6 inches high by 2 feet 3 inches wide, was 57 feet long by the end of the month and had been worked on for 4 days. Gallery 11C, a left branch at 399 feet along 6G and the same dimensions as 11B, was 43 feet long by the end of the month.

On 9th March two attached infantrymen were killed in action. March also saw

a change in the divisions holding the front at the Railway Wood sector. On the 16th of the month, the 16th Infantry Brigade was relieved in the line by the 3rd Guards Brigade of the Guards Division. With the 4th Grenadier Guards holding the line from the Bellewaerde Beek northward to the Ypres to Roulers railway, the 3rd Guards Brigade set about its task of improving and beefing up the defences around Railway Wood. The importance of the position, overlooking the German lines to the north and south was not lost on the men. An effort was also taken to either beef up defences in or incorporate the existing mine craters, in the vicinity of the British front, into their system of defences.

The importance of the role of 177 Tunnelling Company in their defensive and offensive mine workings was given as a brief to the General Officer Commanding the Division, Major General G.P.T. Fielding, on a visit to 3rd Guards Infantry Brigade

HQ just after the relief took place. It was stated that due to the secret nature of the tunnellers' work, only the GOC of the division and his general staff will be made aware of offensive mining schemes. It was of course different for defensive mining operations where it was encouraged that tunnelling officers would brief the Brigade Commander under whom they were working, at least once a week on defensive mining matters. Locally, on the ground, the tunnelling officers in charge of the mining sectors were briefed to inform battalion commanders of units holding the lines of any German mining being carried out and any actions taken by themselves. Orders went down as far as the lowly Tommy holding the front: If any enemy mining was suspected, i.e. heard or sandbags with blue clay seen lining the enemy's lines, then the situation had to be reported with haste.[11] During the Guards Division's tenure at Railway Wood, men from the Pioneer Battalion, 4th Coldstreams, were to be attached to 177 Tunnelling Company for labouring duties, with Lt A. Dickinson and 82 other ranks from the battalion performing that task.[12]

Also that day, 2nd Lt Oscar Earnshaw joined 177 Tunnelling Company. He had qualified as a mining engineer and worked at Hamsterley Colliery, Amble, Co Durham. Leaving behind a wife and two young children he went to war. He had transferred and was commissioned into the RE from the Northumberland Hussars Yeomanry. He described his initial observations of 177's officers, their forward billets (Ramparts Dugout) and the conditions of the Railway Wood sector and the fatal wounding of Lt McFarlane in a letter home to his dad written on the day he arrived:

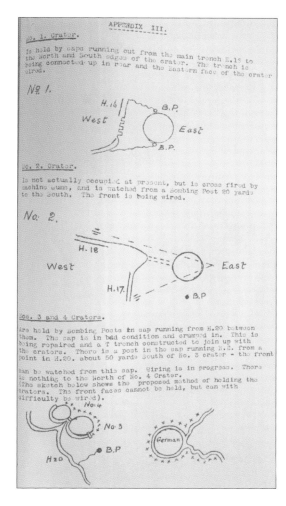

Intelligence report from the Guards Division war diary describing the German utilisation of craters opposite Railway Wood. (TNA. WO95/1191)

"I am at the company billet which is a few miles behind the firing line but not outside the range of shellfire, a few have passed over our heads, but I suppose there is never any dropped here. I shall probably be going up to the trenches either tomorrow or the following day.

The officers here are so far a very decent set of fellows, but all strangers to me, so I won't say too much yet about them. There are three Canadians, one from South Africa and one from China, and also a Dane.

Obituary of Lt
Oscar Earnshaw.
(Author's
collection)

The quarters are most comfortable, each officer has his own cubicle and bed, and the mess is well lit and more comfortable than at the base.

We have a jolly fine gramophone with some glorious records, even some from Griegg, so judging by the taste for decent music, it says something for my brother officers.

I am given to understand, in fact I knew before I came up, that it is practically the hottest part of the line, not at present, but taken throughout the whole war, there has been more

doing here, than in the most of places, but in casualties this company has been extremely lucky. The first actual fatal casualty amongst the officers occurred the day before yesterday and that happened on the road home. He tried to run over open country where a machine gun was playing the deuce."

In a letter written on the 11th he described how he got up to the Railway Wood sector for his first stint as a section officer and what conditions were like in the sector:

"I came up at 6pm on the 8th and stay seven days, and then go down for seven, and so on.

We left camp in motor lorries and came as far as possible, that is, just outside machine gun range, in the dark of course, we would not dare have come so far in daylight, then after dismounting we got into the communication trench, and walked to our dug out.

Our dug outs are very nice indeed, although there are drops of water knocking about just now, yet we are not badly off.

There is quite a lively fusillade going on at present, our artillery are shelling, and of course the Hun is replying on our dug out. The canaries seem to be enjoying it, and are chirping away, I can't say I am.

I had a lively time last night, the Bosche started shelling our communication trench as the relief was coming up, they caused a few casualties, and one man was brought to me suffering with shell shock, and I wishing to steady him up, gave him a tot of rum, after which he got worse, instead of better, and went mad and it took four of us to get him strapped down on a stretcher, and carried back to hospital.

I'm afraid I'd be committing a breach of honour were I to tell you what is going on in the mine, all I can say is that it is well laid out, and I can't think it possible for Fritz to get through, without hearing him, and blowing him to the other end of his workings.

You'd laugh if you could see us now, absolutely no swank; we look more like Corporation men than British Army officers. We wear rubber thigh boots, a leather waistcoat, a black rubber reefer coat, with a tommies webb belt, to which is attached your revolver, also we always carry a smoke helmet in a satchel. We wash about every second day, and shave twice a week, if we are lucky.

We work in shifts of eight hours each, there are a few of us three second lieutenants, and one Lieut in charge. That is the three shift system again. I am in the night shift from 4pm to midnight. It's very interesting work, and when all your 'marrers' are miners, it's not so very dangerous, the great thing to do is to be cool and collected, and never let the men think you have 'got the wind up' and never to allow them to get it up either."

Yet another new working was started by 177 in March. Working number 16, an inclined shaft set in timber 5 feet 6 inches high and 3 feet wide was driven to a depth of 23 feet in a week, including the construction of a small pump chamber and sump for the shaft. This working was located just off Mud Lane communication trench, map

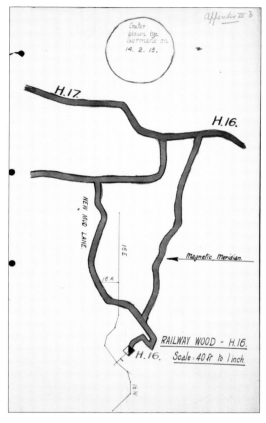

Railway Wood No 16 Workings, March 1916. (TNA)

reference I.11.d.9.7, where it became New Mud Lane communication trench which joined up with Junction trench; a set of two support trenches running parallel separated only by a few yards. In turn this trench joined the front roughly at the junction of trenches H16 and H17. At the bottom of the shaft a gallery was broken away, set in timbers 4 feet 6 inches high and 2 feet 3 inches wide. This gallery known as 16E ran up to the front line, worked on for twenty days of the month it was 180 feet long by the month's end. Gallery 16W, also started from the bottom of the shaft, ran west away from the front. It was set in timbers 5 feet 6 inches high and 2 feet wide and by the 26th of the month was 310 feet long. At the

53

2nd Lt Charles Geoffrey Boothby, seen here in the uniform of the South Staffordshire Regiment. Geoffrey transferred to the Royal Engineers and was posted to 177 Tunnelling Company in February 1916. He was killed on 28th April in gallery 11H with Cpl Roland Brindley and Sapper William Spooner following the blowing of a German Camouflet. Their bodies remain in gallery 11H and the men are commemorated at RE Grave, Railway Wood. (Photo courtesy Arthur Stockwin)

end of this gallery was an inclined stairway leading to the surface. Work along 16W on a series of dugouts also began. A left branch at 112 feet along 16E was started as an inclined stairway to the surface coming out in New Mud Lane communication trench. It was crumped in by shellfire on the 25th March, but repaired and by the end of the month was 16 feet long.

The month also saw the arrival of another officer, recently transferred to the Royal Engineers. Second Lieutenant Charles Geoffrey Boothby, known as Geoffrey, was posted to 177 Tunnelling Company, arriving on 18th March along with Second Lieutenant Montague Wright. When 2nd Lt Boothby arrived at 177 he had not long celebrated his 21st birthday. He had been studying medicine at Birmingham University when the war broke out and had left his studies to be commissioned into the South Staffordshire Regiment. He

arrived in France in July 1915 with the 8th Battalion and it wasn't long before he found himself working with a tunnelling company as attached infantry. He was an officer with the 51st Brigade Mining Section along with Montague Wright, part of the 17th (Northern) Division, initially working with 172 Tunnelling Company. Geoffrey Boothby took to his new work like a duck to water. He was educated at Clayesmore School, and kept in touch with his old Headmaster, Alex Devine. He wrote to Alex Devine, the letter later being published in the school magazine, describing his new job and recent experiences:

"You will be pleased to hear that I have a 'manual labour' billet with a vengeance. All of us here are manual labourers to a certain extent, but I have gone one better. My job is that of Brigade Mining Officer, and, together with another officer and a handful of mud-plastered villains, I endeavour to outwit the wily Bosche underground, and now and again elevate that personage sky high with a well placed charge of powder. The job is rather interesting and affords at long intervals quite exciting little periods as instanced by a short, sharp strafe we enjoyed a couple of weeks ago. We took over several shafts from another Brigade Mining Section and while examining two galleries came upon a microphone, stuck in the wall of an old heading, which was half full of water. Further exploration showed that the Hun had connected his gallery up with ours and had established a listening post at the junction. We found a complicated electrical instrument and a water pump with which he used to pump the water from his gallery into ours. Well, we left these and went to hustle around above ground and get explosives ready. Then three of us, an RE officer, a Corporal and I went down to bag the thing. Mr Hun was ready for us, though, and let off rapid with a revolver at 6 yards range. These galleries are 4 feet by 3 feet, so this was a wee bit unhealthy, especially as the Bosche was completely concealed behind a right angled corner. So after firing one shot with my rifle, I retired ungracefully, to the next corner, where together with the Corporal, I built a barricade and laid a charge, which the RE officer fired. This little job took us four hours and was rather exciting, as the Hun was doing precisely the same thing. However, we got ours off first, and I'm afraid the Bosche was decidedly an 'also ran' on that occasion.

Otherwise mining is a peaceful business. We dig a bit, and listen a bit and everything is very nice … until we hear the Bosche digging too."[13]

By the time he arrived at 177, he was actually an old hand as had been attached to them for five months. He seemed very happy with his transfer to the RE and wrote to his sweetheart, 18-year-old Edith Ainscow:

"I'm feeling awfully bucked tonight. My transfer is through at last & I'm a real RE. I have been posted to the company I have been with for the last five months, so my address will be the same – minus 8th S. Staff attached. Did I tell you that my pay is now as regal as Arthur's*, i.e. sixteen bob a day. I feel a fearful 'knut'**, Royal Engineers, eh what! Think I must start a monocle, but perhaps it would be rather awkward in the mines, so I won't."[14]

*Arthur was a friend in the RFC

**Jocular spelling of 'nut' = 'dandy' 1911. OED

Work over at Hooge continued on the number 21 workings off Grafton Street trench. The 24th Division was relieved in the line by the 3rd Canadian Division. The shaft, 4 feet 6 inches square was sunk in timber to 23 feet deep. A sump and a small stage located up the shaft as a pump relay was also constructed with a vertical ladder to give the tunnellers access. A gallery was broken away from the shaft and labelled 21DO1, which ran under the Menin Road. A right Branch at 50 feet off 21DO1, using the Menin Road above as extra head cover and bursting protection for shells that would strike the ground above, ran another gallery, 21DO2. Dugouts were constructed off this gallery and a total of 10½ days were worked on the gallery and dugouts. Another gallery was broken away from the base of the shaft. Gallery 21A ran north for a short distance and then turned half right and ran north east towards the front. By the end of the month it was 100 feet long and at 27 feet, had met and crossed Lt Cassel's old gallery that led out to the old Hooge mine. When the tunnellers struck the old gallery they had an inrush of water from the old system. As there was only one eight-hour shift per twenty-four hours working on the system, three days of work were lost due to the water difficulties met when they struck

Plan of Grafton Street workings at Hooge, March 1916. (TNA)

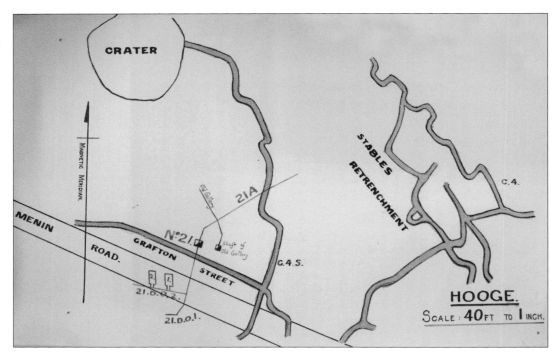

the old gallery. Twenty-five feet of the old gallery was cleaned out and ready to be utilised in the new system.

Within the area of responsibility of the 3rd Canadian Division, 177 were also tasked to assist 175 Tunnelling Company with the construction of shallow workings at Sanctuary Wood. It was a connecting gallery between two shafts known as shafts 1 and 2 under trenches B3 and B4. Like other areas in the Salient, water was a real problem for the tunneller. When the work was taken over from 175 at midnight on 14th March, 177 continued pumping out the workings and carrying out listening work. In some cases the galleries that 177 had taken over required complete retimbering. The system was only 12 feet deep and was set in timbers 4 feet high and 2 feet 6 inches wide. 177 worked in this system for a total of ten days during March digging out a further

70 feet of gallery in the yellow clay. Lt Oscar Earnshaw was one of the section officers supervising the work in Sanctuary Wood. Writing to his father on 20th March he described what was happening and how he had just survived a close call:

"I have already been in two parts of the line, and I am quite given to understand that when I go up again I am going a few more miles further south, but not lucky enough to get out of the Salient.

I had a lucky five minutes the other day. I was coming down the communication trench which the Hun has ranged almost to an inch and he had 'a sausage', otherwise an observation balloon, when all at once, he commenced to straff with a few whiz bangs, which burst quite close to me, Jove you should have seen how I sprinted down the trench, I'm sure

I made a record, for he was following us up with his shell, and we jolly well had to move 'some' fortunately we beat him in the end."

His father had obviously described to Oscar in a letter written to him his own description of what he thought of the horrors of war. This had obviously niggled Oscar as his reply, given by only those who were there can know, and described his own feelings of the conditions and pressure on the men:

"I admire your description of the horrors of war, but it is a long, long way short of the real thing. No one can possibly form even a remote idea of what it is like except those who have actually seen it, it's Hell, or if possible worse than Hell. I cannot possibly describe my feelings on first coming into it. One sees all but must not show his feelings, or what would be the effect on one's men, you've got to shut your eyes and grind your teeth. The whole of the Salient has been fought over time and time again until the whole place is one immense graveyard through which our new lines have been made. Fancy going down a trench and seeing a leg sticking out of the ground in one place, then perhaps walking on and seeing an arm or a hand in another, such sights one sometimes does actually meet with.

We opened an old gallery the other day from which a crater had been blown, what we found is better not described, it was sickly enough to look at and remove, that I DO know.

I have got fairly well accustomed to shellfire now, but familiarity DOES NOT breed contempt, altogether for there comes a time when a man has had so much of it that his nerves get weaker and weaker until he gets worse than he was on his first day out."

Back at 177 Tunnelling Company's HQ opposite the drive to Château Louvie, a shaft, 7 feet by 5 feet was sunk to 35 feet deep, as part of an experimental mine. The work here progressed slowly due to manpower being needed elsewhere at the front. This working would form part of the Second Army Mine School when it was formed and it was used to instruct men in the art of listening.

APRIL 1916

April would be a trying month for 177 Tunnelling Company. Again the issue of manpower was high on the list. At the beginning of the month the company had 21 officers and 323 men on its books with 12 officers and 522 from attached infantry to help with mining and labouring tasks. The British lines were facing constant threat of shell and mortar fire and also trench raiding by German soldiers. One of these raids materialised at the beginning of the month and saw Lt Oscar Earnshaw and a shift of men called into the trenches to aid in the defence of the line. He describes what happened and their defence of the trenches in a further letter to his father on the 4th April:

Dear Dad
I came up to the trenches again on the 30th Ultimo and have just won a glorious attack wherein I had the time of my life, but let me add I'm not too keen

57

for another like it for a few weeks more.

It started last night. I was just going to sit down and scrawl off a few lines to you when our adversaries opened out with a fine display of shells, trench mortars, bombs, rifle grenades, hand grenades and goodness knows what else. Things came down and burst almost as thick as rain and made my dug out rock and rock until I thought it must come down.

Well, I may as well be candid, I did get the wind up somewhat, but managed to keep my head sufficiently to get round and report myself and my noble band of heroes to the OC trench. He asked me to get my men out of the mine, and get to a certain point of the line which I did, as coolly as possible at the time scared to death.

Anyhow we got there and there we lay for 2½ hours solid with this glorious racket going on above and around us, sand bags and all manner of things hurtling about. Gee it was exciting and what made matters worse was the fact that the people occupying the trenches also had the wind up. They were a new lot just out and getting their baptism of fire.

All at once the thing shut up and someone shouted 'Here they come' then we all jumped and got our guns going and bombs and the machine guns didn't forget either. Jove it was fine the way those boys stood up and worked the bolt and the trigger, my revolver soon had to be charged up again.

Well he started over pretty thick but only 15 huns reached our trench, some of them jumped onto a bayonet, and some got it later anyhow. We only got one live prisoner, and the remainder went west. He got the surprise of his life; I guess he thought we would all have been scared stiff.

The excitement was terrible, no one can form the least idea of the feeling that comes over one at a time like that, but the reaction is not so good. Today I'm as jumpy as possible; a bomb fairly scares the life out of one. I hope nothing happens tonight.

Think I'll manage to get home on the 13th alright. Hope everyone is in the pink at home. Love to all.
Your affect. Son
Oscar

It is actions like this that hammer home the old adage that every soldier, regardless of his or her cap badge is a soldier first and a tradesman second.

The experimental mine working system back at 177's HQ near Proven suffered low on the list of priorities and no work was done on it until the 26th of the month. A shaft 7 feet long and 5 feet wide was sunk to 35 feet deep and a gallery driven out 33 feet. Along this gallery was a series of steps descending a further 16 feet. A right branch at this lower level was driven out 10 feet.

177 were also to revisit the Yser Canal with orders to drive a subway under the canal within grid C25. Two shafts, both in steel caissons, 4 feet 10 inches in diameter, were sunk. The west bank shaft was 47 feet deep by 27th April and the east bank shaft was 46 feet deep by the 22nd of the month. These shafts were both sunk from within small chambers a few feet below the surface

and considerable work had to be done to dig the lead in galleries and shaft chambers. As the shafts were sunk they went through the various geological layers experienced by tunnellers in Flanders, running sand, sandy loam, bastard blue clay and then blue clay. Once at depth, both teams broke away from their shafts and commenced digging galleries that would meet. Initially both sides were using timber sets of 6 feet high and 4 feet wide, and as the galleries were driven towards and under the canal the timber sets shrank to 6 feet high and 3 feet wide. This was the third time that 177 had been employed on the banks of the Yser; both previous projects were abandoned mainly due to poor ground and problems with water. This time, with months of experience

behind them, it looked like success may be on their side.

Work continued on the Railway Wood dugouts scheme with tunnellers now able to sleep in the workings as they were constructing it. The scheme began to represent a series of streets off which were numerous dugouts that would accommodate soldiers and house various departments and branches of the units holding and supporting the front lines.

The dugout system would eventually connect with the number 6 workings. During April these workings were extended. At the 50 feet level, gallery 6WK was worked on at odd times by listeners and was 43 feet long by the month's end. Gallery 6ZA, which was the third level of the number 6

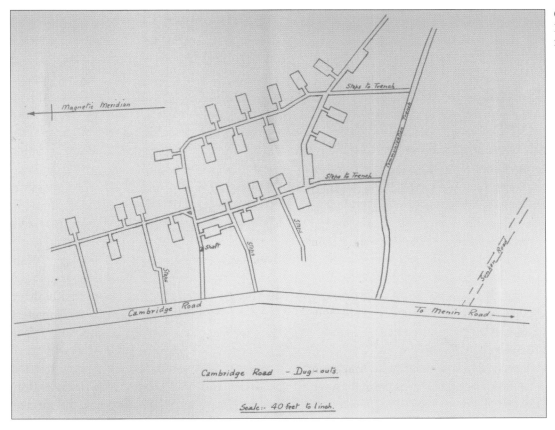

Cambridge Road Dugouts plan for April 1916. (TNA)

workings, 82 feet deep, was driven to 66 feet long in blue clay, by the end of the month. Maintenance and timbering work was carried out in this gallery by listeners during the month as they quietly went about their business listening and waiting for noises of the enemy. On 17th April one of 177's attached infantrymen was killed in action followed by another killed on the 21st April and two more on the 27th.

Gallery 11G, the gallery which connected the number 6 and number 11 workings, was driven out to 234 feet long by the 23rd April. The gallery struck very bad ground and the last 40 feet of it was filled with sandbags filled with spoil taken from a new gallery discussed later, 11H. A small linking gallery was also constructed to link galleries 11G and 11B. This small gallery, 11A, was used to ease the way of the underground trolley used by the tunnellers in galleries to facilitate the removal of spoil. These trolleys, with rubber tyres, running on a wooden mine track, were 'standard issue' to Second Army Tunnelling Companies. Earlier in the war it had been common practice to use trucks running on narrow rails, but narrow though they were, they still took up a lot of the width of the galleries. The wooden mine tracks, ran inside a 10½ inch wooden track. They possessed the great advantage of providing a less obstructed walking way.[15] Gallery 11B was 143 feet long by the 10th of the month. This gallery ran back from the front towards the support lines and was 20 feet deep. At the end of the gallery, a shaft was raised to the surface coming out in the trenches. On the surface a winch chamber was constructed off the trench with 40 feet of the trench being covered to hide it from enemy observation. Gallery 11C

ran in the opposite direction towards the front line. This 4 feet 6 inch high, 2 feet 3 inch wide gallery was driven out to 101 feet long. A 12 feet 'T' junction was constructed at the end of this gallery to be used as a listening post. Gallery 11D was utilised the same as 11C. 11D, a left branch at 148 feet along 11G, was set in timber the same dimensions as 11C. It had been driven out to 115 feet long by the 23rd of the month and a 12 feet 'T' junction placed at the end of the gallery. At 156 feet along 11G was a right branch along which gallery 11F was driven. A short distance into this gallery a chamber 12 feet long and 6 feet wide was dug in order to house another winze. At the end of 11F was a stepped incline up to the surface. The winze was labelled 11W and was a steel shaft 4 feet 10 inch in diameter. By the end of the month this winze was 32 feet deep, a total of 52 feet from the surface. A problem with water was also experienced in the last few feet of sinking the winze. Gallery 11E, a right branch at 236 feet along 11G was the same dimensions as 11C and was 94 feet long by the end of the month. Gallery 11H was a left branch at 245 feet along 11G. On 28th April it was 45 feet long. The gallery was dug to replace the end of gallery 11G, which had hit bad ground.

Just before 7am that morning enemy noises were heard by the tunnellers working in 11H. It was believed that the gallery was probably over a deeper enemy gallery. The suspicious noises were immediately reported to the duty officer, 2nd Lieutenant Alex Wilson, who stopped the work at the end of 11H and went to seek the advice of the OC, Major Bliss. On his way back to the working, 2nd Lt Wilson ran into Geoffrey Boothby and both men set off to investigate, discussing the situation as they went. 2nd Lt Boothby was of the frame of mind not to take any action until they were a hundred per cent sure of the situation. The reported German talking seemed to be unguarded, was this a sign that 177's men had not been heard by the Germans?

On arriving at 11H, both officers met up with Cpl Roland Brindley a 39-year-old, Staffordshire born collier, who had reported the noises initially. Roland had arrived in France with the BEF in January 1915 as an infantryman in the ranks of the York and Lancaster Regiment. He was one of the many miners, already in the ranks of the BEF that made the transfer over to the RE when Norton Griffiths' call went out. Sapper William Spooner, a 46-year-old miner from Cannock, Staffordshire, kept a listening watch whilst Geoffrey Boothby and Roland Brindley went forward. 2nd Lt Wilson, mindful that the gallery was only 4 feet 6 inches high and 2 feet 3 inches wide, stayed at the junction of 11G and 11H, to ensure quietness during the forthcoming period of listening. At 7.45am that morning the Germans blew a camouflet under 11G. The resultant explosion wrecked 11H and the last 40 feet of 11G. Geoffrey Boothby, Roland Brindley and William Spooner were killed and buried in the collapse of 11G.[16] 2nd Lt Wilson and four other ranks in 11G were badly wounded and evacuated. It must have been a huge blow to the morale of the company to lose three men in one day. Casualties of this number, whilst sad, would have been almost insignificant to an infantry unit holding or fighting in the line, to the tunnellers, fighting an almost invisible enemy underground as well as facing death from the usual evil means

on the surface, the loss was heavily felt. The devastating scene, immediately after the blow, 20 feet below the surface, was described by 2nd Lt Wilson in a letter he wrote whilst recovering from his wounds, to Geoffrey's mother, Alice Boothby:

"About half a minute later the explosion occurred and as soon as I could get clear of the wreckage I sent a man back to get help and went in to see the extent of the damage. I found the gallery entirely blocked for almost the whole length with earth and broken timbers, and was almost immediately made insensible by the fumes. From the severity of the explosion and the fact that he was so near the seat of it – apart altogether from the absence of air – your boy's death must have been immediate, and I know he would be ready."[17]

Lt Oscar Earnshaw wrote to his father describing the loss of Lt Boothby and the men:

"Only a sense of duty compels me to write in reply to your letter which I have just received. I certainly do not feel like writing letters as I have today lost my chum.

The Hun has blown a camouflet on us and killed my chum Lieut. Boothby, and wounded another of our officers Lieut. Wilson, also a number of our men have gone down, so I, and in fact, all of us, are somewhat down in the mouth tonight.

Poor old Boothby, he was a priceless chap. He got it full and so far has not been recovered, nor is there any hope of

Railway Wood No 11 Workings, April 1916. Gallery 11H and part of 11G are shaded over signifying the damage caused by the German camouflet on 28th April that killed Lt Boothby, Cpl Brindley and Spr Spooner. (TNA)

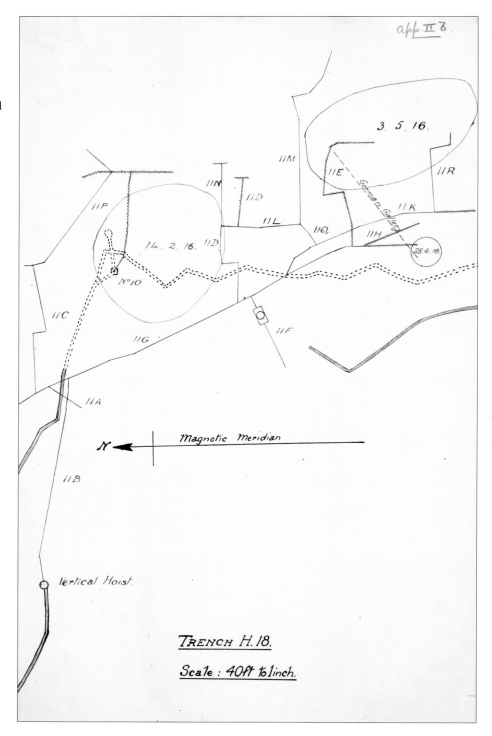

ever getting him out. He was right at the face listening, when the thing blew up. This has been a most disastrous week, we lost a tremendous number of men but all have been by shell or bullet until this lot today."

The OC, Philip Bliss, promoted to Major the month before, described Geoffrey and the impact of his loss in his letter to Geoffrey's mother:

"He was a most likeable man and a very keen and efficient officer, and both I and all my officers feel his loss very deeply, both on the social and military counts."

Work also continued through the month on the number 16 workings. Gallery 16W that ran from the bottom of the inclined shaft, away from the front line, saw a number of small dugouts constructed along it. Seven of these dugouts were finished during the month of which one was utilised as accommodation for officers, one as a store and the other five as other ranks accommodation. 16E, the gallery that ran from the bottom of the shaft, eastwards towards the front line, was 306 feet long by the end of the month. Time had been lost in this gallery due to difficulties with water and also the pump system they had in place to help alleviate the water situation. Gallery 16B a left branch at 203 feet along 16E was started and was a stepped incline to the surface, 5 feet 6 inches high and 2 feet wide, coming out along New Mud Lane communication trench just a few feet away from where it joined with Junction trench. Gallery 16C, another left branch off 16E, this time at 279 feet, was also a stepped

incline to the surface coming out in land between Junction trench and the front line, H17. This gallery had initially been planned to lead to a chamber for a winze off which to sink a lower level of the workings. Due to bad ground being met this was abandoned and the gallery used as a stepped incline instead. The gallery that would serve the chamber and winze was yet another left branch along 16E, at 313 feet. Work was carried out to widen the gallery into a chamber for the winze, but also, at the end of the gallery, to drive a stepped incline to the surface coming out just behind trench H17.

The Grafton Street workings at Hooge suffered, as they did the month previous, with a lack of manpower. Only one shift per

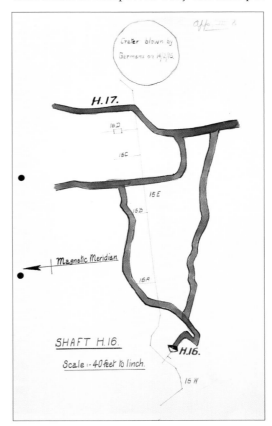

Railway Wood No 16 Workings, April 1916. (TNA)

63

day working seven to eight hours, mainly at night. Gallery 21A which ran out towards the front was 134 feet long by the 9th of the month. At 72 feet along 21A, a left branch, known as gallery 21B, was begun. It had the same dimensions as 21A, 4 feet 6 inches high and 2 feet 3 inches wide. By the end of the month this gallery was 56 feet long, the end of it being a stepped incline to the surface. Along the gallery, widening took place to build a chamber for a winze. Gallery 21C, a right branch along 21A, was driven to 88 feet by the end of the month. Worked also continued on 21DO1 raising the stepped incline to the surface and also with the dugouts under the Menin Road.

Over in Sanctuary Wood, under the 3rd Canadian Division, the company also continued on the works it had taken over from 175 Tunnelling Company the month before. Most of the work here was pumping

and listening but a new chamber, 12 feet long, 6 feet wide and 5 feet 6 inches high, was made within the old workings from which a new shaft was going to be sunk. This shaft, known as number 4, was made of steel caissons, 4 feet 10 inches in diameter and by the end of the month had been worked on for a week and ended up 15 feet deep. As it was being driven down, the tunnellers were going through soft running sand and water causing a great deal of messy slow work. The Section Commander Oscar Earnshaw described 'his mine' in a letter to his father:

"My mine is going well, we are commencing to sink a steel-lined shaft through running sand, which will be a trying and anxious business until we get down on hard ground, as we are commencing from the surface, and

Plan of Sanctuary Wood workings taken over from 175 Tunnelling Company, April 1916. (REL)

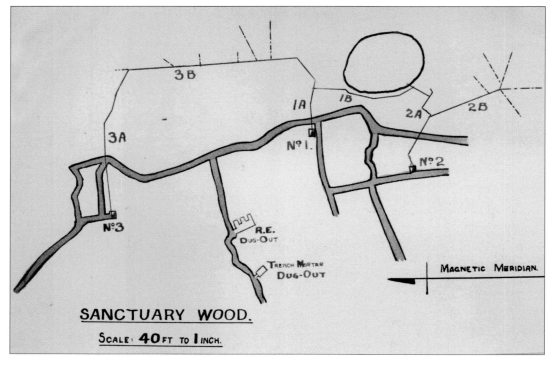

SANCTUARY WOOD.

SCALE: 40 FT TO 1 INCH.

we have difficulty in getting a strong enough way to force the rings down with 5-ton screw jacks. I dare not say any more about it, but will try to tell you all when I see you, perhaps it will surprise Mr Merivale that such a thing is being done in the front line trenches. A steel tubbed shaft 6 feet in diameter. I was at Dunkirk today getting the rings, bolts etc, and will be going to the trenches when the first lot arrives."

The troops also faced hazards in the supplying of material for the construction of the workings. Lt Earnshaw described one such incident in the Sanctuary Wood sector in a letter to his wife:

"By Jove the Canadians are some lads. I must tell you what they did for me one night last week.

I wired the brigade and asked for a carrying party of 120 men to bring up from our dump to the trenches, a matter of two miles, some material. Brigade wired back saying 120 men would report to me at 8 pm that night at the dump. I sent down a guide to lay out their loads and guide them back up. Well they turned up alright in charge of an officer, and the guide asked him to file the men past, and take up their loads straight on. Unfortunately, the sporty old Hun commenced to sling a few bangs there, just at that moment, so instead of 120 loads being taken only 75 filed up past, the remainder, including the officer had vanished, not hit but merely 'mizzled'. Well that wasn't too bad, but when that party arrived at our sap-head there were only ten men and only five had a load, the remainder having followed the officer I think. Well to say I was mad was to put it very mildly, I positively raved and reported the whole thing to my CO. He at once, or rather the following day, went down to Brigade HQ and 'straffed,' the old Brigadier went hairless, and rang up the Colonel of the regiment, where the men came from and gave a terrible dressing down and swore he'd do all manner of things if it happened again, but at the finish up he absolutely spoiled things by saying 'All right Dicky old boy I'll be round tonight and we'll split a bottle or two of scotch.' That's the sort of thing we've got to put up with, and at the same time make good in the pit, they are real hard nuts these sons of Canada."

MAY 1916

The arrival of May saw the weather improve dramatically allowing for the troops of the Guards Division holding the trenches to carry out much needed repair work. One of the main problems faced by them was that trenches H17 across to H19 did not connect. This was due to the weight of fire that had been put down on this area by the enemy and the poor weather over the previous winter had gone a long way to destroy the trenches in place. 177 were involved in discussions at 3rd Guards Brigade HQ in order to try and alleviate the situation. On 3rd May listeners on duty in the number 11 workings picked up sounds believed to be that of enemy miners. Further consultation was taken with 3rd Guards Brigade and it was agreed that 177 would blow a mine between the two trenches and then a raiding party would go over and capture the crater and secure it holding the eastern lip. A wiring party was to move forward and wire the eastern lip whist two working parties would begin to construct trenches from H17 and H19 linking via the crater.[18]

The mine charge, consisting of 2,500 lbs of ammonal was placed at the end of gallery 11E, 20 feet deep located about 100 feet forward of trench H18. It was fired at 8.30pm that evening. The resultant blow formed a crater about 100 feet in diameter and 20 feet deep. The eastern lip of the crater was estimated at being about 70 feet from the German front line. All of gallery 11E, which was located off to the left at 236 feet along 11G, was wrecked with the remaining section of 11G past the junction with 11E. On the surface a large portion of trench H18 was badly damaged, but was repaired at once. The waiting Guardsmen of the 4th Grenadier Guards were not slow to react after the explosion of the mine. Lt Payne-Gallwey, one NCO and ten men of 3 Company stormed the crater forming a covering party on the eastern lip. Lt Nairn, one NCO and ten men also of number 3 Company rushed forwards occupying the near edge of the crater and began placing pre-filled sandbags in position to give some form of cover when digging commenced. Lt Nairn then proceeded to guide in the digging party approaching from trench H17. Capt Layton, OC 3 Coy, after dispatching the three parties, then sent out the wiring party who advanced to a position just forward of Lt Payne-Gallwey's troops. He met up with the wiring party and they began work with the wire being brought to a point immediately in front of the centre of the crater. The Germans sent up flares and were quite visible in heavy numbers lining their trenches, throwing grenades which exploded some distance away from the wiring party although six or seven casualties were sustained by splinters. Lt Sloane-Stanley, OC of 2 Company sent forward a wiring and covering party from trench H19. Their wiring party got to within about 30 yards of the wire laid by 3 Company when they were opened up on by a machine gun and unable to advance the wire further. That night great progress was made and the entrenching teams succeeded in linking trenches H17 to H19. The next morning GOC 3rd Guards Brigade, Brigadier General F.J Heyworth CB, DSO,[19] visited the work done the previous night and was greatly pleased. He forwarded on a letter of congratulations to the 4th Grenadier Guards:

"… I myself personally inspected the crater this morning, and was enabled to walk through the trench which was dug and which now connects H17 with H19.

The work done last night reflects the greatest credit on those officers and men who took part in it, and more especially on the wiring party who for sometime had to work under the most trying circumstances as the Germans turned a machine gun on them, and it was in this party that all the casualties occurred.

… The defence of this sector has been considerably strengthened by this new trench."

Work continued during the month with an attached infantryman killed in action on 8th May. In the number 11 workings, gallery 11P located at the end of gallery 11C, was driven out to 114 feet by the end of the month and in doing so ran into the old number 10 workings from 1915, these being 3 feet higher that the number 11 workings. Gallery 11N, an east running gallery located at 68 feet along 11D, was 55 feet long by 14th May with an 11 feet long 'T' junction built across the end for listening. 11L a south running gallery, 80 feet to the right off 11D was pushed out to 55 feet and joined up at a junction with gallery 11Q, described shortly. 11K was a branch to the left at 182 feet along 11G which ran out and turned right running parallel with 11G. At the 87 feet mark it ran into the smashed enemy gallery, about 3 feet lower than ours, from which the camouflet was fired that killed the three 177 men on 28th April. On 25th May a flow of mud rushed into 11K forcing it to be barricaded at the 120 feet mark. At 55 feet along 11L and to the left ran gallery 11M. By 28th May it was 137 feet long. 36 feet to the left along 11K was gallery 11Q, a short gallery which connected at the junction of galleries 11L and 11M. 11R, a left branch at 117 feet along 11K, was 40 feet long by the month's end. The steel shaft located in a chamber along 11F was worked on for three days during May and was 40 feet deep by the end of the month.

The number 16 works were also continued during May; Gallery 16E saw an inrush of running sand early in the month with 20 feet of the gallery being lost prior to the gallery being barricaded. Along the gallery a right branch, gallery 16F, was 81 feet long and then had a 13 feet 'T' junction built on the end for listening. 16G, a left branch at 11 feet along 16F, ran into very bad ground between the 40 to 50 feet marks and was barricaded and left. 16I, a right branch at 353 feet along 16E, was 74 feet long by the end of the month. Another

listening gallery, 16J, located 74 feet along 16I to the left, was out to 70 feet and had a 15 foot 'T' junction built across the end. A section of a cross-cut gallery at 13 feet along 16C which connected into 16E at 243 feet into the gallery, was widened to 6 feet for 12 feet of its length to prepare for a winze to be sunk to a lower level, known as 16S Winze.

A lower priority during the month was the workings off Grafton Street trench at Hooge. Only one shift of men for five hours of the day worked on the system. Dugouts were constructed along 21B and a stepped raise to the surface was driven up from this gallery. Along 21C a dugout was constructed in preparation for housing a winze. More dugouts were worked on from along galleries 21DO2, 21DO3 and a stepped raise to the surface started from gallery 21DO4.

Over at Sanctuary Wood under the 3rd Canadian Division, maintenance work continued on the works. Great difficulty was experienced due to bad ground and also the ferocity of enemy shelling. The number 4 shaft, located off trench 63, was fitted with a smaller diameter of metal rings in order to strengthen the shaft.

On 20th May began the relief in the line of Guards Division by the men of the 20th (Light) Division. The 2nd Guards Brigade, which had been holding the Railway Wood sector for a few days, were relieved by Brigadier General Hon L J P Butler's 60th Infantry Brigade. Considerable progress was made behind the lines along the canal bank on the various galleries being driven under the canal. Back at 177 Tunnelling Company's Headquarters near Proven, work continued on an underground working designed to be a school for instruction in various military mining techniques. This system would be vital in training those miners who would become the 'ears' of the company, a vital link in the defence of the troops holding the line above.

On 29th May Lt Montague Wright, a section officer with 177, was badly injured in an accident whilst climbing up a shaft while the ground above was under heavy German shellfire. A platform gave way and he fell 25 feet banging his head as he fell on a piece of angle iron supporting the platform. He was knocked unconscious, remaining in that state for twelve hours. He was evacuated to the UK via Number 10 CCS, Poperinge and Number 7 Stationary Hospital, Boulogne, where he remained on sick leave for two months prior to rejoining the company.

JUNE 1916

177 Tunnelling Company was 337 officers and men strong at the beginning of the month. Their work at Railway Wood in the dugouts and sector mining schemes had really branched out since their arrival almost a year before. This can be seen by just how many attached personnel were with 177 at this stage of the war. The miners were being used for the technical phase of their work both above and below ground and also for the protection through listening that was constantly taking place underground. The attached personnel were there for the inglorious yet vital task of labour. The removal of spoil, transportation of wood needed to line the galleries and many more often forgotten yet important tasks. Without these attached men none of the tunnelling companies could have functioned as they did. 893 of these men, from a variety of

units, were attached to 177 at the beginning of June. Their number would increase during the month to over 1,000. All of the workings under the trenches in the vicinity of Railway Wood were now down more than one level deep. Two had been sunk to medium level, about 50 feet and there were plans afoot to go even deeper. The tunnellers were to accompany the infantry on a trench raid on 13th June when the 7th KSLI were to raid the German lines along the southern face of the German Salient opposite Railway Wood. 177 would supply men to search out, reconnoitre and destroy German mine workings. The raid was called off at the last minute due to the devastated nature of the ground made worse by recent rains.

The number 6 workings, which had remained fairly quiet during the previous month, saw some action early in June when a camouflet, fired as a defensive measure, was blown from gallery 6WK, a right branch 94 feet along 6WE. This gallery was situated 50 feet down on the medium level of the number 6 workings. It had been very cautiously advanced over the past few months with lots of time spent listening, which now had paid off. The whole of gallery 6WK had been tamped in preparation for the camouflet, a charge of 100 lbs of ammonal. For some time afterwards it was not known what the outcome of that camouflet was. German prisoners taken on a trench raid to be discussed later, said after their capture that one of their shafts was so badly damaged it was rendered useless. As this small camouflet was fired from a medium level, it was believed that the shaft mentioned by the prisoners could well have been a winze connecting their workings to a deeper level. Firing a

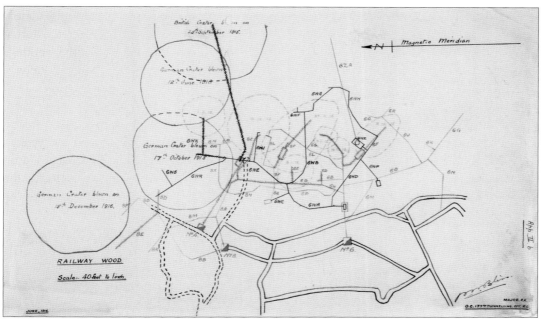

Railway Wood Nos 6 and 8 workings, June 1916. (TNA)

defensive camouflet from this intermediate level was always going to alert the Germans to your location. A revenge strike was almost inevitable and occurred on 12th June at 2.30am when the Germans blew a mine. All of gallery 6WK and part of 6WE were wrecked. Three men from number 3 section were buried by the collapse of the galleries. Rescuers got to work immediately, led by the Section Commander, 2nd Lt Agner Dalgas, recovering one of the buried men, 41-year-old Sapper Fred Cheeseman, a Yorkshire miner from Masborough,[20] who unfortunately had been killed by the collapse. Sapper Thomas Dawson, a 30-year-old Durham miner from Crook[21] was rescued 22 hours later after 20 feet of untimbered gallery had been driven. He died of his injuries later that day. The third man, 34-year-old Sapper Michael Carter, another Staffordshire miner from Tipton, was never recovered.[22]

Normal work resumed in the workings throughout the month, all of it being done on the 50 feet level. Gallery 6WR, a left branch at 88 feet along 6WE, was driven out to 84 feet by the 28th of the month, its end rising into gallery 8P of the number 8 workings. Gallery 6WS, a right branch at 64 feet along 6WR, was 25 feet long by the end of the month. Gallery 6ZA, 85 feet deep on the third level of the number 6 workings made its way eastward towards the German lines. By 30th June it was 94 feet long.

Work continued in the number 11 workings under trench H18. The first underground level of this working was fairly shallow, with a system of galleries at 20 feet deep. 11W, a 5 feet diameter, steel shaft, had been sunk down another 57 feet to a second level 77 feet deep. An attempt had been made by the tunnellers to break away a gallery higher up the shaft, but bad ground was experienced and they continued to go deeper into the blue clay. Gallery 11WA was the gallery broken away and driven eastwards towards the German lines, from

Railway Wood
No 11 workings,
June 1916. (TNA)

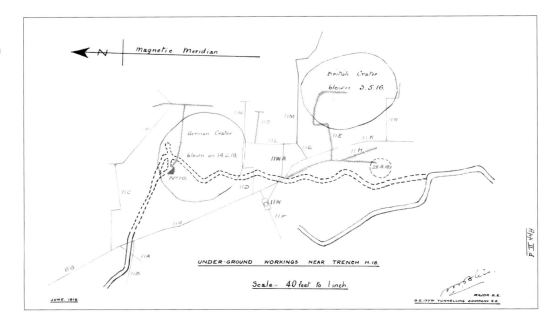

the bottom of 11W. This gallery, set in timber 4 feet 6 inches high and 2 feet 3 inches wide, was 47 feet long by the end of June.

Similar work continued in the number 16 works. A steel shaft was sunk from 20 feet down within gallery 16S. Once this winze was down 38 feet, to a total of 58 feet, a gallery, 16WA, was broken away and started, being 47 feet long by the end of June.

The Grafton Street and Sanctuary Wood workings were only worked on for a day or two in June, when early afternoon on the 2nd June, the area fell into the hands of the Germans as they drove home a small localised offensive stretching from Sanctuary Wood across to Hooge. Tragedy struck the company on this day when Second Lieutenant Oscar Earnshaw and 4 attached infantrymen were killed in action in the German push.[23] The German offensive was designed to take

Railway Wood No 16 workings, June 1916. (TNA)

Mount Sorrell and also high points within Sanctuary Wood. With the German Army involved in heavy fighting to the south in the Verdun sector and preparing for another attack soon to be made against them on the Somme; the Germans used troops based locally for this strike. Initially the Germans took the ground from Mount Sorell to Tor Top. The Canadian defenders pulled back and, worried about being flanked by the Germans from Hooge, withdrew further. Caught up in the unexpected attack that day, visiting the front, was the GOC 3rd Canadian Division, Major General Malcolm Smith Mercer CB, MiD and his 8th Infantry Brigade Commanding Officer, Brigadier General Williams. Both men were wounded and Mercer later killed by shellfire, with Williams being captured by the advancing Germans.[24] Major Bliss wrote to Oscar Earnshaw's family later in the month, describing his loss:

16/6/16

Dear Mr Earnshaw

I am exceedingly sorry to have to tell you that there can be no doubt, but that your son, Oscar, was killed on the 2nd instant.

We hoped against hope that he might have survived, though he was missing, but yesterday we received by an indirect route his identity disc and signet ring. These I am sending to his widow. They were taken from off his body by a Lieut Forbes, machine gun officer of the PPCLI who was himself wounded, and handed over to the RAMC who passed them to us through another RE unit. Lt Forbes stated there was no doubt as to his being dead.

I am afraid that things are still so confused up there that we cannot hope to recover his body for separate burial. Lt Forbes may be in England & possibly able to give you more information.

I cannot close without asking you to accept the very sincere sympathy of myself & my officers, who were all extremely fond of Oscar. His loss is deeply felt by us, both on the social and the service side, as he was a very efficient officer.

Yours sincerely

J M Bliss

Major RE

Another attached infantryman was killed in action on 3rd June. On the 6th the Germans blew four mines in a row in the Hooge area and captured our former positions including the Grafton Street workings. The Canadian Corps Commander, fresh into his role, Lieutenant-General Sir Julian Byng, realised the importance of counter-attacking to seize back Tor Top and Mount Sorrell. Hooge didn't fit into the picture, just yet, it could wait. On 13th June the Canadians counter-attacked and retook their positions, ejecting the Germans from their gains of the 2nd June. Hooge, however, remained in the hands of the enemy and the Grafton Street workings were lost.

This didn't stop 177 from working in the Hooge area. Just down the Menin Road, slightly west of Hooge, at Birr crossroads, test boreholes were made as a prelude to underground workings. On 13th June a shaft was begun and by the end of the month was 28 feet deep. The ground here was lower and exposed to the enemy holding the higher ground, so work only took place at night when the conditions above ground allowed. The shaft here would eventually lead to a system of deep dugouts under the Menin Road.

Work on the attempt to tunnel under the Yser canal at grid C25 also hit problems in June. Towards the back end of May, a huge weight forced itself onto the east and west bank workings breaking the timbers of the galleries and closing them in. Fortunately for the miners working on this project, none were killed or injured. The miners worked out the probable reason for the incident being that they were working too near the surface of the blue clay layer, above which was a heavy layer of water-filled sand, causing the problem. If they had been deeper in the blue clay, this may not have happened, but time was not on their side. The scheme was abandoned but four tunnels with dugouts off them, in the West bank of the canal were started, as were causeways across the canal.

Back near Proven at 177's HQ work on an experimental mine using push tubes, also moved forward. It was the responsibility of 177 to run both the Second Army Mine Listening and Rescue Schools. Both were run from 177's company Headquarters location near which was also located a small section of infantry practice trenches in a wooded cul de sac just north of Zoom Farm. On 20th June 1916, 177 blew a 1,550 lb practice mine from these trenches. The likely reason for this mine to blow well behind the lines at practice trenches was to allow for the infantry to practice the capturing, holding and reinforcing of mine craters within his lines.

At the Railway Wood sector on 30th June, a few minutes after midnight, a raid on the German front local to trench H16 to H20 was made by 84 men of the 6th KSLI, 60th Brigade. The raid had been preceded with a fierce bombardment of the German

Canal Tunnels plan for June 1916. (TNA)

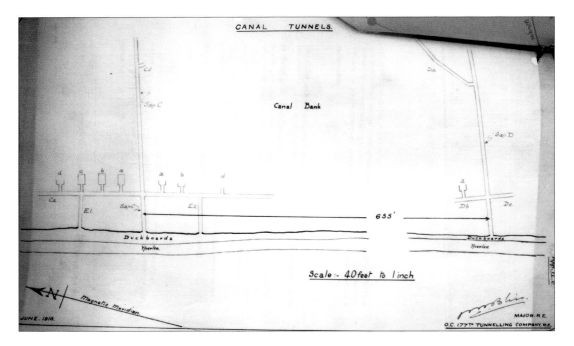

front lines. Accompanying the infantry were parties: Sappers from 177 Tunnelling Company, 83rd Field Company RE and Special Company of the RE. The task of the 177 men was to try and find German dugout and mine entrance locations. The raiders were split into two parties, A and B. A Party would raid the German Salient just opposite Railway Wood with B party raiding the German front line, Idiot trench, just east of crater 1a. Each raiding party, once in the German trenches, split into sub-sections to carry out their raid. The attached 177 personnel discovered no enemy workings on the raid, this being put down to the difficulty in locating the enemy's mineshafts due to the destructive nature of our artillery had over his ground. It was agreed that the accompanying parties of RE would withdraw just before the infantry made their own withdrawal back to our own lines. In the vicinity of crater 1 Lt McKimm of the 6th KSLI was commencing his move up a German sap head heading back to friendly lines. He then came across a German shaft about 4 feet square topped with a winch but had no means to destroy it due to the tunnellers being withdrawn. Grenades were thrown down the shaft before his retirement was completed. The casualty figure for the raid claimed at least 80 Germans killed with 13 being brought in as prisoners. The raiders suffered 2 killed, 1 missing and 9 wounded.

1   Mining notes number 51, from series issued by IOM, GHQ, 1916 – 1918. RE Library Chatham.

2   86953 LCpl John Anthony Hayward is buried in Nunhead (All Saints) Cemetery and commemorated on the screen wall panel 89.

3   Lt Eric Archibald McNairs VC citation reads: "For most conspicuous bravery. When the enemy exploded a mine, Lieutenant McNair and many men of two platoons were hoisted into the air, and many men were buried. But, though much shaken, he at once organised a party with a machine gun to man the near edge of the crater and opened rapid fire on a large party of the enemy who were advancing. The enemy were driven back, leaving many dead. Lieutenant McNair then ran back for reinforcements, and sent to another unit for bombs, ammunition and tools to replace those buried. The communication trench being blocked he went across the open, under heavy fire and led up the reinforcements the same way. His prompt and plucky action and example undoubtedly saved the situation."
Lt McNair died in Italy in August 1918 and is buried in Staglieno Cemetery, Genoa.

4   9th Royal Sussex war diary February 1916. WO95/2219 and 73rd Infantry Brigade HQ war diary February 1916. WO95/2216

5   139138 Sjt H Byles' DCM was gazetted into the London Gazette on the 21st June 1916. His citation reads: "For conspicuous gallantry and good work on several occasions, notably when he tried to rescue some men in a wrecked shaft under heavy shellfire, and when he volunteered to take rations up to the trenches, also under heavy shellfire."

6   Page 146, Beneath Flanders Fields, Barton, Vandewalle and Doyle.

7   Lt MacFarlane is buried at Lijssenthoek Military Cemetery, plot V, row A, grave 2.

8   6th Division "Enterprise Report No 9." 16th Infantry Brigade war diary, March 1916.

9   Report in Appendix 3, 16th Infantry Brigade war diary for March 1916

10 16th Infantry Brigade war diary for March 1916

11 Appendix 523, titled "Mining" Guards Division HQ war diary, March 1916.

12 4th Coldstreams war diary, March 1916

13 Letter from Geoffrey Boothby originally to his old Headmaster, Alex Devine and published in the Old Clayesmorian magazine of December 1916. The account is of an underground action that took place at The Bluff on 5th October

1915. 172 Tunnelling Company was active in this sector at the time and from the relevant entry in its war diary (WO 95/244) reference the incident it appears the RE officer that Geoffrey mentions is Lt Williamson.

14 Letter from Geoffrey Boothby to his sweetheart Edith Ainscow. Published in "Thirty-Odd Feet Below Belgium" edited by Arthur Stockwin. Parapress limited 2005. ISBN-10: 1-898594-80-5

15 Second Army Mine Note No: 80 Standard Mine Tracks. RE Library.

16 Lt Geoffrey Boothby, Cpl Roland Brindley and Sapper William Spooner are all still buried under the ridge and are listed in memory on the RE Grave Cemetery memorial to 177 Tunnelling Company. Lt Wilson was awarded a Military Cross for his actions in trying to save Boothby, Brindley and Spooner. His citation reads "For conspicuous gallantry. When wounded by the explosion of an enemy camouflet, he made repeated gallant efforts to rescue an officer and two men who were nearer to the explosion than himself under very dangerous conditions."

17 Sections of letters both printed in full in "Thirty-Odd Feet Below Belgium. The book is a series of letters from Geoffrey to Edith, and hers to him. The book tells a very human and emotive love story between two young sweethearts separated by the war. After the war Edith married and had a son Arthur, who discovered the letters a few years after his mother died, in 1983. What I find very poignant is that although Edith moved on in life, married, raised a family and had a successful career in medicine, she still continued to visit Alice Boothby until her death.

She took her son, Arthur, with her a few times and he remembers seeing Geoffrey Boothby's memorial plaque set into the living room mantel piece but was then unaware of the link between Edith and the Boothby's. The book is thoroughly recommended reading for those studying the Tunnelling aspect of the war and for those interested in the human side of the war. Letters kindly reproduced with the permission of Arthur Stockwin and Parapress Ltd.

18 3rd Guards Brigade Operational Order number 34, May 1916.

19 Brigadier General Frederick James Heyworth CB DSO, GOC 3rd Guards Brigade, died of wounds received in action just a few days later on the 9th May whilst heading up the trenches near Hooge to inspect a mine blown by German miners at 4.10am that morning. He is buried in plot 2 row C grave 2 of Brandhoek Cemetery.

20 132897 Sapper Fred Cheeseman is buried in Plot 1, Row C, Grave 27 of Reservoir Cemetery, Ypres

21 102406 Sapper Thomas Dawson is buried in Plot 7, Row C, Grave 34 of Lijssenthoek Military Cemetery, Poperinghe

22 132856 Sapper Michael Carter is commemorated on the RE Grave memorial.

23 Lt Oscar Earnshaw's body was never identified or recovered in post war clearance of the battlefield. He is commemorated on Panel 9 of the Menin Gate.

24 Major General Malcolm Smith Mercer is buried in Plot 6, Row A, Grave 38 of Lijssenthoek Cemetery. He remains the highest ranking serviceman to die in the Ypres Salient during WW1.

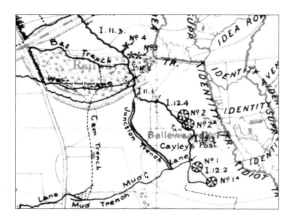

Bellewaerde Workings. (Courtesy Great War Digital)

CHAPTER THREE

JULY 1916

July started with the British 4th and French 6th armies launching a major offensive in France in the Somme region as an attempt to smash the German stranglehold in the area and also to relieve pressure off the French forces fighting in the Verdun area. The offensive opened with the British sustaining 58,000 casualties on the first day of fighting. It is sometimes hard to grasp that for such high casualties there were successes on the first day and these were exploited by the British as the offensive progressed. Although most of the British effort was now focused on the Somme offensive, the static way of life continued in the Ypres Salient. 177 Tunnelling Company suffered a tragedy on the 1st of the month when one of the section officers, 38-year-old Lt Andrew Stuart Holms was killed in action.[1]

The month saw 177 Tunnelling Company continuing underground work on the number 6, 11 and 16 workings under the Railway Wood sector, with gallery 6WR stepped raise to gallery 8P of the number 8 workings finished after some troublesome work in connecting the two galleries. 177's deepest working, the 6ZA gallery was pushed out to 319 feet by the end of July. 225 feet of ground was driven over twenty-nine days worked in this deep gallery. Two or three days were spent doing repair work to the gallery. At this depth the workers were hindered with bad air. In the number 11 workings listeners picked up noises on 2nd July and a charge was put in gallery 11M 15 feet from the end and then tamped. Careful

Original grave marker of Lt Andrew Holms at Vlamertinghe Military Cemetery. (Author's collection)

continuous study was made of these noises by those on listening watch but they were eventually traced to harmless surface noises and on 10th July the charge was removed. Gallery 11WA, 77 feet under trench H18 was driven out to 249 feet with 202 feet of spoil removed over twenty-nine days. At 58 feet under trench H16, gallery 16WB was worked on for twenty-four days of July. By the 26th it was 220 feet long but time was lost here due to patches of bad ground being experienced by the tunnellers. German shellfire also blew in the Proto House, the chamber containing the breathing apparatus that would be used in the case of entering gas-filled galleries. Lack of manpower due to work on other workings, meant that by

75

the month's end work on this working was stopped. Meanwhile up on the surface the 60th Infantry Brigade was relieved by the 61st Brigade through the night of 10th/11th July. The 61st Brigade continued to hold the Railway Wood sector until the 20th Division was relieved in the line by 29th Division on 18nd July.

Where Cambridge Road and Union Street met the Menin Road, the location was known as Birr Cross Roads and it was during July that 177 got to work in the area of the 3rd Canadian Division on a dugout system under the road. The cobbled nature of the road 26 feet above the dugout allowed for extra burst protection in the case of shelling.

Railway Wood Nos 6 and 8 workings, July 1916. (TNA)

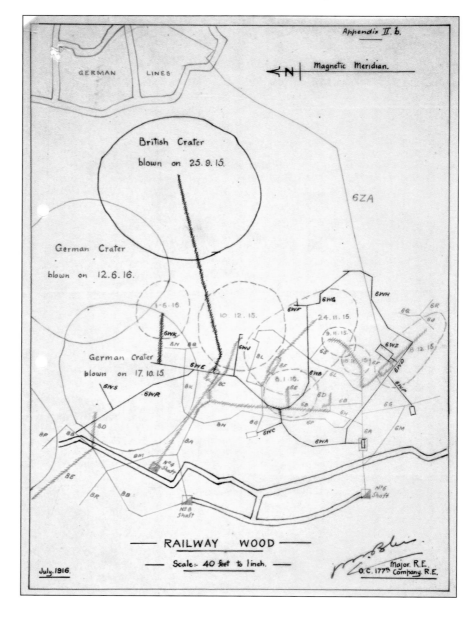

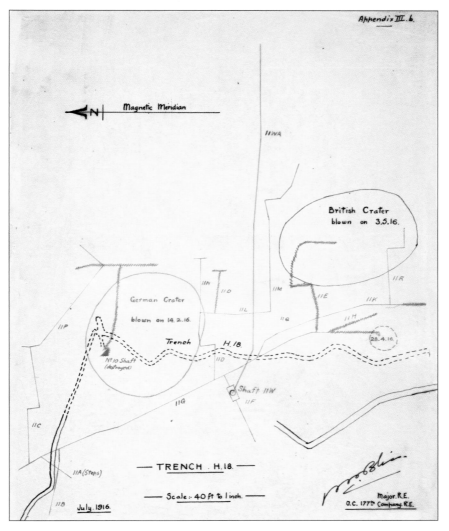

Railway Wood
No 11 workings,
July 1916. (TNA)

A timbered shaft, 4 feet by 4 feet at map reference Sheet 28 NW I.17.b.25.85 served the dugout which was known as working 1. An incline stairway 5 feet 6 inches high and 2 feet 6 inches wide was driven to the surface from the base of the shaft and known as 1A. A gallery, 1B ran eastwards from the base of 1A and was 18 feet long by the 18th July. Tunnellers in this working encountered soft ground at the face, heavy shelling on the surface and difficulties in removing bags of spoil due to the area being under constant German observation. A right branch along 1B, known as 1C was driven out to 80 feet by the month's end and two small dugouts 11 feet 6 by 5 feet 6 constructed along the gallery. At 48 feet along 1C another gallery, 1D was 36 feet long and stepped to the surface by the end of the month. It came out along Cork Street communication trench. A west running gallery from the base of 1A was also driven out during the month. 1B was 38 feet long by the 31st July.

Railway Wood
No 16 workings,
July 1916. (TNA)

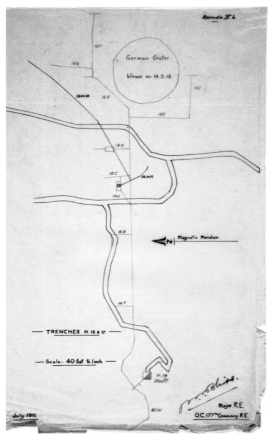

Where Cork Street communication trench met the Menin Road there was a culvert. During the month, 177 attempted to step down an incline under the Menin Road to allow for soldiers to pass safely. This work was only possible at night due to the road being under observation from the German front. Their work here was hindered by shellfire, the incline twice being damaged.

In the XIV Corps area, work rapidly continued on the extensive system of dugouts along the Yser Canal bank. Work-ing some distance behind the front, the miners were more able to work freely not constricted by the need for silence found in workings under the front line. A total of 1,925 feet of tunnel and dugouts were driven in the Canal bank during the month, with a total of 33 new dugouts completed. The system also included in its plans an old gallery from a previous attempted working known as Miner's Rest. This was 113 feet long already when it was incorporated into the Canal bank system and during the month was extended to 156 feet, connecting either side of the Canal bank making a ventilation tunnel.

Back at 177's HQ near Proven, the Second Army Mine Rescue School was now co-located with the Mine Listening School. Skills and arts that miners honed and perfected under the front needed continuous training and re-examination, especially in the important subjects of listening and mine rescue. The responsibility running of both schools under the collective heading of the

Birr Cross Roads
dugout for July
1916. (TNA)

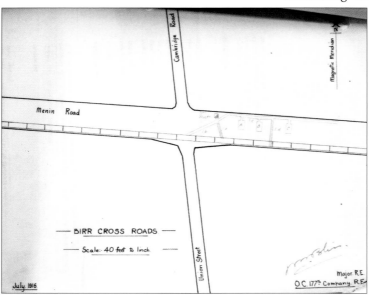

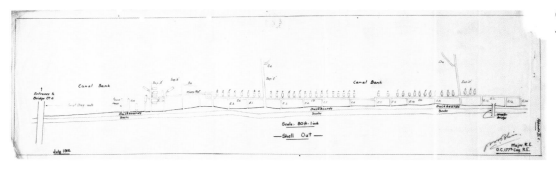

Canal Dugouts, July 1916. (TNA)

Second Army Mine School was given to 177 Tunnelling Company and was no mean feat.

July 1916 ended with the announcement in the *London Gazette* of a Military Cross to Lt Agner Dalgas for his actions in directing the rescue of Sappers Cheeseman and Dawson and the attempted rescue of Sapper Carter on the 12th June. His citation read:

"For conspicuous gallantry and promptness on many occasions, notably when, after the enemy had exploded a mine and damaged a part of our galleries, he directed rescue operations with great coolness and skill, and rescued two out of three men."

AUGUST 1916

At the beginning of August the company was 400 officers and men strong. Also working with the company were 532 officers and other ranks from attached infantry units.

Men stood outside the Canal Bank Dugouts, Ypres. (Photo courtesy of Peter Barton)

Drawing highlighting a British tunneller on listening duty picking up the sounds of German mining. Note the duty officer of the mining section at his side investigating. (Drawing courtesy of Jonathon Porter)

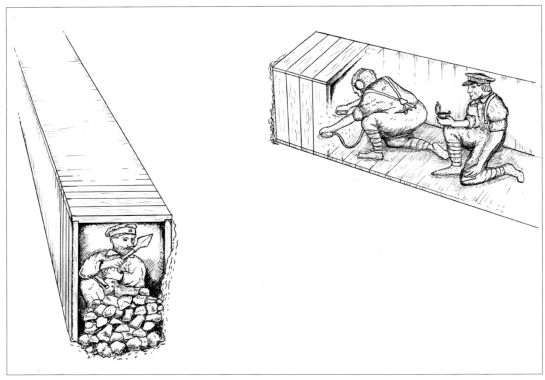

August would see the company increase its sphere of influence in the Ypres Salient where it was detailed to construct a number of dugouts to the north of its normal area of operations. Mining work within the Second Army's area of responsibility was at an all time high. The grand Messines offensive scheme was in the process of being realised and developed south of Ypres and there were now at least eight tunnelling companies at work under the command of the Second Army. 177 Tunnelling Company would have no direct part to play in the Messines mining operation. It was, however, one of the most important tunnelling companies at work in the Salient. It helped defend the troops holding the apex of the Ypres Salient. The important feature of Railway Wood that gave British troops a valuable height advantage over the Germans needed defending. Height was not something the British had a lot of in the Salient during 1916 and every patch of high ground owned by the British needed defending both above and below ground.

The mining scheme under the Railway Wood sector gradually grew during August as the 29th Division went about their business on the surface. Holding the line, maintaining the trenches and harassing the enemy all played a part in the infanteers' daily schedule. Under his feet, under trench H20 the number 6 working was coming along nicely at both the 50 feet and 82 feet levels. At 50 feet in the number 6 working gallery 6WT was driven connecting galleries 6WD to 6WE and a wooded track laid for the disposal of spoil. In the deep 82 feet level of the number 6 working a great deal of repair work took place in gallery 6ZA. This gallery was now well under the German lines. Work digging the gallery stopped when it was 361 feet long. Two 3 feet long branches were constructed each side of the gallery 4 feet from its end. A total of 6000 lbs of ammonal was then placed at the end of the gallery and in the two branches. This charge was then tamped up using spoil dug from two 10 feet branches dug each side of the gallery 120 feet back from the charge.

To the right of the number 6 working, under trench H19. lay the number 11 working, similar in nature to the number 6 working; number 11 was also on two levels. The main level was fairly shallow at 20 feet deep with its deeper part at 77 feet deep. On the 14th August a listener in gallery 11M, which ran east under No Man's Land had picked up a noise, possibly that of a German listener opposite 11M. Sounds were also heard overhead in the deeper gallery 11WA which ran parallel to 11M. Work stopped temporarily in 11WA as specially trained listeners took over. On the 21st August orders came down from company HQ to continue driving 11WA. This gallery was already 285 feet long and working its way out towards the German lines. On 23rd August, in view of what was suspected above them, the miners in 11WA started construction of a left branch at 287 feet along 11WA. This gallery which would parallel 11WA, was labelled 11WB and was to be used to store a charge for emergency use. However, on 25th August

gallery 11WB ran into bad ground and an inrush of mud filled it up together with 15 feet of 11WA before the tunnellers could dam and stop the flow. A second gallery was then started as a right branch at 277 feet along 11WA, known as 11WC and it was this gallery that was used to push onwards towards the German lines.

The number 16 working suffered with lack of work in August compared to its number 6 and number 11 companions. The number 16 workings lay to the right of the number 11 workings and the majority of the

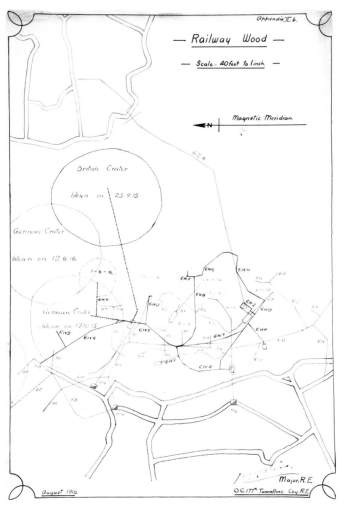

Railway Wood Nos 6 and 8 workings, August 1916. (TNA)

Railway Wood
No 11 workings,
August 1916.
(TNA)

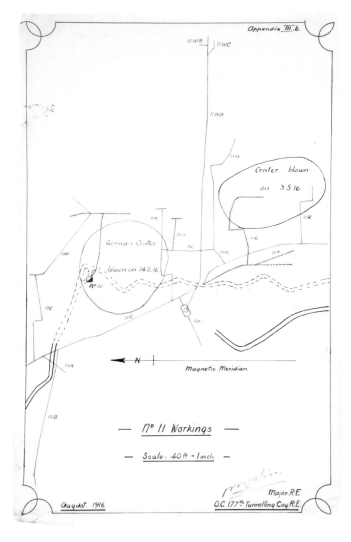

serving the 26 feet level was put down another 19 feet in order to start a deeper second level of the dugout which would eventually become a very well known dressing station. Three stairways off the Menin Road served the upper level of the dugout and along the main 26 feet deep gallery three more dugouts were completed. An inclined stairway serving the deeper level of the system was started along Union Street with a gallery 1G running north to connect to the rest of the system. By the end of the month this had been driven 135 feet. A good deal of water was experienced due to the bad nature of the soil and a pump chamber was also constructed. From the base of the shaft, at 40 feet, a second drive was started. This lower level drive was labelled 2A and was 48 feet long by 16th August. At 45 feet along 2A a left branch was started, known as 2B and 4 feet along 2B, a further left branch 2C, was started which was stepped up into 1F on the upper level. At the end of 2B, to the right, a room 5 feet 6 inches high, 6 feet wide and 14 feet long was constructed, to be used as an operating theatre. Running westwards from the theatre was a 7 foot long passage which connected into another room 5 feet 6 inches high and 8 feet wide and 21 feet long which would be used as a ward. To the north of gallery 2B a small Medical Officers' dugout was also constructed. Work in the Birr Cross Roads dugouts was not without its pitfalls through

month was spent in gallery 16WB at 58 feet deep. In 27 days 168 feet of the gallery was driven and a great deal of bad ground was experienced with much spiling necessary. This gallery ran northwards and was built to connect the number 16 workings to the rest of the workings under the ridge. By the end of the month 16WB had been stepped up and connected to gallery 11R.

The Birr Cross Roads dugout system also saw expansion during August. The shaft

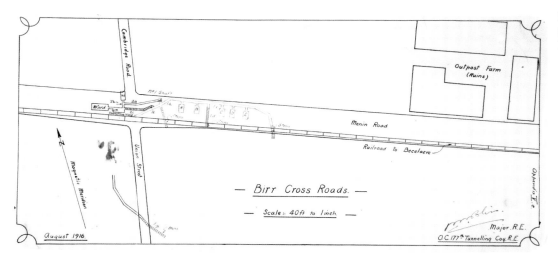

Birr Cross Roads dugouts, August 1916. (TNA)

the month, lack of fatigue parties in help-ing to remove the spoil and bring up the wood required for the construction of the dugout hampered work, as did the high numbers of gas alarms experienced throughout the month.

The small tunnel under the culvert, which was started the month before, was only able to be worked on under cover of darkness. The ground experienced by the tunnellers here was very bad. That, coupled with the fact the road was always under shellfire, forced the tunnellers to abandon this project during the month.

The Canal bank dugouts project really took shape during the month. A total of 2,400 feet of ground was driven in the system including the construction and completion of 36 dugouts, an engine room and stepped inclines to the surface.

Work was also started on other dugout systems in the Ypres Salient. These new projects designated as Strong Points would all be hampered by the nature of the ground and water table, frequent gas alarms and work was carried out on them at night only.

Mill Cottages were two ruins which sat just off the Ypres to Zonnebeke road about 150 metres short of where Cambridge Road joins the Zonnebeke Road. A dugout was started from the cellar of the southernmost ruin. Some days were spent clearing the cellar of debris prior to sinking the shaft. By the end of August the 4 feet by 4 feet timber shaft had been sunk to 30 feet.

In the small village of Wieltje which sat

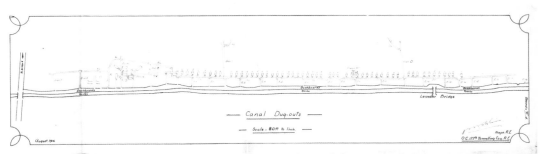

Canal Dugouts, August 1916. (TNA)

right on the British front line to the north east of the Salient was the next location of a dugout project for the company. Work began on what would become very extensive system of dugouts. The dugouts, which would have the ominous name of Hades, commenced on 17th August. Work started on two entrances, a shaft and a stepped incline. The shaft was sunk from the cellar of a ruin in the village about 170 metres behind the front line after two days was spent clearing it of muck. A standard 4 feet by 4 feet timber shaft was sunk and the tunnellers were soon into the Bastard Blue Clay. By the month's end the shaft

had been sunk to 12 feet deep. The stepped incline was driven down from the northern end of Monmouth trench in timber 5 feet 6 inches high by 3 feet wide.

Work also began at Wilson's Farm just off Bent Road, east of the Yser Canal and just northwest of the hamlet of La Brique. On the 16th the tunnellers began to clear the cellar of the ruined farmhouse of debris prior to having to cut through a concrete cellar floor. Then the standard 4 feet by 4 feet timber shaft was sunk. By the end of the month it was down to 24 feet deep.

The final of the new dugout projects started during August was at Hill Top Farm

Hades dugout location, Wieltje. (Courtesy Great War Digital)

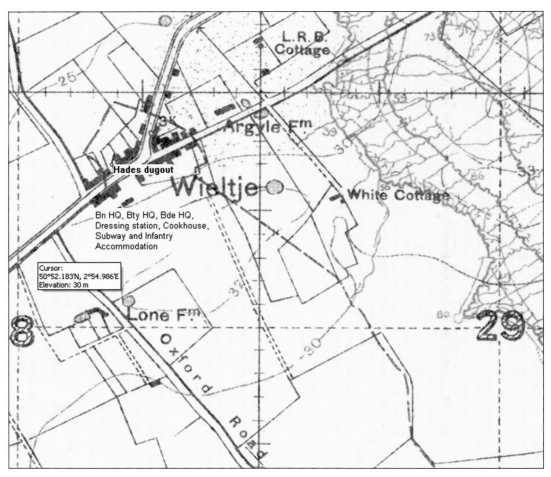

located about a fifth of a mile west of the British Front Line and just north of Buffs Road. Considerable work was carried out in clearing the cellar and cutting through its concrete floor before a 4 feet square timber shaft was sunk. By the end of the month it was 23 feet deep.

Time was also spent in August in expanding the Cambridge Road dugouts under Railway Wood. By the 16th a dressing station had been constructed attached to the system consisting of two dugouts 15 feet long and 6 feet wide. Attached to this was a small dugout for the Medical Officer, a small well and all connected by 30 feet of gallery. The dugout was to be connected to the front and during August plans were drawn up for a gallery to be driven eastwards to the front line. This gallery would be used to support infantry as well as to drain the old number 6 and number 8 workings and would have dugouts along it for electric power and lighting plants. Plans were also afoot to continue the dugout at a newer deeper level. The main gallery of the dugout was continued with both a dugout constructed along its length as a shaft house from which a raise was made to the surface coming out in the sunken road that runs up the southern face of Railway Wood. A steel tubbed shaft 4 feet 10 inches in diameter was started and by the end of the month it was 22 feet deep.

On 28th August 177 blew a practice mine of 8400 lbs of ammonal at the Second Army Central School in Wisques, northern France as part of a demonstration for GHQ.

SEPTEMBER 1916

With the sun now over the yard arm for 1916, the company was 363 officers and

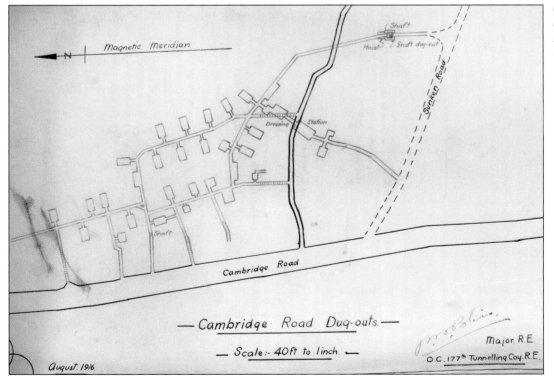

Cambridge Road dugout plan for August 1916. (TNA)

men strong at the beginning of September. Whilst the battle further south on the Somme front slogged on, and preparations for the 'big blow' that would precede the start of the Messines offensive continued further north along the foot of the Messines Ridge, 177 continued to exercise its part in the grip that the BEF had in the Salient holding the apex of this shattered land. In the continuation of its work it had 713 men attached as labour working with the company at the start of the month.

During the month 10 feet of the gallery in the 50 feet level of the number 6 workings was blown in by enemy trench mortar fire and subsequently repaired. Most of the month was spent conducting listening operations from this level of the workings and also a lot of time was spent pumping out the galleries as part of the continuous care and maintenance shown to the galleries by the tunnellers. In the deeper level of the working repair work continued throughout the month.

To the south of the number 6 workings lay the number 11 workings and September would prove to be a busy time in this sector of the line. For some weeks listeners in gallery 11M, a shallow east running gallery at 20 feet deep, heard regular sounds now highly suspected to be those of a German listening team relieving each other after a stint of subterranean duty. Within a number of feet of 11M lay defensive galleries 11S, 11T and 11V all of which were there to provide defensive listening positions. Sounds had also been picked up by British listeners in 11V and 11N confirmed to be that of the enemy working nearby. These active listening galleries were providing a lot of protection for the deeper east running

offensive gallery 11WC, itself a smaller branch off the longer 11WA. This was now deemed threatened by the tunnellers. HQ 177 firmly believed that the positions from which the enemy noises had been heard were connected with a lateral gallery that ran across the German line. It was believed that this lateral passed just 50 to 60 feet horizontally from the junction of 11WA and 11WB and about 30 feet above the deeper British working.

Major Bliss voiced his concerns to the Controller of Mines and authority was granted for 177 to take action against the German miners.

4000 lbs of ammonal explosive, in tins, was placed at the end of gallery 11WC. The charge, 70 feet down at map reference I.12.a.25.03, was fitted with number 8 and number 13 detonators wrapped with 13 ounces of guncotton explosive. Following the placing of this charge which would have been done silently in these adrenalin-charged galleries, the gallery was tamped of 85 feet with solid tamping. At 4pm on 8th September the camouflet was blown. The resultant explosion ripped through the German's galleries in the vicinity of 11WA. The explosion did not crater the surface and the ground remained unbroken. But observers reported seeing an object and smoke rise upwards from a sap above where the charge lay. It was believed to be a stairway from the German subterranean position leading to their surface trenches. Artillery supporting the 29th Division then commenced firing on the German front line but no retaliatory action was forthcoming. Damage from such a blow was not just limited to German galleries. 11WA was wrecked back to the 200 feet mark. No further sounds were heard underground. The camouflet had done its job.

Contact with the enemy underground in the vicinity of the number 11 workings was made again during the month when, at 11am on the 18th, gallery 11S, whilst being driven eastwards, 25 feet deep, came into contact with the wooden timber setts of an German gallery. The section working at the time was 3 Section commanded by Lt Agner Dalgas.

Both he, Sgt Jenkins and one other man from 177, were at the face of gallery 11S and after a period of careful listening were ready to explore the German gallery that lay beyond. Equipped with Webley revolvers the men gained entry to the German system, Dalgas moved off to the right down the German gallery with Jenkins exploring off to the left. Not far into the enemy system Dalgas came upon tamping and a 4 feet by 4 feet wooden shaft with grenades placed in storage spaces, no doubt to ward off intruders! Jenkins in his careful reconnaissance came upon a party of Germans but was not seen. Both men then made their way back and met up with each other where they were then seen by German tunnellers. Shots were exchanged between the parties which must have been a terrifying experience given the small dimensions of the tunnels both parties were in. Lieut Dalgas believed that they

accounted for two Germans dead. The British party withdrew back to Gallery 11S where a portable charge was prepared for detonation, but this failed as it had become damp. Not to be outdone, the men went forward to 11M and blew a 150 lbs charge of ammonal that had been laid some weeks previous. The resultant explosion wrecked both the 11M and 11S galleries, but no casualties were sustained by the British.

The following day at 6 am the Germans blew a charge estimated to be fired not far from the end of gallery 11S. The resultant blow caused no damage or casualties to the 177 workings under the sector and no damage was seen on the surface, although troops holding the trenches reported the

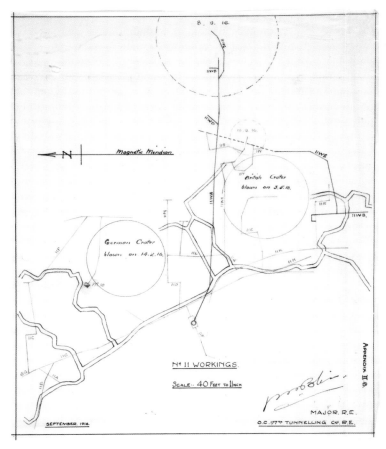

Railway Wood No 11 workings, September 1916. (TNA)

trenches shaking and smoke rising from in front of the front line barbed wire. With the excitement for September now over in the number 11 workings, the remainder of the month was spent on repairing the system particularly the first 200 feet of the deep gallery 11WA.

The deeper part of the southernmost workings under the Railway Wood sector, the number 16 workings, under trench H16 continued to expand. Towards the end of the month gallery 16WA was 164 feet long and off that ran 16WC and 16WE, both south east defensive galleries. These being 100 and 92 feet long respectively by the end of the month.

To the north west of the number 11 and 16 workings lay Railway Wood and 177 were hard at work underneath it on a series of dugouts and a main gallery that would be driven eastwards connecting to the offensive mine systems worked on by the company. During the month 102 feet of the main gallery was driven by the tunnellers, this main gallery lay at the bottom of a steel shaft and during the month a sump was sunk at the base of the shaft at the end of which was constructed a pump house. 177's work on the dugouts and dressing station under Birr Crossroads was finished on 19th September and the system handed over to field engineers attached to the 29th Division.

The canal bank dugouts suffered with a lack of manpower during September when 200 attached infantry were withdrawn. With this reduction in manpower only one day shift was able to work on the system with fifteen men. Notwithstanding the reduction of men at least twenty-nine of the existing dugouts were extended to 20 feet long, another 20 feet long dugout was constructed, 23 feet of surface trench that would serve the system was dug and

Birr Cross Roads dugout plan for September 1916. (REL)

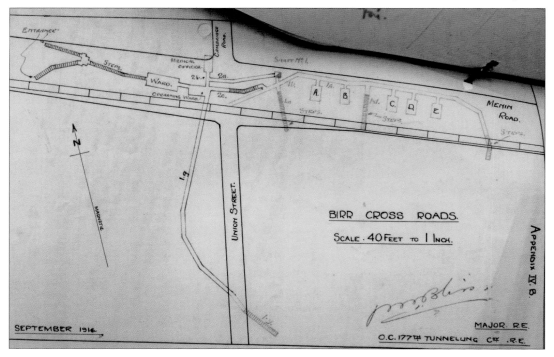

two exits to the surface near the canal and bridge 4 were made.

The strong points started by 177 in the previous month also took on new shape as work progressed. For tactical and manpower reasons for the most part, work was only done at night but from 10th September this changed at the Wieltje and Mill Cottage dugouts and from 24th September at Wilsons Farm dugouts whereby such progress was made that a day and night shift was now able to work on them. Mill Cottage shaft was down to 36 feet by 6th September and a gallery designated 'A: Main Drive' was started. This gallery, 5 feet 6 inches high and 3 feet wide, was 84 feet long by the 27th of the month. At 17 feet along 'A' a second gallery was begun labelled as 'B' which was a set of stairs that led up to a machine gun emplacement. A series of 6 feet wide dugouts were also started during the month.

Just north of Mill Cottages lay the ruins of the village of Wieltje. Running north to south at the eastern tip of the village lay the front lines, established here by the limit of the German advance at the end of the Second Battle of Ypres the previous May. The name given to the Wieltje dugouts aptly described what life for many was like on the surface here – Hades. The dugout, 35 feet deep, would follow the direction of the main street running through the village above, using the cobbled road as extra bursting layer, protection against shellfire. An inclined stairway had been started the month previous from the surface but this had to be temporarily discontinued owing to drainage problems. This did not deter the workers who simply started an incline from 35 feet below that then linked into the one

started from the surface. The main gallery that would serve the dugout, off which would be located dugouts was labelled as 'B' and by 27th of September was 67 feet long with three dugouts already constructed along its length.

At Hill Top Farm the 4 feet by 4 feet timber shaft was down to 40 feet deep by 10th September. Three galleries, A, B and C were started from the base of the shaft set in timbers 5 feet 6 inches high and 3 feet wide. By 20th of September, gallery A was 20 feet long, Gallery B was 21 feet long by the 24th of the month and Gallery C was 8 feet long by 27th September.

At Wilsons Farm the shaft was also down to 40 feet by 10th September, a single gallery was driven out and by the month's end was 54 feet long.

OCTOBER 1916

With the onset of October work on the number 6 and 8 workings under the Railway Wood sector was minimal, nine days work throughout the month was carried out in gallery 6ZA and this consisted of pumping, listening and repair work only. On the surface, the 55th (West Lancashire) Division relieved the 29th Division on the night of 4th October with the 165th Brigade initially moving into the Railway Wood sector. As the year progressed through autumn to winter the weather conditions deteriorated and the rain, coupled with harassing artillery fire, played havoc with the conditions of surface trenches. Flooding and collapsing of trenches were frequent. Many of the infantrymen occupying these trenches worked both night and day to get them into an acceptable condition that could be both lived in and defended. In the number 11 workings under trench H19, on the upper level of the workings where gallery 11M met the German gallery that was entered in September, the junction of that meeting of galleries was raised two feet. In the deeper levels, down at 77 feet, gallery 11WD, which ran northeast off 11WA at the 200 feet mark, was driven out to 90 feet long by 8th October. On the 3rd the Germans had blown a camouflet in the vicinity which damaged about 10 feet of 11WD, but no casualties had been sustained and the damage was quickly repaired. A charge chamber was made along 11WD and filled with 4000 lbs of ammonal but not tamped. Gallery 11WE, a right branch off 11WA, was started and was 47 feet long by 11th October running parallel with the damaged section of 11WA.

In the number 16 workings a pump chamber 6 feet long and 4 feet wide was made at the foot of 16W, the winze that took miners from the upper to the lower 58 feet deep part of the workings. The two main galleries that sprouted out of this deeper level were 16WA and 16WB running north east and south east respectively. Along these galleries further galleries ran their way under No Man's Land. 16WF, a right branch at 167 feet along 16WA, was 47 feet long by 18th October. Gallery 16WG, a right branch at 50 feet off gallery 16WE, was 38 feet long by 28th October and 16WD, a right branch at 250 feet on 16WB, was 125 feet long with a 12 foot 'T' section built across the end by 27th October. In the upper levels of the number 16 workings, the floor of gallery 16E was lowered to allow for water collection prior to being pumped.

The month also saw the company working with a unit not long arrived on the Western Front. The Australian Electrical and Mechanical Mining Boring Company (AEMMBC), affectionately known as the 'Alphabet Company' had arrived on the Western Front in May 1916. Under the command of Major Richard Morse they provided the infrastructure to support the various mine workings and dugouts under construction in the BEF's area of responsibility. Their jobs included the powering of mining systems with generators to provide a multitude of tasks such as the lighting, pumping and ventilation of systems. They also conducted thousands of bores across the British lines in order to see what ground was suitable for mining tasks. Their first task on the Western Front was the installation of a generator at the 2nd Army Mine School. By November they were working in teams all along the front and 177 Tunnelling Company's relationship with these men started on 10th October 1916 when ten men from the Alphabet Company were attached to 177 to light, power and maintain generators in the Ramparts and Canal bank dugouts.

The Cambridge Road dugouts grew in size during the month after numerous dugouts were constructed for various tasks. The dugout was becoming of a size that necessitated for it to be powered by an electrical generator ably fitted by the men of the Alphabet Company. This dugout was also now on two levels, 30 feet and 20 feet. In the main gallery C1 at 30 feet, two 3 feet deep manholes were made in the wall of the dugout as passing places. By 31st October C1 was now 407 feet long. Along the shallower level of the dugout, construction had commenced on machinery, electricians and Drying Room dugouts and 52 feet of the older section of the dugout was expanded from 4 feet 3 inches by 2 feet 3 inches to 6 feet high by 3 feet wide. At 307 feet along C1 left and right branch galleries were started labelled C5 and C6 and were 17 and 45 feet long respectively by the month's end.

Work on the canal bank dugouts suffered during the month in that only one small shift was available for work per day. Over 379 feet of 3 feet by 2 feet ventilation tunnel was constructed during the month with seventeen dugouts connected to the system. 22 foot long urinal recesses were also constructed by the shift throughout the month.

The various strongpoints being constructed by the company also took shape in October. The main gallery of Mill Cottage dugout was 473 feet long by the end of

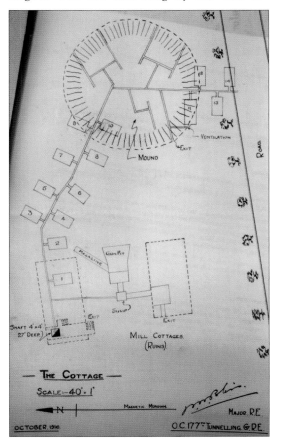

The Cottage dugout plan for October 1916. (REL)

Railway Wood Cambridge Road dugouts, October 1916. (TNA)

the month and fourteen dugouts had been constructed along its length including 8 feet of ventilation shaft for a cookhouse dugout within the system.

In Wieltje the Hades dugout had a stepped incline to the surface as well as a shaft. Gallery 'C' was 177 feet long by the end of the month and Gallery B 201 feet long. Thirteen dugouts in the system had also been completed.

Hill Top Farm dugout was only worked on at night and its Gallery C was 72 feet long by the 11th October and Gallery D was 76 feet long by the end of the month. Wilson's farm dugout again was only worked at night. By the months end Galleries A, B and C were a total length of 108 feet and Gallery D had been driven 62 feet. Construction on

Wieltje dugout
plan for October
1916. (REL)

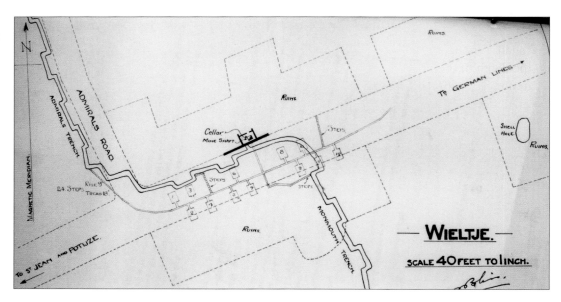

dugout chambers for both dugouts was also underway.

On 22nd October 37-year-old 132805 Sapper James Dennis of 177 was killed in action.[2]

NOVEMBER 1916

With the onset of winter life under the Railway Wood sector continued unabated during November 1916. Pumping, repairing and listening work was carried out in the number 6, 8, 11 and 16 workings. The only other mention for these workings in 177's war diary for the month was that shaft 16W was deepened by four metal rings in preparation for making a sump for the soon to be installed electric pump.

Whilst life under the front may have been quieter than the norm during November, it certainly wasn't the case under Railway Wood. The Cambridge Road dugouts were worked on feverishly during the month. By 17th November gallery C1 was 594 feet long and now connected through to gallery 6A. An 8 foot borehole at the end of the gallery connected through to the number 6 shaft to allow for drainage of the system. It was now possible to enter this large dugout at Cambridge Road and work one's way up to the front connecting into the number 6 underground mine working which in turn connected with other mine workings stretching under the Bellewaerde Ridge without exposing oneself to the Germans and all other dangers above ground. Gallery C5 of the Cambridge Road system was driven out to 157 feet long by the 17th of the month and twelve dugouts 11 feet long and 6 feet wide were constructed along its length. The AEMMBC also provided another team of six men to install and power the dugout. 157 feet along C5, a left branch C5A was 68 feet long and stepped to the surface by 24th November. C5B, a left branch 34 feet along C5, was 24 feet long by the 24th. Gallery C6 and a branch gallery off C6 labelled C6A, were both stepped inclines driven to the surface coming out in Crater trench, a second line trench running parallel with the surface. Gallery C8, a left branch at 491 feet along C1, was 106 feet long by 29th November and connected to the shaft serving the number 8 working. As the depth of the tunnellers here was not accurately known they drove this gallery 4 feet 3 inches high. Once connected to the number 8 workings 85 feet of the gallery was increased to 6 feet high to grade the gallery correctly for drainage purposes. Gallery C9, a right branch at 401 feet along C1, was 137 feet long by the 29th of the month. By 24th November a generator had been installed into the dugouts ready to power electric lighting.

More useful intelligence was gathered on German workings during the month when on 29th November an 'all volunteer' party of three officers and 83 other ranks from the 1/6th Kings Liverpool Regiment, 165th Infantry Brigade, carried out an extensive trench raid and reconnaissance on the German front line opposite Railway Wood. The section of German front line, Idea trench, chosen for the raid ran for 130 metres from map references I12a2.4 to I.12.a.0.5. The raiders had been out of the line practising for the raid for some eight days. Zero hour had initially been fixed for 4.50pm on 28th November but had to be postponed due to fog. The raid was given the go ahead for 4.50pm on the 29th and for 65 minutes before the raiders went over, British artillery commenced a bombardment that fell some distance behind the German lines and then crept forward with the idea it would move any troops caught in front of it forward as well. Trench mortar batteries also opened up on the German front line on orders to try and cut the wire. The raiders gathered in crater 2a just behind the British Front and during the preparatory bombardment,

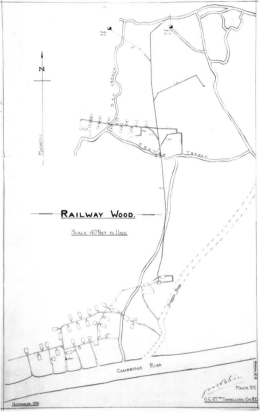

Railway Wood Cambridge Road dugouts, November 1916. (TNA)

Bangalore torpedoes were placed through the British wire and fired during the bombardment so as to cut through the British wire giving a path out into No Man's Land. The preparatory bombardment which consisted of 4,400 x 18 pounder and 900 x 4.2 inch shells and 1,186 trench mortar bombs was a resounding success; the infantry commenting on the "obliterated condition of the trenches". During the raid 17,500 rounds of machine gun fire was put down over the attacking infantry onto the German's communication trench network so as to stop any advance forward. Although no sappers from 177 accompanied the infantry on their raid, eight sappers from the 1st/1st West Lancashire Field Coy went forward as demolition experts finding no

93

use for their skills as the artillery had done its job so well. During their exploration of the German fronts they came upon a concrete dugout, wood lined and a deeper mined dugout under the German parapet. The deeper system was bombed with four prisoners taken from it. The description given by the raiders of the German trenches in this area was that they were about 7 feet deep and 4 feet wide, well built, with a sandbagged parados and parapet. They were revetted with fascines and brushwood, were wooden floored and comparatively dry in comparison to the British front line. Eleven German prisoners were taken during the raid with British casualties standing at 4 men killed, 13 wounded and 1 missing.

At the canal bank dugouts system work continued throughout November ventilating a further sixteen dugouts and extending a further nine dugouts to 20 feet long. There was a lot of work on the surface as well as underground as a slide occurred that necessitated the rebuilding and shoring of the Yser Canal bank.

Work progressed on the strongpoints with Cottage strongpoint at map reference I.5.a.0.7 being provisionally handed over to the infantry as a dugout with machine gun emplacement on 2nd November. Further work was required on the dugout and this was carried out between the 13th to the 21st of November before being finally ready for handing over to the infantry following

Map showing the trench raid carried out by 1/6th Bn, King's Liverpool Regt on 29th November 1916. (TNA WO95/2901)

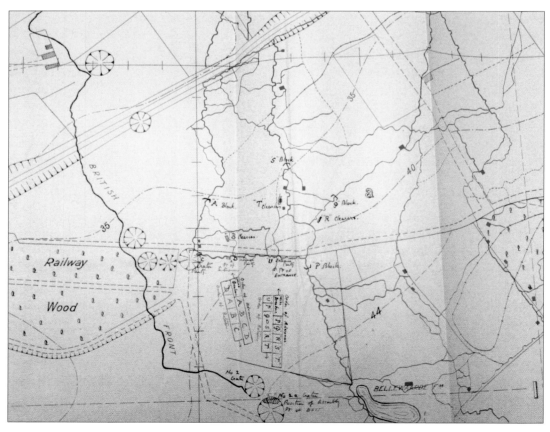

an inspection by the Commander Royal Engineers of the 55th Division whose infantry would be the first to utilise the dugout and machine gun emplacements. The dugout was used by the 1/4th Royal Lancashire Regiment as a Battalion HQ in a 200-man trench raid that took place on 23rd December. At Wieltje, B gallery of the dugout was driven out to 257 feet long by mid-November. By the 29th of the month nineteen dugouts 11 feet 6 inches long and 6 feet wide had been completed along the gallery. An all important ventilation gallery 3 feet high and 2 feet wide was 10 feet long by the end of the month and on the surface, just behind the front, a few shell holes were chosen to be fortified into machine gun emplacements that would connect with the dugout by means of inclined stairways leading underground. At Hilltop Farm in the northeast of the Salient, the main gallery, D, was 148 feet long by 29th November with seven dugouts along its length. Another Gallery, E, was started which ran southeast and led to a planned machine gun emplacement. At Wilson's Farm, Gallery D was 120 feet long with five dugouts along its length by 29th November. An inclined stairway that led up to a surface machine gun emplacement was 38 feet long by the end of the month. Work was greatly hindered due to lack of timber available for both Hill Top and Wilson's Farm dugouts during the month, with between five and seven days lost due to the shortage.

DECEMBER 1916

December saw an increase in activity under the Railway Wood sector. Harassment by German artillery and trench mortars coupled with the deteriorating weather conditions played merry hell with the surface entrances of many of the workings necessitating many hours being spent on repair and maintenance. Adding to the problems this month was the onset of a serious shortage of timber being supplied to the tunnellers via wood depots behind the lines. In most cases this delayed, and in one case, stopped work on workings altogether. If weather and supply were a hindrance to the company during December, manpower levels remained fairly good. Company strength at the beginning of the month was 343 officers, NCOs and men with 723 officers, NCOs and men attached to the company.

In the number 6 and 8 workings under the Railway Wood sector work remained the same as the previous month with repairing, pumping and listening being the norm. The number 11 workings however, were very active during the month. A regular pattern of sounds were being picked up by listeners both in the shallow and deeper levels of the number 11 workings in galleries 11M and 11WD. Action was needed and authority granted from Major Bliss to camouflet the enemy. As a camouflet charge was prepared and planted, disaster struck when a particularly heavy German trench mortar bombardment caused two heavy falls in 11WD cutting off the camouflet charge and blocking the gallery. The idea of reclaiming the charge was abandoned when listeners picked up sounds thought to be those of German miners working within 20 feet of the 30 feet mark of 11WD. Clearing out the collapses, repairing the gallery and preparing the charge for firing would have been almost suicidal with the enemy that close. A camouflet of 2000 lbs of ammonal with an accelerant of guncotton all primed with electric detonators was planted at the 30 feet mark of 11WD. The gallery was then tamped with 35 feet of solid tamping, a gap of 10 feet to allow for an air cushion and then a further 20 feet of solid tamping backed by a 2 foot thickness of timber. 11WE was also tamped with 15 feet of solid tamping. At 1715 hrs on 10th December the camouflet was fired. It was deemed that the result was 'probably successful' against the Germans, but the British did not get away without any damage to their own workings. Galleries 11WD and 11WE were completely destroyed by the camouflet and a leakage of gas came back into the upper levels of the 11 workings, believed to have leaked via the German galleries discovered and linked up to a couple of months earlier. Ten casualties were sustained as a result of the gas which included eight men attached to 177, who were killed as a result of exposure to this deadly, noxious air. 6318 Private William Tilsey and 6246 Private Ernest Magnall both from the 1/4th Loyal North Lancs attached to 177 Tunnelling Company both attempted to get back into the workings to rescue men overcome by the afterdamp gas but were forced to return empty handed.[3] 11WA was wrecked back to its 50 feet mark and on the shallower level 11M was wrecked with 11D and the end of 16WE being shaken up. It was believed by many that the camouflet also detonated the lost 4000 lbs charge along 11WD which in turn led to the release of the gas that caused the casualties. The situation on the surface was also busy in that four two-minute shoots, combining machine gun and artillery fire targeting roads, trench railway and communication trenches behind the German lines took place at 4.55pm, 6.05pm, 7.25pm and 9.35pm.

At 6am on 17th December the Germans blew a series of small charges between craters 2 and 2a running eastwards. One of the blows occurred directly below a section of the British trench damaging about 30 feet of it but not destroying it as it was prepared and protected against blows of this nature. The blows caused no damage to 177's underground workings and it was believed the purpose of the blows was to destroy or damage surface trenches or shallow galleries. The blows left a row of small craters and it was deduced that they had probably been a series of bored mines, charged at intervals, and set so that they would blow upwards. The German infantry on the surface then began frantically to work on the craters in the vicinity of their own trenches consolidating them into their own defences. Opposite, British infantry of the 55th Division on the surface, set about repairing the damage immediately and in his Mine Explosion Report Major Bliss stated that work would commence to destroy the underground position from where the enemy detonated their charges. Witness evidence gathered from the infantry on the surface is recorded as stating that some remembered the blows as a series of explosions and others remembered hearing a sizzling noise prior to the blows.

In reaction to the work the Germans were doing in consolidating the small craters on the surface, a 250 lb camouflet charge was prepared and laid at the end of gallery 11P which was then tamped with 30 feet of solid tamping. The 250 lbs was in tins and primed with gun cotton and electric detonators. Authority to prepare and fire the charge came from the Section Officer on the ground at the time and the charge was fired at 3am on 21st December. The resultant explosive shockwave was believed to have passed down the German galleries in the vicinity of the blow. 11M stood up to the blow fairly well with only a few feet of gallery behind the tamping being damaged. No gas or flame was reported in any of the British galleries and no gas or flame reported on the surface.

Thirty minutes after the blow, however, a fissure caused by the blow allowed water in crater 2a to flood into our workings which made its way back through the Cambridge Road dugouts flooding out the pump at the foot of the steel shaft of the dugout!

With most of the focus of 177's work being in the number 11 workings during the month, work still continued in the

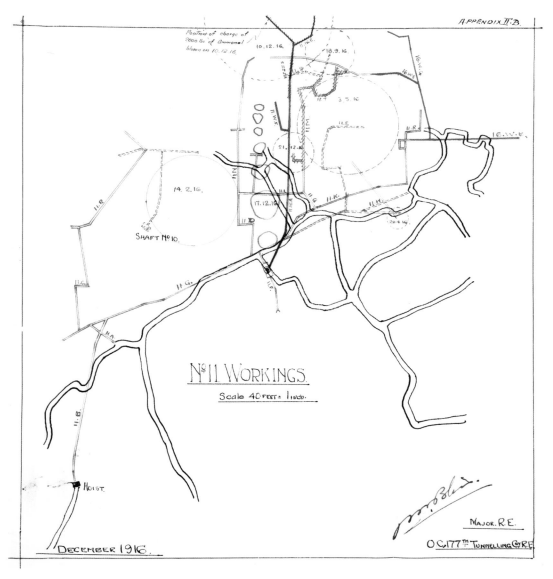

Railway Wood
No 11 workings,
December 1916.
(TNA)

adjacent number 16 workings under trench H16. Gallery 16WH located off to the left at 16 feet along gallery 16WB, was 16 feet long by 27th December. 16WS, a gallery in the deeper 58 feet level of the number 16 workings, was 81 feet long by the 17th of the month with 50 feet of the gallery reset lower to aid drainage. A pump dugout into which 16 was connected was also constructed.

Work on the Cambridge Road dugouts during December was hampered by a number of reasons, chiefly the shortage of timber available to the company but also by the gas and the flooding of the system as a result of the camouflets blown on the 12th and the 21st December. Three stepped inclines to the surface were completed during the month, C5b, C5b1 and C9. A shaft dugout was started, to facilitate a proposed new steel shaft at 550 feet along gallery C1 of the dugout.

During December ten dugouts belonging to the Canal bank dugouts system were ventilated and six dugouts extended to 20 feet long.

At Wieltje, the Hades dugout continued to grow. Gallery E was 187 feet long by 27th December and was raised in steps to the surface. The ventilating gallery to serve the cookhouse of the dugout was 30 feet long by the 4th of the month. An inclined stairway up to a machine gun emplacement was worked on whilst an inclined stairway up into Monmouth trench was discontinued due to bad ground. Work continued on the dugouts in the system with three more being added including three urinal recesses being added to the living dugouts. The Engine Room dugout had been completed and the AEMMBC added an electric lighting plant to power the dugout.

At Hill Top Farm Gallery D was 194 feet long by the 20th of the month. Five days was spent working on a 24-feet long stairway to the surface which was completed by 20th December. Another stairway leading to a machine gun emplacement was 53 feet long by the 17th and stepped to the surface. Gallery E was 190 feet long by 27th December with a stepped incline to the

Wieltje Hades dugout, December 1916. (TNA)

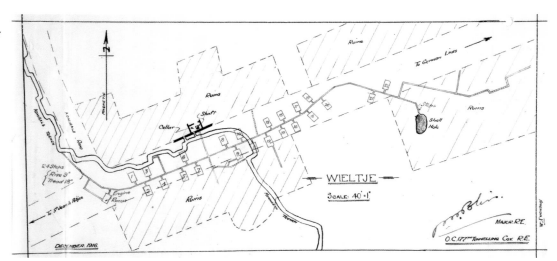

surface. Eleven dugouts 6 feet by 3 feet in size were also completed along galleries D and E.

Wilson's Farm suffered during December with the lack of timber, with work finishing on the 8th. Some work was done prior to this nuisance with a stepped stairway to a machine gun emplacement being worked on and six dugouts being completed.

---

1   Lt Andrew Stuart Holms is buried in Vlamertinge Military Cemetery plot II row D grave 18.

2   Spr Denis is listed by SDGW as being killed in action but the exact location of his death is unknown. He is buried in Vlamertinge Military Cemetery

3   6318 Pte William Tilsley was awarded the Distinguished Conduct Medal for his actions on the 11th December 1916. His citation reads:

"For marked gallantry and devotion to duty at Railway Wood on December 11th, 1916. On that day eight men were killed in a mine by after-damp. Private Tilsley immediately went down the mine shaft, but was forced to return. He then put on his box respirator and made another attempt, but found the respirator of no avail. This man has always worked well and shown a good spirit under all circumstances."

His colleague that day, 6246 Private Ernest Magnall was mentioned in Dispatches. His citation reads:

"For great devotion to duty at Railway Wood on December 11th 1916. On that day, when eight men had been killed in a mine as a result of 'after-damp', he offered his services, and attempted, with Private Tilsley, to go down the mine. He has at all time done good work, and has been most useful to his company commander, owing to his good spirits under all circumstances."

CHAPTER FOUR

Image 7. 1917 Aerial photograph of 177 Tunnelling Company HQ and the 2nd Army Mine School near Zoom Farm, Proven. Practice mine craters, one of which was blown by 177, can be seen to the centre left of the photograph. (Author's collection)

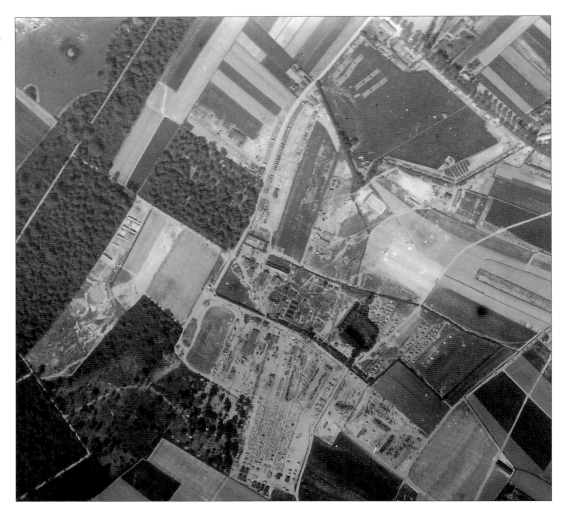

Located at the headquarters of 177 Tunnelling Company was the Second Army Mine School. The school consisted of a listening and mine rescue school and taught subjects that were vital to the safe operation of tunnelling companies at the front. GHQ had detailed 177 to set up the school which had to be up and running for its first courses from July 1916.

The listening school was under the command of Major James Pollock, a 50-year-old professor of physics from Sydney University, who had been transferred to 177 from the Australian Mining Corps at the beginning of June. On the surface, the listening school consisted of a large shed 40 feet long and 20 feet wide, used as both a repair workshop and lecture hall.

Underground, the school consisted of two galleries, one at 18 feet deep and the other at 30 feet deep both connected by an inclined stairway and vertical shaft. Off these galleries were listening chambers that tapered away from each other the further into the gallery you went. Between the two galleries was a working gallery at both 18 and 30 feet depth connected by both shaft and inclined stairway. The instructors used the working galleries to replicate the different types of sounds that would be heard by listeners under the front line. Major Pollock attached principle importance to the sound of falling dirt. It was the least variable sound and the one most likely to be picked up by listeners, regardless of what tool was being used by opposing miners. The distances from the listening chambers to the working galleries differed from 5 feet to 60 feet. At the opposite end of the listening galleries a further gallery ran off in the opposite direction. At the end of this gallery a chamber was dug. It was from this chamber that push pipe trials were carried out, possibly to see how much ammonal per foot was required in the pipes if they were going to be used to blow underground galleries.

Officers and men going through training in mine rescue would also receive 2½ hours instruction and practice per day in estimation of distances for all regular sounds and direction. In addition to men temporarily detached for courses, the school was able to train a further two officers and ten men per day from the tunnelling companies, in the art of listening.

The importance of listening and being proficient in it cannot be underestimated. It was an art rather than a subject. The pressure on an individual, listening at a gallery face or from a 'T' junction, again cannot be understated. From the time a listener commences work underground, under No Man's Land, his nervous system is in a state of tension, couple with this, the deadly monotony, loneliness of the work and the necessity for absolute silence.

"It is difficult to realise what silent working means, and to estimate the strain on the men, more especially as they were carrying out hard work all the time. The slightest noise might result in such serious consequences, and have such far-reaching effects, that every man had to concentrate his attention on working, in perfect silence; and, as you all know, concentration causes fatigue to be felt more quickly." [1]

Men either had the 'gift' of being a proficient listener or not and this would be discovered during training at the Listening School. The pure psychological pressure on the listener was huge. The buck rested with you. Here you were in this tiny 4 feet 6 inch high by 2 feet 3 inch wide gallery, deep beneath the ground, in total silence, trying your best to protect the soldiers on the surface and your comrades underground from enemy mining. The enemy would be doing the same to you, listening and waiting. The slightest noise, muffled or otherwise could be the enemy. What state was their mine working at? Were they going to blow first? What is that noise? Have you missed them and have they tunnelled past you? Do you report that slight noise or not? Listeners would keep a log of their shift. It was found out very quickly during the evolution of listening on

101

the Western Front that the shift time for a listener to be on duty had to be short. Thirty minutes was identified as a good time span. With the pressure on the listener and with wearing a Geophone, after some time it was commonplace to confuse your own heartbeat with that of the noise of a pick striking the face of a gallery or a tool sliding into the clay. The slightest innocent noise could be misinterpreted by a listener on the edge of panic. Lt Geoffrey Boothby experienced nervous miners on periods spent on duty before his death in April 1916:

"This mining is not without its dangers, rather unexpected ones at times. It is rather trying on the nerves, listening for Huns burrowing and expecting them to blow you up at any minute, as witness to what happened last night in a shaft where the Corporal in charge had the wind up badly. He was down the shaft going along one of the galleries when suddenly he came upon two Bosches round a corner. He drew back (all this is his own account) & heard them say (in English) 'It's only 10 feet to the bottom of the shaft.' So entirely convinced was he that they were wily Bosche that he let fly with his revolver several times, then retired rapidly & reported to the officer at the top, who went down & of course found nothing. Naturally we are returning this imaginative fellow to his Regiment. I have no fancy to be mistaken for a Hun by any fool who has the jumps. In another case a miner listening in one of the galleries swore he could hear the Germans quite near, talking in one of their galleries. An officer and two men he said. He could tell it was an officer, for in spite of the fact that he couldn't speak German himself, he could easily detect the cultured accent of the officer! These are not 'cum grano salis' stories, they're facts."[2]

The tools used by the listener to carry out his work went from the 'Heath Robinson' to the technically innovated. Earlier in the war all sorts of listening contraptions were used. Lt Col A Hacking, CO of the 8th Notts and Derbys witnessed just this as his men held trenches near Kemmel in 1915:

"My men were Nottinghamshire miners some of them reported to me they were sure the Bosche were working below our trenches. Some Sappers came along to investigate and said it was highly unlikely as the ground was too wet. However, my mining boys rigged up a contraption consisting of an 18lb shell case into which was inserted a bayonet running through the base. The lid was the tin of a cigarette case, connected up by wire to the top of the shell case and the contraption was put on the floor of the trench. My fellows spent hours holding the tin to one ear and the lid to their teeth and were absolutely certain that mining was going on. During my next spell they told me that all was quiet which was suspicious and I got authority to move my platoon, at night, to a trench 50 yards or so behind and sure enough our forward trench went up with a bang accompanied by trench mortar fire. My casualties were few. A full story was put up to Brigade but I gather the RE were not impressed with our home-made mine detector."[3]

At times an empty biscuit tin, minus the lid was sunk flush with the gallery floor. Filled with water a miner could place his ear in the water to pick up magnified sounds, or a lit candle floated in the tin, the flickering flame or ripples in the water alerting listeners to nearby work. The most common instrument used, similar to a doctor's stethoscope was also used by water companies in peacetime to locate underground fissures in water supply systems. It was undoubtedly the best instrument devised for determining direction whilst listening. There were different types of geophone in use; their role was to magnify noise. The geophone consisted of a mercury filled mica disc encompassed in a wooden pot, which would magnify the noise. The listener wore a contraption similar to the stethoscope. If using only one disc, this would only magnify noises detected by the listener. It could not determine direction. When two discs were used at the same time, together with a compass, a direction of the noise detected could be attained:

123

Instrument.	Use.
Geophone	Determination of Direction.
Western Electric Detector ...	Determination of Distance.
Seismomicrophone	Central Listening Stations. Listening in gassy galleries. Tamping in with charges.

(The notes that follow were written immediately after the war (December, 1918), by CAPT. H. STANDISH BALL, R.E. (T), *and must be read with due regard to that fact).*

20. THE GEOPHONE.

The Geophone (*Plate* XX. and *Photo* III.) is undoubtedly the best instrument yet devised for determining direction.

One of the chief factors which determined its universal use is the true reproduction of sound obtained by its means.

Constructed on the principles of the ordinary stethoscope, the sound waves are transmitted from the ground through the instrument to the listener at an intensity approximately two and a half times greater than would be obtained when listening with the ear alone.

Several different types of instrument have been made, all based on the same principle; a description of the Geophone and its use will suffice for all.

Plate XXI. shows its method of use. Its construction is simple, consisting of a mass of mercury enclosed on either side by a mica disc, the whole contained in a wooden frame. On the exterior of the pot are two small nipples to which are attached the rubber tubes and ear-piece—if two Geophones are to be used, one nipple is blocked up by means of a small rubber plug.

Single Geophone.—One Geophone only is used when it is desired to magnify the sound only, and no direction is required—it is used generally by listeners who have not been trained in double Geophone work, but at the same time can be relied on for their accurate knowledge of mining sounds. It is impossible to obtain direction by means of the single Geophone; its use, however, is of the utmost value for sound magnification, and all mining sounds can be heard over a considerable distance by its means, as is seen later in the table of sounds.

Double Geophone.—For the successful use of two Geophones in the determination of direction, experience shows that the listener must be possessed of unimpaired hearing, and have been thoroughly trained at a School of Instruction and have obtained a creditable pass.

Working on the principle that the Geophones are two highly sensitive ears, the listener manipulates them to and fro on the ground until the sound is reproduced equally in both ears. When

Notes on the use of the Geophone from *The Work of the Royal Engineers in the European War 1914 to 1919* (Military Mining). (REL)[4]
See also pages 104–108

103

that condition is satisfied, the source of the sound will be in a direction at right angles to the line joining the centre of the two pots.

Plate XXII. shows the principle of working. Assume that the two Geophones are placed on the ground, about $1\frac{1}{2}$ ft.–2 ft. apart, their position at starting being L1 and R1, L1 being the left Geophone and R1 the right one. If the source of sound is as shown by the arrow in the diagram, the sound will strike the left ear first, pointing to the fact that L1 is too far round and is nearer the source of sound than R1. The Geophones will now be shifted to position L2, R2; the first impact of sound is immediately transferred to the right ear, showing the fact that R has been brought too far round, and the fact is now established that the correct position for L is somewhere in the arc L1–L2, and that for R between R1–R2. After a little bracketing backwards and forwards, a position L3–R3 will be found, where the sound will be heard simultaneously in both ears.

On the Geophone Compass being placed between the pots, the direction of the arrow pointing to the source of the sound is read and booked. Thus it will be seen that in *Plate* XXII. the direction of the working place is 41° W. of N. If a direction determination has been made from the end of a listening-post, a further determination is made either from an adjacent post or from a point further back in the gallery; on the two directions being plotted in the plan, the intersection should give to a close degree of accuracy the position of the working face. The Geophone may be used in a similar manner to ascertain the level of the working. The Geophone pots are placed against the side of the gallery, one above the other—if the sound is on a higher level, it will strike the upper pot first, if on a lower level, the bottom pot. When making a determination, great care must be taken that the pots are resting on a solid foundation, and are not on any foreign matter such as sandbags or straw. If the condition of the ground is such that it is difficult to find a suitable foundation, a ledge must be constructed in the side of the gallery large enough to allow of the free movement of the pots.

When listening, all leather equipment or articles liable to produce any creaking sound must be removed; the slightest noise disturbs the listener and leads to the production of inaccurate results.

On moving the Geophones around, the body should be made to follow them as far as possible, the shoulders being kept close between the pots.

Silence is naturally an essential feature of a listening-post, and on no account should more than two listeners be allowed in together.

Standard listening forms should always be used for booking results, Army Form W.3379 being used for this purpose.

125

Mine Listening Report.   A.F. W. 3379.

Listener's Name—Sapper Evans.   *Date*—27/11/17.

Name of Gallery.	Time.	Sounds heard.	Estimated distance in feet.	Estimated direction.
" A "	2 p.m.-4 p.m.	Picking and Shovelling.	40	N.30°W.

Compass.—The compass should be mounted in a wooden frame about 18 in. long, into the ends of which the Geophone pots will fit. The compass is graduated in 36 segments, each segment representing 10°, and reads from 0 to 18 to the right and left of the arrow respectively. This arrow always points directly at the source of sound, and its position is recorded E. or W. of Magnetic North, *e.g.*, 30° W. of N. or 150° E. of N.

Care of the Geophone Set.—Great care must always be taken of the set, the listener being taught to regard his Geophone in the light that an infantry man should regard his rifle.

The following are practical points which should always be tested by the listener when examining his set :—

(i).   The rubber tubes must be of an equal length.

(ii).   The pots must be a pair, and must correspond with the numbers on the box.

(iii). The tubes, ear-piece, and Geophone nipples must be free from any obstruction.

(iv). The compass must be in the box.

Each side of the Geophone must be tested, as it sometimes happens that one side may be rendered useless and not the other.

Geophones have lately been constructed containing lead in place of the mercury mass. This type is quite satisfactory, but gives a slightly different reproduction of the sound from the mercury type —hence care must be taken that only one or the other is used ; if one mercury and one lead were used in combination, difficulty would be experienced in determining the final point.

21. WESTERN ELECTRIC MINING DETECTOR.

This instrument consists of an earth-wave detecting apparatus which is capable of transforming the energy received from earth-waves originated by mining operations into electrical impulses, when supplied with current from a battery placed in circuit ; and of reproducing those noises in a telephone receiver. In circuit with this detector is an apparatus capable of reducing all received sound to one level, called the " Zero Sound," by the introduction of variable resistances into the circuit, thus altering the current. The amount by which the apparatus has to reduce the received sound to attain this zero limit can be measured ; and, by means of suitable calibration curves, such measurements can be expressed in feet.

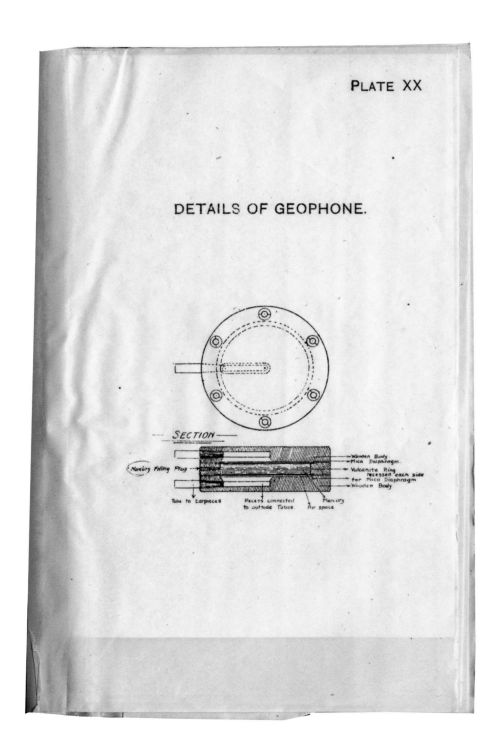

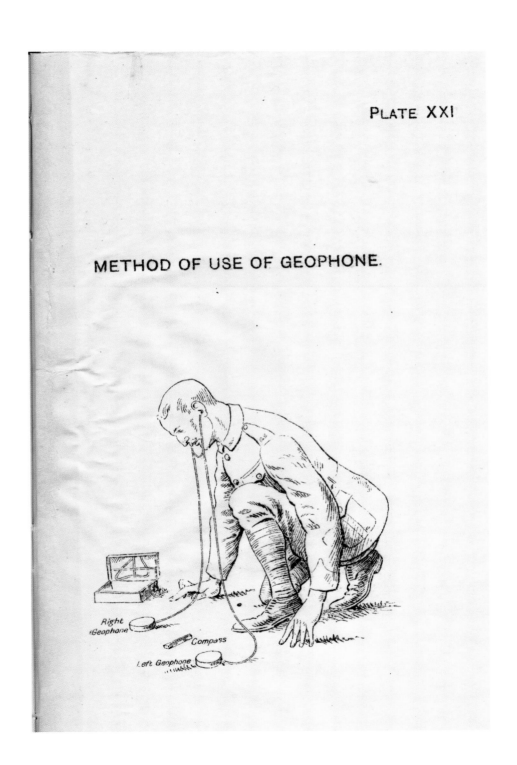

PLATE XXI

METHOD OF USE OF GEOPHONE.

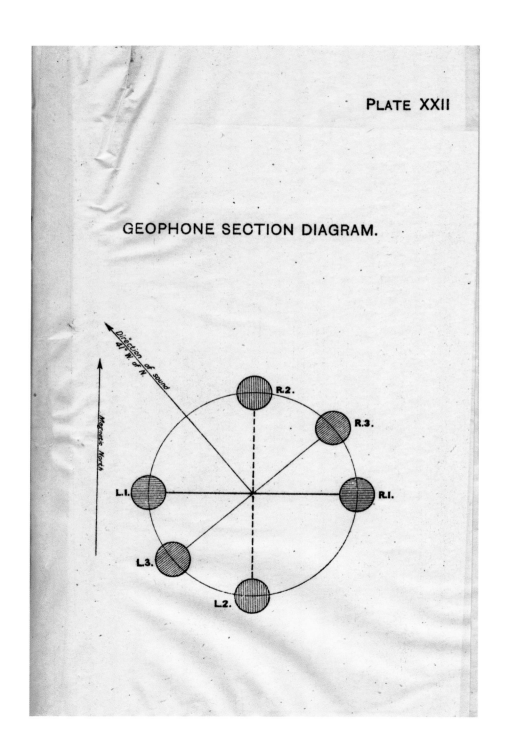

The drawback of the geophone was that it required a person to be at the face of the working. This amounted to a lot of men when consideration is taken into account of the amount of galleries, at various depths, operated by 177. This is where the Seismomicrophone came into play. This piece of equipment allowed listeners to carry out their duty remotely. One can almost sense the despair of a listener at the face in an area where the enemy are expected to blow any minute, or having to spend any time in a gassy gallery following a blow. With the Seismomicrophone, a greater economy of manpower was obtained. The remote detectors were put into watertight boxes and placed in the galleries. An underground chamber, in a dugout system, behind the front could be utilised as a switchboard allowing listeners to listen in their multitude of mine workings. This device could also be placed onto the tamping of a mine charge and left for as long as needed.

Trials were carried out to determine distances over which different types of sounds could be heard and with what instruments. The geology of the Western Front played its part in determining the ranges sought after. The clay and sand geology found in Flanders contrasted completely with detection made in the chalk found further south in the British area of responsibility. The main noise that would be picked up in mining in clay, if done carefully, would be the timbering work required to support the galleries. Some average listening distances trialled in the varying geology, with the geophone and with the unaided ear produced interesting results:

With Geophone	Chalk	Blue Clay	Sand and Loam
Picking	250 – 300 ft	50 – 70 ft	30 – 40 ft
Dirt Falling (Careless)	60 ft	25 – 35 ft	8 -12 ft
Walking (Enemy)	55 ft	10 – 15 ft	8 – 10 ft
Dragging Sandbags	55 ft	10 – 15 ft	8 – 10 ft
Talking	30 ft	4 – 6 ft	3 – 5 ft

With unaided ear	Chalk	Blue Clay	Sand and Loam
Picking	100 – 150 ft	35 – 45 ft	20 – 30 ft
Grafting	Nil	10 – 15 ft	8 – 12 ft
Dirt falling (Careless)	35 ft	10 – 15 ft	4 – 6 ft
Walking (Enemy)	30 ft	5 – 8 ft	5 – 8 ft
Dragging Sandbags	25 ft	6 – 10 ft	4 – 6 ft
Talking	12 ft	3 – 4 ft	2 – 3 ft [5]

Men from all the Second Army tunnelling companies would pass through the Listening School under Major Pollock's careful instruction. On 9th April 1917 he was mentioned in Despatches for his efforts.

THE MINE RESCUE SCHOOL

The Second Army Mine Rescue School was the original school of instruction in the subject. Once the policy of military mining was determined and work increased on a tremendous scale underground within the Second Army area, these big scale operations brought with them an ever-increasing risk of detection and blowing by the enemy. The deadly nature of gases existing after an underground blow were realised early. Army requests for portable breathing apparatus and men trained in the usage of such equipment met with instantaneous response.

It became apparent that a school was needed, completely detached from the tunnelling companies at the front so as not to interfere with their mining work. Lt Colonel David Dale Logan DSO, then a captain, was appointed to GHQ as an advisor in mine rescue matters. Under his supervision a number of Proto breathing sets were sent out and training in their usage began. From May until October 1915 Mr A Clifford was sent out to instruct in the usage of Proto sets. He was solely responsible for the training of men in mine rescue work during this time. Initially requested to train 3,000 men in the usage of Proto, in a month, with only 36 sets available in the country, training began in earnest at Strazeele, in the yard of the Royal Engineers Park. In July the Second Army school was moved to Armetières, whilst here Lt Oscar Earnshaw of 177 Tunnelling Company, a qualified mining engineer, was sent on a course. He described his experiences in a letter to his father:

> "Well I've managed to get down the line again after a spell of 12 days, which was rather long to be stuck in a dugout in the front line, and I appreciated my bed in camp after a good bath and a change of underclothing. I almost had to peel my socks off and also my trousers; they were pretty well soldered to my legs.

> The unfortunate part of the business is, instead of letting me rest as I think I deserved they bumped me off to Armentières to a proto School, and now here I am listening to the same lectures and wearing the same apparatus as I did at Elswick Rescue Station a few years ago. I told them I'd gone through it before but they said, 'Yes but not an ARMY course!' which they think is something wonderful, but never mind, I suppose I'll get over it alright. I see the Australians are here in this spot, so I think that according to their bombast and swank we may expect the war to finish at any moment now."

Clifford's intimate knowledge of the apparatus and his devotion to the work of training the men especially when training later increased on a considerable scale merited the highest praise. He was awarded the Meritous Service Medal in recognition of his valuable service in 1917. In October 1915 the School moved to Nieppe. It suffered difficulties in the supply of apparatus and material. Here it was placed under the wing of 171 Tunnelling Company who set about the first real attempt to set up a training centre more in keeping with the scope of the work. The demand for more skilled mine rescuers grew and as the value of the training in mine rescue was greatly realised the school moved once again, in June 1916, this time to Proven where it was co-located with the Mine Listening School. Here both schools fell under the wardship of 177 Tunnelling Company. The new school location provided better facilities for the accommodation of officers and other ranks and there was considerably more room for the expansion of the school.

As well as being responsible for the training of tunnellers in their area in mine rescue the school was also responsible, to the Controller of Mines, in the maintenance and efficiency of the Proto men in the Second Army area. Each tunnelling company OC would submit weekly reports to the Mine Rescue School detailing the number and disposition of the various types of breathing apparatus in their possession. The OC of the Mine Rescue School then collated the weekly reports from the Second Army tunnelling companies and forwarded them, with a weekly statement of the week's work at the school to the Controller of Mines. The information was then sent further up the chain to GHQ and the Inspector of Mines.

The OC of the Mine Rescue School, in addition to his supervision and running of the school, was responsible for the efficiency of all the company mine rescue organisations. On a regular basis he would visit tunnelling company HQs and mine rescue stations. In each tunnelling company there was an officer responsible to the OC Mine Rescue School, for the efficient training of men in mine rescue carried out away from the school. This type of detached training consisted of artificial respiration and an alarm practice where a team would enter the saps in which they were working wearing their breathing apparatus. The company officer responsible for the training would be assisted by a specially trained and selected SNCO. Details of the companies' training would be submitted on a special form to the OC Mine Rescue School.

As well as being responsible for the training of men in mine rescue work, the school would also supervise and lend staff to a company that may be carrying out rescue work at the front. The school staff were there to advise on rescue work and to supervise the use of apparatus especially where prolonged use of it occurred underground. Staff from the school were deployed to companies only on a few exceptions. Each company organisation was sufficiently strong to battle through its bad times unassisted. In June 1916 near the Petit Bois at Wytschaete, 250 Tunnelling Company were driving a gallery under the German front as part of the Messines offensive scheme. The Germans blew a camouflet that collapsed a large part of the British gallery trapping twelve miners below ground. A rescue operation got underway that lasted for six days, finally getting through to the trapped men. Unfortunately all eleven of the men were dead with the exception of one, Sapper Bedson. This rescue has been well documented elsewhere and although no proof can be found, it is believed that this is one of the few operations that the staff from the rescue school became involved in a mine rescue operation. The school was also responsible at times for tunnelling units belonging to the Second Army. Prior to the start of the Third Battle of Ypres, the Fifth Army took over a part of the Second Army area and for a period of time the Second Army Mine Rescue School was responsible for the maintenance and efficiency in mine rescue work of seven Fifth Army companies along with the eight companies belonging to the Second Army.

At the school, the principle was adopted that it would be better to train and keep in practice a small number of men per company rather than training a larger number. More difficulties were foreseen by trying to keep proficient large numbers of men. By early 1916 officers were receiving basic instruction at Chatham in mine rescue work before deployment to tunnelling companies. This course would not make them experts, but would give them good grounding in the subject prior to further training either in the field or back at the Second Army Mine Rescue School. There were a fixed provisional number of forty other ranks per tunnelling company to be trained in the use of Proto breathing apparatus. This number for many was seen as a minimum number per company. In reality, far greater than forty per company would have to be trained many as battle casualty replacements. Other ranks attended the Mine Rescue School courses as volunteers. They were given very rigid medical inspections by their own tunnelling company Medical Officer prior to starting courses. Great emphasis was placed on checking that the men had no cardiac or bronchial weakness and were fit for all aspects of work put to them. On arrival at the school all candidates had to produce a medical certificate stating that they were clear of any cardiac or bronchial issues. Anyone suspected of suffering from these ailments went straight in front of the 177 Tunnelling Company MO for a further rigorous examination. Prior to donning breathing apparatus on course, students' pulse rates were taken and noted again after each practice. During the courses, men who showed signs of strain or unwillingness to continue training were struck off the list of 'Proto Men' held by the school. Cases of unwillingness to continue training were few and it was nearly always the school that insisted on men not coming up to the standard required to stop training mainly due to strain or shell shock. Basic

psychometric evaluation was made on the students to confirm suitability for the job and certain types of men invariably rejected. For example, those who were very keen but easily excitable and those who were incapable of understanding the necessary theory of the various apparatus and the reasons for taking necessary precautions in mine rescue work. In these cases it was considered that men falling into this category would be a danger to men on a mine rescue team and also to those they may be rescuing.

Proto breathing apparatus was the equipment of choice for mine rescue operations. At the time it was the simplest and most efficient mine rescue apparatus on the market and was well suited for mine rescue work. For tunnel reconnaissance and work of less than thirty minutes duration underground the Salvus apparatus was used. In all cases it was the simplest and most foolproof material that was used in mine rescue.

The staff of the school consisted of an officer, a sergeant, a corporal and two sappers. One of the sappers was also the officer's servant and was not always available for work within the school due to other duties he had to perform. The staff carried out all instruction and supervision tasks on courses and were also there to carry out repairs, recharging and cleaning of apparatus as well as keeping on top of all clerical work. Students attached to the school for courses were lodged and fed by 177 Tunnelling Company to which the school was attached for messing and disciplinary purposes. The school was located alongside the Poperinge to Proven road just opposite the driveway to the Louvie Château. The school consisted of a main hut 90 feet long and 16 feet wide in which there was a room for charging and storing apparatus, a lecture room, a very small office, a staff billet and a repair room. A washhouse for cleaning out bags and for disinfecting apparatus was attached to the apparatus room. In addition the school had an oxygen cylinder store, a general store, an issue store and four training galleries of which two were above ground and two underground. The two surface galleries were used as a fresh air gallery and a gallery filled with smoke or gas to replicate conditions the students may face when underground.[6]

Apparatus held by the school varied according to the nature and area of the work being done by the tunnelling companies. The amount of apparatus held by the school may seem excessive but it must be remembered that in cases of emergency demand for spares were at times heavy and forthcoming from more than one company. It would never be safe, and was not practiced, robbing one company spares to loan to another. In the field, companies lacked the adequate facilities in which to clean and recharge their apparatus after use and therefore it was standard operating procedure that once apparatus had been

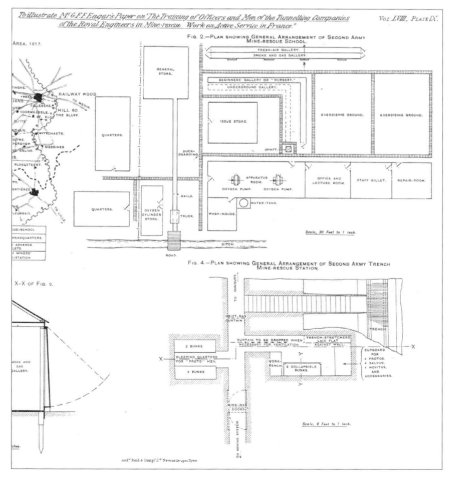

Plan of the underground workings at the Second Army Mine School near Proven which were used to train tunnellers in the art of listening. The entrance to this system is still visible today. (TNA)

used, sets were returned to the school for cleaning, maintenance and refilling. Only in cases of urgent necessity were SNCOs of the company rescue teams able to carry this out on location. Instructions on the use and care of the apparatus were printed and a note pasted in the lid of every apparatus box. A record was kept of dates of examination of equipment and the date when it was to be returned to the school.

As well as training focusing on breathing apparatus, it was also necessary for students to be tested with equipment in the various types of tunnels they would construct underground. Much time was spent with students practising ascending and descending mine shafts whilst wearing breathing apparatus. In the deeper shafts existing at the front it was common for tunnellers to construct a platform every 10 to 15 feet down a shaft. Every platform would have a hole in which the ladder took you down to the next level. In order to accustom men wearing breathing apparatus to getting through these narrow holes on the ladder ways, holes of 18 inches square were constructed around the ladders. Each practical exercise the men carried out at the school began and ended with ladder climbing and descending. Time was also spent in training men to evacuate wounded men from tunnel systems. Men were trained in the use of 'Mine Stretchers' developed especially for the use of tunnelling companies. Its size allowed it to be winched up and down mine shafts. First aid training, including training in artificial respiration, was also carried out on every course. The first course run by the Second Army Mine School at its location near Proven commenced on 24th July 1916. By the spring of 1918 over 2,500 courses of training had been carried out by the school. After initial courses men returned at intervals of three to six months for refresher courses, with officers every six to nine months. Special courses for non-tunnelling personnel were also held. One hundred and fifty officers and men of the Machine Gun Corps were trained in the use of the Salvus breathing apparatus, discontinued in 1916 with the advent of the box respirator. Special lectures were given to men of the Royal Army Medical Corps on the treatment of men suffering from carbon monoxide poisoning, the biggest killer of men underground. The lectures also focused on maintaining continuity of correct treatment after mine gas poisoning cases had been evacuated through the casualty evacuation chain. The training of tunnelling officers and men in rescue work differed in that officers were discouraged from carrying out strenuous work whilst on rescue operations. This was because in the field they were 'Mine Rescue Team Captains' and were there to oversee and manage operations. Officers attending the school would spend the morning over at the Mine Listening School with the afternoon at the Rescue School. A normal class at the school would consist of eight officers and sixteen other ranks. A separate course focusing more on the maintenance and repair of equipment was held for those officers who were detailed as in charge of company organisation of mine rescue work. Their course also focused more on the managing of rescue operations.

With the training of NCOs and men, heavy focus was attached to the familiarity with all parts of the apparatus and sufficient understanding of the theory of apparatus, satisfying simple questions as to the reasons governing the design and dispositions of parts of portable breathing apparatus and the causes of gas poisoning. Lectures for other ranks were given in the simplest possible language with practical demonstrations to press home theory. There was practically no difference in courses for beginners or refreshers but the examination held for the latter was more comprehensive. During the course of training men were actively encouraged to describe cases which they knew or puzzled them. These would be then discussed by the class at large.

Instruction for NCOs in charge of company mine rescue organisation also differed slightly from the normal. Heavy emphasis was placed on making them absolutely familiar with every part of the various apparatus and thoroughly accustomed to methods of examining and testing their apparatus. These SNCOs were specially selected from the most efficient and intelligent of the men from each company who attended the school. Their courses coincided with those of other ranks and during practical training they would be responsible for looking after the class. In turn they would attend all lectures given to refresher courses.

Following the successful passing of a course all ranks were issued with a proficiency certificate. No one was allowed to operate apparatus without holding the certificate. Additional certificates were issued to those attending refresher courses and the men were marked as to their capabilities in each subject. On average the total failure rate of officers and men that passed through the Second Army Rescue School was about 8 per cent. The main causes of failure were due to students being not suited for the work in hand due to lack of education or over excitability of temperament when under pressure.

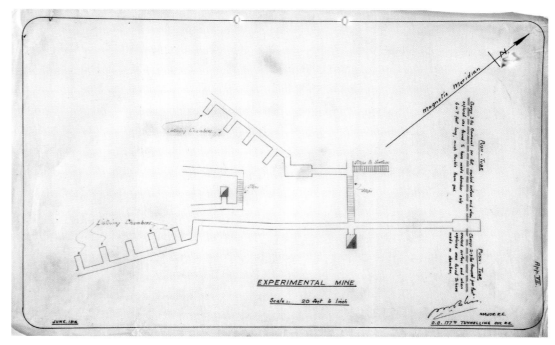

Experimental push pipe mines bored at the 2nd Army Mine School near Zoom Farm, Proven. June 1916. (TNA)

Practice Mine blown by 177 near the 2nd Army Mine School in July 1916. (TNA)

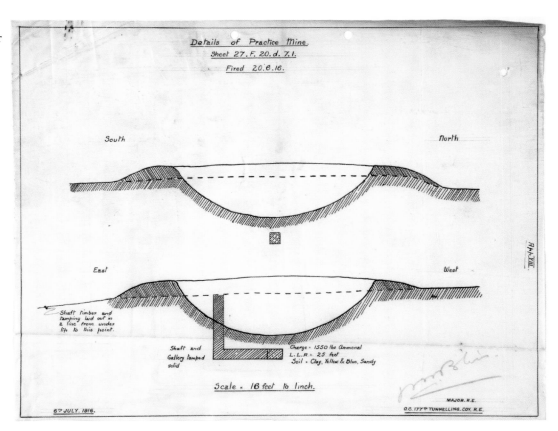

1 "The difficulties and dangers of mine rescue work on the Western Front" Article by Lt Col D Dale Logan DSO written for institute of mining Engineers.

2 Letter to Edith from Geoffrey dated 27 September 1915. Published in "Thirty-Odd Feet Below Belgium" edited by Arthur Stockwin. Parapress limited 2005. ISBN-10: 1-898594-80-5

3 Transcript of interview with Lt Col Hacking and Alexander Barrie. RE Museum

4 The Work of the Miner on the Western Front 1915-1918 by H Standish Ball, 1919.

5 Mining note number 12, dated 23rd April 1916, issued by GHQ.

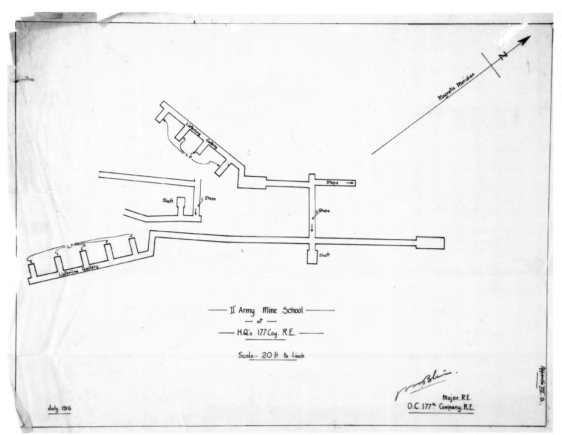

Plan of the 2nd Army Mine School at Zoom Farm near Proven. The entrance to these practice listening tunnels still exists. (TNA)

CHAPTER FIVE

JANUARY 1917

The New Year dawned with 177 Tunnelling Company 344 men strong with 679 infantry attached, still hard at work below the Railway Wood sector. On 9th January 177 lost their first man of 1917 when 32-year-old 121983 Sapper Aurthur Nettel MM, a miner from Repton Derbyshire, died of wounds behind the lines.[1] During the night of the 16th and early morning of the 17th the 164th Infantry Brigade of the 55th Division was relieved in the Railway Wood sector by troops of the 116th Infantry Brigade of the 39th Division.

Temperatures dropped and snow fell on the ground freezing some of the wet trenches. It was conditions like this that could cause worry to the tunnellers. Their underground workings tended to stay at a constant temperature which, during the winter, was higher than the outside temperature. Steam often rose from entrances to the workings and care had to be taken that it wasn't observed from the German lines attracting very unwelcoming artillery fire.

In the number 6 and 8 workings under trench H20 the work carried out during January was limited to pumping, general repair and listening. There was an increase of German artillery fire on British positions in the local area during the month requiring more repair work, especially to entrances, during the month. In the deeper 77 feet level of the number 11 workings, gallery 11WF, a left branch at 124 feet along 11WA, was 152 feet long by the 24th of the month. Gallery 11WG, a right branch at 124 feet along 11WA, was 105 feet long by 31st January. In the shallower 25 feet level, 11Y, a continuation of gallery 11P, was 14 feet long by the 10th and gallery 11N was 146 feet long, also by 10th January.

The action for the month took place in the vicinity of the deeper level of the number 16 workings 58 feet under trench H16. As the month progressed consistent

Railway Wood No 11 workings, January 1917. (TNA)

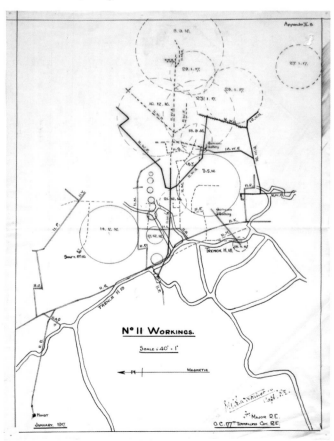

No 11 Workings.

Scale 40' - 1'

118

sounds were picked up by listeners working in gallery 16WG. Further investigation believed the sounds to be that of German tunnellers in the process of driving a forked gallery. One of the forks had holed back into their old shaft, now part of 177's workings, and sounds of pumping had been heard. The other fork was believed to be in the process of being driven in between galleries 16WD and 16WG. 550 lbs of ammonal, in tins, with gun cotton primers was placed at the end of 16WG and tamped with 30 feet of solid tamping, 10 feet of air and 20 feet of solid tamping. With the frequency of the noise of the Germans working increasing and the belief that they were only 15 feet away, the charge was blown at 4.20am on 23rd January. The blow caused no damage outside the tamping and the estimated radius of rupture was 40 feet. The blow caused no surface crater and no gas was detected in 177's workings. Listeners, following the blow, picked up sounds of hammering and pounding which continued until 10am then stopped, no further sounds being heard from the Germans. The sounds could have been from trapped German tunnellers trying to dig themselves out of their collapsed system as their air supply dimished or could have been of a German pioneer rescue team trying to get through the blockage caused by the camouflet blow.

The Germans struck back at 4.20am on 27th January by blowing a camouflet of their own. The estimated weight of the charge was 250 lbs and the location of the blow was well to the front of galleries 16WH and 16WD. There was no damage whatsoever to 177's workings, the only effect felt by 177's tunnellers was a listener's candle being blown out in gallery 16WD; nor was there

any damage to the surface as a result of the blow.

Two further German camouflets were blown during the month, both on 29th January. The first was blown at 1.20pm in the vicinity of gallery 16WD at an estimated depth of 50 feet. There were no surface effects or gas detected in 177's workings. A section of the company, working in 16WH were shaken up by the blow with one man slightly wounded but managed to get out of the gallery without serious injury. 15 feet of 16WH was damaged by the blow but repaired almost immediately. The second German camouflet of the day was blown at 6.20pm that evening. It was believed that the camouflet was blown from the same German gallery as the day before, from an estimated depth of between 40 to 50 feet, although it was believed the charge was smaller than the one used earlier. Questions arose as to the objective of the German blow, but could not be answered. No damage or injuries were sustained by 177 to its men or its workings. Perhaps German listeners had misinterpreted sounds heard from their galleries?

Normal work in the number 16 workings continued throughout the month with gallery 16WH, a right branch along 16WG, was 36 feet long by 31st January. The last day of the month saw work start on an inclined stairway located at the junction of 16WG and 16WB, heading towards gallery 11K.

Heavy shelling of the area caused a large number of repairs to be done to the Cambridge Road dugouts under Railway Wood during the month. Work continued in the dugout at the 30 feet level. A branch to the left at 10 feet along C5a became another entrance to the system and was 21 feet long by the 3rd of the month. Gallery C5 was now known as Leicester Lounge and where it met and crossed gallery C1 it was named Leicester Square. C1 was named Coventry Street and the main system of dugouts in the system, located along Cambridge Road was now named Burlington Arcade and Albany. A gallery for an auxiliary sump was started and labelled as CB and another new gallery was also started along which more dugouts would be constructed. This was labelled as C11. Those dugouts included stores, a dugout for a fuel tank and a set of latrines. Off Coventry Street a set of dugouts was started as a company HQ for infantry holding the surface. Coventry Street ran eastwards and connected with the number 6 workings shaft. Another gallery was started in the vicinity of the number 6 shaft, off C1, labelled as C10. A dugout was started along C10 which would be the chamber for a new shaft to feed the number 6 workings.

At the extensive Canal bank system of dugouts work was at the finishing stages with 108 feet of ventilating gallery constructed during the month linking five more dugouts. A further four dugouts were extended to 20 feet long.

Work also continued on the dugouts and machine gun emplacements to the north of 177's main location in the Railway Wood sector. Owing to manpower shortage and lack of timber, no work was done at Wilson's Farm during January. But at Hill Top Farm the dugout work continued with the main galleries D, F, G and H being driven out to 60, 101, 70 and 63 feet respectively. Gallery H was a connection to F off D gallery. Twenty-three dugouts were constructed along D, E and H galleries, one of them as an engine room to power the dugout. A sump gallery, 14 feet long was constructed from the bottom of the shaft that fed the dugout. It ran 6 feet below the dugout level and would be used to collect standing water.

At Wieltje, the Hades system had suffered at the end of December when heavy rains partially flooded the dugouts and galleries. To combat this ever present nuisance an electric pump was installed and a

Railway Wood Cambridge Road dugouts, January 1917.

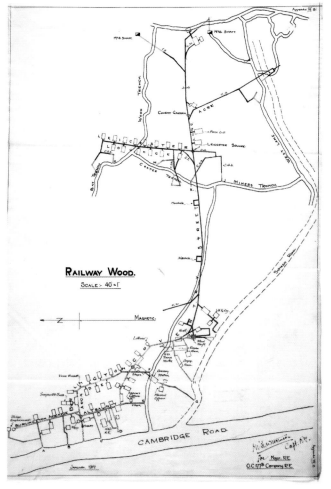

sump gallery was constructed just north of the shaft, 6 feet below the dugout level to collect standing water prior to pumping out. Work on the system was further hampered during January by enemy shelling, delaying the disposal of the sandbags full of the Bastard Blue Clay and requiring much repair work to entrances on the surface. F gallery was driven out to 126 feet during the month with two new galleries started off it. G gallery ran north east with H gallery running south east, both would run out to machine gun emplacements, and were 24 and 53 feet long respectively by the month's end. An exit gallery and stairs from No 12 dugout up into Monmouth trench was 110 feet long and a set of exit stairs from the machinegun emplacement between dugouts 10 and 12 was 69 feet long by the end of January.

Work was also started on a dugout system at Lancashire Farm, sheet 28NW, at map reference C.13.d.9.3. Day work was all that was carried out as there was insufficient manpower to work constantly on the system. Two surface dugouts and a grass roof covered shallow sap to a shaft house were worked on during the month. The shaft was 6 feet diameter steel tubbed and was sunk down to 38 feet by the end of the month with the plan to have the dugout at 44 feet.

FEBRUARY 1917

Both the weather and German shelling caused delays in the workings under the Railway Wood sector during February. Life at the helm of 177 Tunnelling Company changed on 2nd February when Major Edward Marie Felix Momber DSO, MC took over command of the company from Major Bliss upon his promotion to Lieutenant Colonel and subsequent posting. Edward Momber was born in Biarritz, France in 1886 to a French father and English mother. His father was a veteran of the Crimean War who lost a leg during the siege of Sebastapol. Momber joined the British Army and was commissioned into the Royal Engineers in 1907. He arrived on the Western Front in December 1914 then serving as a Captain with the 25th Fortress Company, RE. Upon the formation of the tunnelling companies in early 1915 he had formed and commanded 176 Tunnelling Company which had spent a good part of its early life working under Vimy Ridge and the surrounding area. It was here that Momber would be awarded the MC in December 1915 and a DSO in May 1916. He also had one of the many craters adorning Vimy Ridge named after him. He came to 177 as an experienced commander of a tunnelling company. Major Norton Griffiths, who had long chastised Bliss for not enough offensive mining work, was now at home in the UK. He would have been happy to know that someone of Momber's character had taken over the helm of the tunnelling company protecting the very apex of the British defences around Ypres, but at the same time he didn't understand that Bliss realised at such an early stage in the timeline of mining on the Western Front just what was required from his company. By the time of Momber taking command of the company it was primed and ready under the Railway Wood sector to play its part as an important cog in the great wheel that would eventually roll back the Germans from the area. His command would be short, tragic but very successful.

German shelling of the Railway Wood sector was much heavier than usual in both the first and the last weeks of the month and delayed the removal of spoil filled sandbags from the workings as well as causing many more than necessary repairs to entrances than usual. With temperatures plummeting well below zero a keen frost also caused delays to works. The tempo of German active mining on the ridge was also up during the month with two major mine blows by them. The first occurred at 1.10am on 3rd February when an explosion ripped through the ground just east of the number 1 crater at map reference I.12.c.25.75 killing one of the attached infantrymen to 177. The infantry holding the line here, M Company of the 12th Royal Sussex, had been warned as to the dangers of enemy mining, but no blow had occurred in this part of the sector since 9th May 1916. This fresh blow caught everyone off guard as nothing had been detected in the days leading up to the mine explosion. Fifteen casualties were sustained by the infantry holding the line here. The crater blew in part of the outside lip of crater number 1 but did not open a passage of communication. Although caught off guard by the blow, the 12th Royal Sussex who were holding the right section of the Railway Wood sector, were quick to react. A platoon from the right supporting the company along with a crater consolidation party arrived on the scene to find a smoking hole in the ground 25 feet deep and 75 feet in diameter. They seized the crater and commenced to consolidate the fresh crater into the British line. Although there was no attempt by the Germans to seize the crater they poured a steady stream of rifle grenades onto the consolidating party. Retaliation was rapid and 12 x 18 pounder shells were fired onto the German lines in the vicinity of the

crater. The party also dug out a man buried by the blow from a surface listening sap. Through the rest of the night two bombing posts and a Lewis machine gun post were constructed and about three quarters of the front was wired. The big problem remained that the crater was isolated from the British front line and daylight was approaching fast. All men were ordered back to the British front line in time and during the nights of the 3rd/4th and 4th/5th February the crater was fully wired into the British front line and connected up to an existing trench. The job was no mean feat due to the close proximity of the German lines in this part of the line and whose troops did not let the work go by without harassment from machine gun fire and rifle grenades. No casualties were sustained underground by the mine blow, but 16 feet of gallery 16WA was damaged. In the mine explosion report filed by 177 after the blow it was ascertained that the probable objective of the mine was to blow the outside lip of number one crater.

On 4th February at 3am 31-year-old 102808 Sapper Thomas Bird of 177 Tunnelling Company died of wounds he had received a few hours earlier. He was being treated at the 133rd Field Ambulance behind the lines near Poperinge for bullet wounds to his thigh and knee.[2]

On 15th February another of 177's attached infantry was killed in action. That night, the 165th Infantry Brigade of the 55th (West Lancashire) Division returned to their old haunts and relieved the 39th Division in the line. The Division would stay at the front in this part of the line until mid June.

Pumping, listening and repair work was carried out on all three levels of the number 6 workings throughout the month. Steel setts were placed into gallery 6ZA at the 75 feet deeper level of the working and it must have been almost impossible to have kept as quiet as possible working with metal underground. At 5.10am on 25th February 177's worst fears were realised when the Germans blew a second mine. The blow occurred opposite the number 6 workings at map reference I.11.b.90.35 forming a crater on the surface, in No Man's Land, 100 feet in diameter and 30 feet deep. Underground, the mine damaged about 320 feet of galleries on all three levels of the number 6 workings. Worse still, two attached infantry in the number 6 workings were killed and three wounded. One of the dead was 25970 Private Thomas Edward Davies, 17th Royal Welsh Fusiliers, from Denbigh, Wales.[3]

There was no attempt by the Germans to capture the crater and the site was just observed. It became apparent to 177, in their

analysis of why this mine was blown, that the Germans had more than likely heard the repair work going on in the deep 6ZA level. The repair work stopped on 23rd February and this must have led the Germans to believe that the British miners were charging a mine, so the familiar race was on to see who could blow first. It was presumed that the Germans had a charge already in place, estimated to be at between 50 to 60 feet deep, as no sounds were detected of them charging and tamping. With this opinion, and the fact that German infantry made no attempt to take the crater, it was believed the mine was a hurriedly arranged defensive mine. The reconnaissance of the crater was carried out by a patrol of men from 1/6th Kings Liverpool Regiment. The patrol led by 2nd Lieutenant George Coleman successfully recced the crater, getting back to British lines as daylight broke.

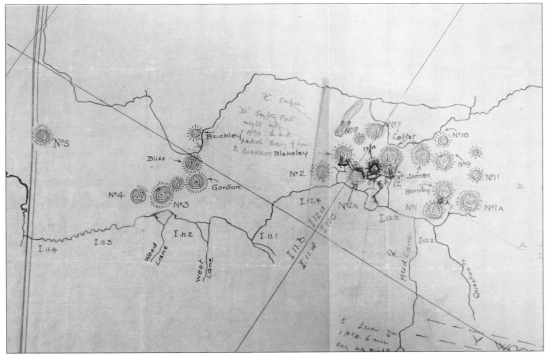

Trace from the 55th (West Lancashire) Divisions HQ war diary from April 1917 showing the various mine craters that existed in the Railway Wood sector. (TNA WO95/2902)

With the tempo in underground warfare gradually increasing, coupled with a seemingly never ending daily exchange of artillery fire, the sector held by the troops on the surface now resembled a lunar landscape of mine craters and shell holes. Almost three years of static warfare had literally churned up the soil, the picture of which must have resembled nothing short of a small glimpse into Dante's inferno. An increasingly difficult task for infantry commanders on the ground was keeping tabs on what crater was blown where and when. This was made more difficult when multiple mines were blown throughout the month. To date, both British and German mine craters in the sector had been numbered on mine plans, this seemed fairly straightforward. But now the situation arose where fresh mine craters had been blown in between existing mine craters and the process of further numbering of the craters was stopped as it was thought it would lead to confusion on the ground. An idea to name British mine craters in order to ease the confusion was submitted for approval by the staff of the 55th Divisions HQ to the General Staff of VIII Corps on 27th February. Approval was immediate from VIII Corps and the process of naming the craters in the sector now began. The crater, located between craters 1 and 1a, which came about as a result of the blow on 3rd February was named Hornby after the GOC 116th Infantry Brigade, Brigadier General M.L. Hornby and the crater formed as a result of the blow on 25th February was named Gordon after the CO of the 1/6th Kings, Lt Col Stanley Gordon.[4]

In the remainder of the workings under the Railway Wood sector, work continued as normal as could be. In 11K, a set of stairs that connected the number 11 workings with the number 16 workings, a dugout was completed. A week's worth of repair work was carried out in the 77 feet galleries, 11WG and 11WK. Here also, steel setts were used in the galleries. All of the work for the month in the number 16 works took place on the 55 feet level of the working. Galleries 16WC and 16WD, both south east running were 172 feet and 68 feet long respectively by the month's end.

In the Cambridge Road system under Railway Wood many repairs to entrances damaged by shellfire were carried out. Steel track was laid in gallery C1 (Coventry Street). This would allow for the transport of material and equipment to and from the front, below ground. C11, the new gallery for dugouts started the month before, was 246 feet long by the end of the month and off it was started a dugout named 'The Criterion' after a famous opulent London restaurant! A well dugout was also completed along gallery C11 and the well, for drinking water, was sunk. Starting at 25 feet deep it was sunk to 40 feet, the shaft being 3 feet by 3 feet wooden timbers. A machine gun emplacement off Leicester Lounge was also started through the month.

At the Yser Canal the work of driving venting galleries for the dugouts continued through February with the vents to five dugouts completed with 98 feet of venting. Two new surface 'Elephant' dugouts were completed and considerable work done on revetting the bank they were sunk into and covering the dugouts.

February would see the completion of the Hill Top Farm dugout and machine gun emplacement. As with elsewhere, work was hampered by frost and German shelling with a considerable amount of repair work being done to the trenches leading up to the dugout entrances. An ammunition dugout was completed along D gallery. E and H galleries were driven out to 127 feet and 48 feet long respectively by 21st February. The sump gallery dug below the level of the dugout to catch standing water was completed by mid month and a small connection between E and H galleries was finished prior to the handover of the dugout to 55th Division later in the month.

The extensive machine gun and accommodation dugout under Wieltje suffered the same delays as the others but considerable work was done during the month. G gallery, which ran north east off F gallery to a machine gun emplacement, was 77 feet long by mid-February and H gallery, which ran south east off F gallery to a machine gun emplacement, was 63 feet long by the 7th. Gallery NL which would run towards a Lewis machine gun post was 111 feet long by the 28th and gallery RB, an exit gallery for bombers, was 49 feet long by the end of the month. Work on two sets of stairs to a surface trench from between 10 and 13 dugouts and also opposite the power dugout, continued throughout the month. Slow progress was made with these as the tunnellers had to cut through brickwork and concrete foundations of ruins of houses on the surface.

Work at Lancashire Farm suffered a setback from the weather and shelling as well as damage from a German trench raid on the night of 24th/25th February. The steel shaft was down at its 44 feet target by 7th February. The main gallery of the system,

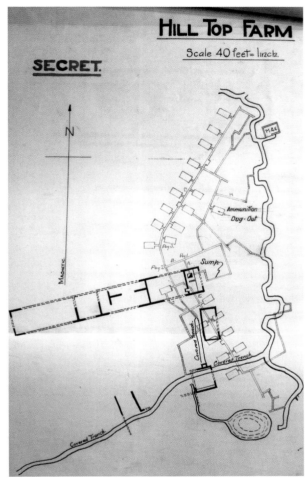

Hill Top Farm dugout, February 1917. (TNA)

6 feet high and 3 feet wide was driven out to 134 feet long by the month's end. The lip of the shaft was concreted and ladders laid to platforms down the shaft. Narrow gauge track was also laid up to the ruins of the farm.

On 26th February, Major Momber wrote a report to Brigadier General E.L. Ellington in charge of the general staff at VIII Corps HQ. His report outlaid what his manpower strategy was for the company in order that it would be able to complete the mining tasks given to it. The priority for the company was the completion of the

Wieltje Hades dugout, February 1917. (TNA)

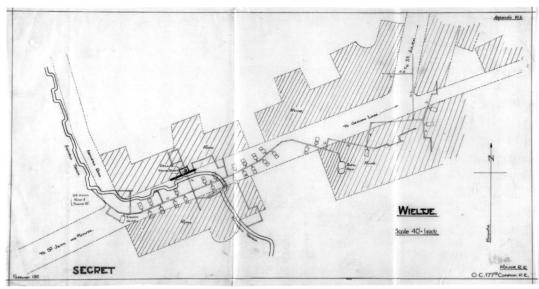

deep levels of the number 11 and number 6 workings. Major Momber was under no illusion that the Corps Commander wanted the work completed as soon as possible and had to swap and change manpower levels on other projects being carried out by the company. His work was not made easier by the increase in German mining under the Railway Wood sector, and the delays caused by damage repair. A classic example of this type of delay was the blow that took place on 25th February damaging over 300 feet of the number 6 workings. As well as the work under the sector taking place another of 177's priorities was the completion of the Wieltje dugout system. Not aiding the situation, Major Momber was then notified that on 27th February he would lose 51 of his attached labour as they moved off to be attached to the 1st Australian Tunnelling Company. Momber mentions in his report that the loss of these men would mean that work on the Hill Top Farm dugout would almost cease as sandbagged spoil could not be stored or removed. Major Momber

intended to use the men currently employed constructing the various strongpoints, for working solely on the Wieltje dugout. He estimated that he needed 100 men for the completion of the Wieltje system but warned that these men would not be available for any other mining work if the system was to be completed on time. Although the report clearly shows that 177 were under an increase in pressure to get their work done, not helped by fluctuations in the manpower statistics, it is written in a very matter of fact way and shows that Major Momber certainly had his finger on the pulse.

MARCH 1917

As February drew to a close, the tempo of mining activity under the Railway Wood sector increased dramatically. This would necessitate additional work in repairing galleries and the digging out and rescuing of listeners temporarily entombed following German mine blows. There was no let up on the surface with German bombardment and the routine repairing of dugout and mine entrances damaged by shellfire continued. First to strike a blow underground this month was 177 Tunnelling Company. This blow came as the local Corps Commander; Lieutenant General Sir Aylmer Hunter-Weston wanted the mine to be blown in order to cause maximum effectual damage to the Germans in this part of the line. An artillery barrage by corps and divisional artillery would precede the mine and would attempt to shepherd the Germans into the area above the mine charge where it would be blown. Lt Gen Hunter-Weston sought advice from the Controller of Mines at Second Army HQ, Lt Col A Stevenson CMG and was advised that the estimated crater would be at least 60 feet in diameter with a 5 to 6 feet high lip. The time for the mine to be blown was left in the hands of Major Momber and the 55th Division General Staff. At 11.30pm on 1st March the mine was blown under the German lines at map reference I.12.a.60.42. The mine, 6,500 lbs of ammonal in tins, was fired from the end of gallery 6ZA, 65 feet deep. It had been placed there during August 1916. The gallery had been tamped with 200 feet of solid tamping. The reason for the mine was that noises perceived to be those of enemy miners, had been heard from galleries 6WF and 6WH for a number of days before the blow. It was also believed that the enemy had a gallery running about 25 feet above gallery 6ZA. Just a few days before on 25th February the Germans had blown a mine which had damaged a substantial amount of the number 6 workings. It was hoped that this mine blow would destroy the main German gallery and lateral in this sector cutting off his listeners. With these dealt with, it would help with the repairing of the

number 6 workings as 177 would be able to work in relative safety. With an act of offensive underground action being carried out against the Germans, Major Momber was more than aware that this would lead to a reaction from the enemy. In fact it was what he was hoping for as it would force the Germans to show their hand. The standard request to blow the mine had come from Major Momber and had been approved at corps level by the Controller of Mines. The mine was believed to be a much undercharged mine with an estimated radius of rupture of 100 feet. On the surface only a heave of earth was seen to rise as a result of the blow forming a crater about 60 feet in diameter. A fighting patrol from the 5th King's Liverpool Regiment, 166th Infantry Brigade went over immediately following the blow to carry out a reconnaissance of the ground. Led by 19-year-old 2nd Lieutenant William Shield of the 6th Kings, they made a complete circuit of the crater observing that there was no attempt by the Germans to capture and consolidate it. The patrol came under fire on its return to British lines. 2nd Lt Shield and 201497 Pte Frederick Bigley from the patrol were nowhere to be seen. Commanding a reserve party back at the British lines was 2nd Lieutenant Cameron Macintosh who immediately on learning that two of the patrol were missing, took a party into No Man's Land to search for them. Accompanied by Sgt John Gaffney they led no fewer than four search attempts that night but sadly returned without finding the men. Major Momber in compiling his Mine Explosion Report stated he doubted the infantry reconnoitred the correct crater. The following night, 2nd Lt Macintosh went out himself to reconnoitre what was now known as Buckley crater, named after the then CO of the 5th Kings, Major A. Buckley. 2nd Lieutenant MacIntosh and Sgt Gaffney were both awarded the Military Cross and Military Medal respectively for their actions.[5] Underground there was no leakage of gas reported in 177's workings.

In turn, with the increase in mining activity throughout March under the sector, Major Momber, drawing on his experiences at Givenchy and Vimy, arranged for a series of lectures to be given to all COs and Divisional Officers on the importance of crater consolidation. It was received very well by the 55th Division.

Work continued in the number 6 workings throughout March. Gallery 6WD was driven out to 43 feet by mid March. Gallery 6WH was 158 feet long by the 21st, gallery 6WJ was 80 feet long by the same date. Gallery 6ZA that had contained the mine was repaired and was 130 feet long by the end of the month. A new shaft, housed in the shaft house that had been built the month before where the Cambridge Road dugouts met the number 6 workings, was started. The head of the shaft was already 30 feet below the surface. Labelled as 6Y, the shaft was steel ringed, 6 feet in diameter and was 77 feet deep by the month's end.

177 did not have to wait long for the anticipated German response. At 7.15pm on the 4th March the Germans blew a mine opposite the number 16 workings. It was estimated that the mine was fired from about 30 to 35 feet depth just to the front right of crater 2a. No casualties were reported on the surface or underground as a result of the blow. With the probable objective of the German mine to destroy British workings, it was also believed the mine was fired to form a bombing post close to the British line. German infantry were hot on the heels of the mine and advanced forward capturing and consolidating the crater. Two attempts by men of the 1/6th Kings, led both times by 2nd Lieutenant George Coleman, attempted to drive the German consolidation party out of the crater. But they were driven back on both accounts. British casualties were three men killed and eight wounded. 2nd Lt George Coleman was awarded a Military Cross for his actions that night and also for his daring reconnaissance made on the 25th February.[6] The crater was named Cotter Crater, after Lt Col (Acting) Edmund Brian Cotter, the OC of 275 Brigade, Royal Field Artillery, whose bombardment three days previously had shepherded the Germans into the area above Buckley crater.

The stressful pace of life continued unabated below the ridge with listeners from 177 picking up sounds of German mining very close to gallery 16WC. They had estimated the Germans were working within 20 feet of them and they had interpreted their detected sounds as being clay falling in a gallery with a sandbag being dragged down the gallery. It was an obvious course of action that a camouflet was needed. Authority was granted by Major Momber to blow and 600 lbs of ammonal explosive, to be fired electrically by two sets of gun cotton primers, was laid in 16WC. The gallery was tamped with 30 feet of solid tamping, 10 feet of air and 20 feet of solid tamping. At 3pm on 8th March the camouflet was fired. It was presumed that the camouflet did its job in destroying the German gallery. No casualties were reported underground in 177's galleries although slight traces of gas were discovered and 65 feet of gallery 16WC was lost. No crater was reported on the surface. A heavy shoot by divisional artillery on Cotter Crater also took place on 8th March. About 300 heavy 6 inch HE shells and 30 x 18 pounder HE shells were fired at the crater in an attempt to destroy what the Germans had done in consolidation work. The bombardment was a complete success. The forward lip of the crater was flattened by 3 feet with trench revetment and duckboarding seen to be flying into the air. The success of the bombardment would be short lived however as they were back in the crater pouring deadly enfilade fire into British crater consolidation parties the next day.

German revenge came swiftly when at 6.45pm on 9th March they blew a mine opposite the number 11 workings. It was believed this mine was fired to destroy and damage as much of the number 11 workings as possible in the vicinity of the blow. 290 feet of number 11 galleries were damaged with galleries 11P, 11N, 11WG and 11WF being those chiefly effected. 132967 Sapper Sidney Firth, a 24-year-old miner from Morley, Leeds, was on listening duty at the end of gallery 11N when the mine blew. With the ferocity and close proximity of the blow there was nothing he could have done and was more than likely killed instantaneously. 75 feet of gallery 11N was destroyed by the blow and Sapper Firth's body was never recovered.[7] Two more sappers from 177 were temporarily entombed for thirty hours in gallery 11WG but were rescued without injury. It is interesting to note that Major Momber notes in the Mine Explosion Report compiled after the blow that these two men stated that they owed their lives to being close to one of the steel setts recently put into some of the British galleries, which withstood the effects of the blow. On the

surface the mine formed a crater 150 feet in diameter and 40 feet deep, between craters 2 and 2a with the nearest lip of the crater being only 40 yards from the British front line trenches. Just 50 yards away from the crater was 240713 Pte Edward Nicholls of the 1/5th Kings Own Royal Lancashire Regiment; he was manning a Lewis machine gun position and got his gun into action, flanking the crater, before the earth ceased falling from the blow! His effective fire kept back German infantry and he continued firing until he was wounded.[8] Two consolidation parties of men from the 1/5th Kings Own Royal Lancashire Regiment, under the command of 2nd Lt TS Blakeley and 2nd Lt Appleyard went forward to the crater. 2nd Lt Blakeley was wounded almost immediately, his position being taken by 2nd Lt Ronald MacDonald, but both parties fought their way to the crater under heavy German fire, eventually consolidating its near lip. German harassing fire was intense for the first thirty minutes after the mine blow with Minenwerfers, 77s and trench mortars. Two wiring parties were also sent out and managed to wire both flanks of the new crater from its lip back to the existing British front line, and also across the crater. Casualties in the two parties were very high with 1 officer and 10 other ranks killed, 3 officers and 17 other ranks wounded and 2 other ranks missing. Five of the wounded other ranks would die of their wounds at the dressing station.[9, 10, 11] The large proportion of casualties in this consolidation operation was put down to effective enemy sniper fire from Cotter Crater. On all future plans the crater blown that evening was now named 'Blakeley Crater' after 2nd Lt TS Blakeley. The mine crater that resulted from 177's very first blow under the ridge on 25th September 1915, at the eastern tip of Railway Wood was also named during the month on the same request form that Saw Cotter and Blakeley craters named. The former OC of 177 Tunnelling Company now had his mark left in the sector when the crater was named in his honour, Bliss Crater.

The next day at 6.20pm the Germans blew a camouflet opposite the number 16 workings shattering the last 20 feet of gallery 16WA. Luckily there were no casualties sustained by 177 or attached workers. The camouflet destroyed one of the companies' listening positions from where sounds of dropping water had recently been picked up. As a result of the increase blowing of mines and camouflets by the Germans under the ridge around this time of day, 177 had started to withdraw listeners from galleries towards the end of the day. This change of normal routine certainly saved a few lives.

On 19th March disaster was again narrowly averted when at 6.05pm the Germans blew a mine which in turn probably detonated a 600 lb charge 177 had waiting in gallery 16WG. The mine caused considerable damage to the number 16 workings damaging at least a 100 feet of galleries 16WG, 16WJ and 16WL. A lot of gas was encountered in the rest of the number 16 workings but was cleared and declared safe by 11pm that night. Luckily, again there were no casualties due to the withdrawal of listeners just five minutes before the blow. It was believed that the camouflet was a push pipe or earth auger as sounds resembling the use of that type of charge had been detected over the past few days.

On 26th March at 8.30pm a small mine was blown by the Germans in front of the number 11 workings at map reference I.12.c.36.87. A small crater resulted from the blow which was reported by an infantry patrol. There were no casualties as a result of the blow and the reasons for the blow were not known. There was no follow up action by crater consolidation parties as the crater was deemed too near to the German lines.

The sound of German voices was picked up by listeners in the number 16 workings, in gallery 16WG (right). The voices could be heard with the naked ear and were estimated as to be as close as 10 feet from the listeners. It was believed that the Germans were hard at work beefing up their defence of Cotter Crater both above and below ground. 177 acted rapidly blowing a camouflet in 16WG (right). The charge, 250 lbs of ammonal with a gun cotton primer was blown at 1pm on 31st March. With 50 feet of tamping in place there was no damage whatsoever to the gallery behind the tamping and no gas reported as a result of the blow. The camouflet caused no crater or action on the surface, but careful listening took place after the blow and plans were afoot to blow the German's rescue attempt. The result of the blow was believed to be successful.

During these times of high tension as the mining tempo increased during the month, time was found to carry on work on the number 16 workings. Galleries at the 55 feet level were further evolved during the month and work started on a new gallery which would hold dugouts and stairs to the surface. Over 400 feet of gallery was dug throughout the month.

Just behind the lines the never ending repair work continued on the Cambridge

Road dugout now a real behemoth of underground streets. Messes, accommodation, trench mortar and machine gun dugouts and emplacement were part of this huge system. All dug under an almost continual bombardment of German shells.

Work behind the lines on the Canal bank dugouts suffered due to the increase in mining under the Railway Wood sector during March when the workforce was detached temporarily to the front. Some work was done including repairs to the system, the fitting of extra cover to elephant dugouts and the maintenance of a track that ran from the Canal bank to the Lancashire Farm working.

Heavy shelling caused no end of delays to the Lancashire Farm working. This necessitated a lot of repair work to the entrances to the system and the surface trenches and tracks around it. Bad running ground was also encountered, during the construction of a stairway to the surface, causing more delays.

At Hill Top Farm pumping work continued for the first week of March when the dugout was then taken over by the infantry.

In Wieltje, the Hades system also advanced during the month. Here the shellfire had been lighter than elsewhere in 177's area of operations and caused only few delays in comparison with other workings. Work continued underground in building dugouts for various purposes such as fuel storage, fire prevention and accommodation. Galleries and stairways leading to machine gun emplacements were also further developed.

APRIL 1917

As April dawned, Major Member's 177 Tunnelling Company was 307 men strong with 708 attached infantry working with them. The fast pace of mining continued under the Railway Wood sector with the Germans making the first move. On 4th April at 4.30am they blew a small mine which left a crater the size of a shell hole, about 10 feet in diameter, just outside Hornby Crater at map reference I.12.c.3.7. The mine caused no damage to 177's workings at all and the reason for the blow was unclear as there had been no underground work in the area for some days. Just a few days later on 6th April, 177 had another attempt at disrupting the German's underground defences at Cotter Crater. At 2am, on the authority of Lt Gen Hunter-Weston they blew a camouflet containing 100 lbs of ammonal and 102 gun cotton primers. The blow was made from the end of gallery 16WD (left) at a fairly shallow depth of 12 to 15 feet. German voices had been detected by listeners not long before the blow and it was estimated that they were just 10 feet away. The charge was tamped with 20 feet of solid, 10 feet of air space and a further 20 feet of solid tamping. No gas was detected in 177's workings and no damage to their galleries was reported outside the tamping. On the surface there was no infantry action as a result of the blow. The camouflet had been destined to blow in conjunction with a small mine at the end of gallery 16WH but this second charge of 800 lbs of ammonal, in boxes with gun cotton primers, failed to activate due to a faulty exploder. A little later at 4.45am it was fired successfully. It was designed as a fougasse mine, one that is set to blow in front of an objective and shaped so that the earth thrown up as a result of the blow would bury and fill enemy trenches and positions. The

131

authority for this mine was the same as the earlier fired camouflet and its objective was to destroy enemy workings, consolidation work and to shake down the lip of Cotter Crater. The mine damaged about 70 feet of 177's own workings past the tamping but the surface effects were deemed to be successful. A crater was believed to have been formed but not observed as it was in Cotter Crater. Infantry of the 1/6th Kings holding the front in that sector, heard the sound of falling earth following the blow and observed flames shooting up from the interior of Cotter Crater. When the light improved, allowing for better observation, it was noticed that the lip of the crater had been slightly lowered. There was no surface infantry action as a result of the mine blow.

The Germans responded with a fatal blow on 9th April. This small camouflet was fired at 12.50pm opposite the number 16 workings. It damaged 29 feet of gallery 16WD (right) beyond repair, killing 22-year-old 18795 Cpl Daniel Evans from Dowlais, Glamorgan and 39-year-old 19105 Private Richard Roberts from Bethseda, Bangor. Both Welshmen were from the 16th Royal Welsh Fusiliers, attached to 177 Tunnelling Company. They were probably working in the 29 feet of unrecoverable 16WD as their bodies were never recovered.[12] The blow also wounded three other men. There were some slight traces of gas as a result of the blow but it cleared rapidly. The tragic aspect of this blow was that the Germans had been heard about 9.30am that morning and an officer and team from 177 stood by with a temporary camouflet charge ready to set up if needed. The sounds of the Germans then ceased, no more sounds being detected until the camouflet was fired. It states on the Mine Explosion Report, compiled by Major Momber shortly after the blow, that it was probably due to the very wet condition of gallery 16WD (right) that the noise of the Germans had not been detected earlier. The second blow of the day.

Just over 50 miles south of the Salient on 9th April the British First and Third Armies launched the Arras offensive. This short, 39-day long offensive was launched as part of the Allies' attempt to break the German stranglehold on the Western Front. It would be the smaller of two offensives launched during April; the second, would come a week later further south when the French army under the command of Robert Nivelle would deliver the fatal right hook. In preparation for the offensive many British and a New Zealand Tunnelling Company had spent a number of months digging and developing underground subways that led from the rear areas out into trenches close to the front. Many ancient underground quarries were explored and linked together providing living accommodation, headquarters and dressing stations for many thousands of men. The first 24 hours of the Arras offensive bode very well for the British Army with the biggest single advance seen since the war began. But as was so common at this stage of the war the offensive slowed down and, although the British saw some success in operations, they failed to break through the German lines. The Nivelle offensive to the south was also unsuccessful. Failing in its promise to break through the German lines in 48 hours, they suffered about 120,000 casualties in five days. The Arras offensive remains the costliest offensive for the British Army, in terms of daily casualties.

Back in the Ypres Salient, most eyes were now pointing towards the Messines ridge as eight tunnelling companies continued work on what would be the 'Tunnellers' Finest Hour'. Although not directly involved in the offensive, 177's job of supporting troops holding the Railway Wood sector, was important enough in its own right. In just under two months after the start of the Messines offensive operations would start in an attempt to drive the German army back. Just over two years of static warfare was almost at an end. 177 had to make sure that the troops that would advance eastwards above had advantage on their side.

On 10th April at 9.05pm the Germans blew again, firing what was perceived to be a defensive mine in their own wire, opposite the number 16 workings west of Cotter Crater. The blow damaged 30 feet of gallery in the number 16 workings and formed a surface crater about 25 feet in diameter. No sounds had been reported in this area by listeners since the blow four days previously. 177 were still in the habit of withdrawing listening teams for a period of about three hours each evening normally between 6pm and 9pm give or take a few minutes each way. This routine habit ensured that no underground casualties were sustained. A small party of German soldiers was observed by surface troops moving

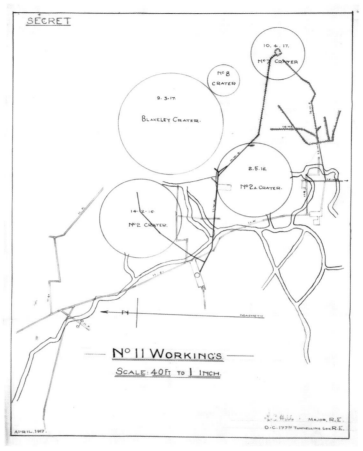

Railway Wood No 11 workings, April 1917. (TNA)

towards the fresh crater but these were driven off rapidly by effective Lewis gun fire from the 1/5th South Lancashire Regiment. This crater was now marked on British plans as number 7 Crater and shortly afterwards became known as both New Cotter Crater and Cotter West Crater.

On 11th April at 10.05pm the Germans fired another small defensive mine just south of Cotter Crater. There was no damage to British underground or surface workings and a small party of infantry from the 1/5 Kings Own Royal Lancashire Regiment went forward to reconnoitre the crater. They found a small crater 33 feet long and 30 feet wide and then withdrew as they

Railway Wood
No 16 workings,
April 1917.
(TNA)

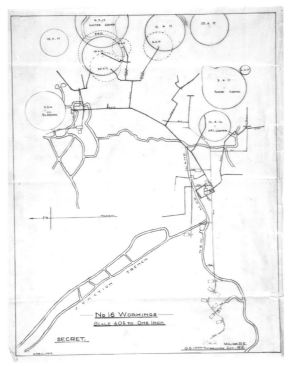

came under grenade attack. In the Mine Explosion Report following the blow, Major Momber added that it was believed that the enemy fired their mine from the same gallery as the mine fired the day before. It is also worthy of note that the marking of this mine on future mine plans would be slightly erroneous. It was always marked as having exploded on 12th April, not the 11th. There is also no record of the mine being fired written in the war diary of 177 Tunnelling Company although a copy of a Mine Explosion Report exists attached to the diary marking it fired on the 11th. War diaries of the 55th Div HQ, 166 Infantry Brigade and the 1/5 Kings Own only show record of the mine fired on the 11th, with no record of any mine being fired on the 12th. On future plans this mine would also become known as James Crater after Lt Col CP James, CO, 1/5th South Lancashire Regiment.

The main focus of 177's operations under the ridge at this moment was the destruction of German positions around Cotter Crater and the constant harassment of attempts to repair them. The German positions were able to enfilade British troops

Tunnel plan
showing the
Cotter Craters
mentioned in
April 1917.
(TNA)

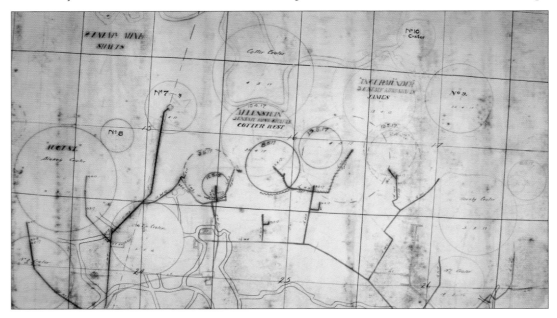

moving forwards towards the German lines, and this needed neutralising. On 18th April at 2.30am a further attempt by 177 to do just that was made when a camouflet containing 4500 lbs of ammonal was fired from the end of gallery 11WG, at 70 feet deep. The charge, in boxes, fired just a few feet north of Cotter Crater ripped through the German defences, shattering underground workings below the crater and on the surface. Although gallery 11WG was tamped with 50 feet solid, 10 feet of air and 65 feet of solid tamping, the blow wrecked a further 20 feet of 16WD left and right and had an estimated radius of rupture of 90 feet. The force of this heavy camouflet shook the surface and blue flames were observed leaping into the night sky from both Blakeley and Cotter Craters followed by a series of small explosions by troops of the 1/5th Kings holding the British front line.

On 25th April at 3.20pm the Germans fired a camouflet which damaged 10 feet of both galleries 16WD (left) and 16WG (right). The blow killed two listeners attached to 177 Tunnelling Company, 31-year-old 358513 Private Edward Poulton from Ardwick, Manchester and 30-year-old 358564 Private Robert Henry Blair from Hulme, Manchester. Both men served with the 55th Division in the 1/10th Kings otherwise known as The Liverpool Scottish.[13]

Listening results showed that no reports of noises had been heard in the vicinity of the blow for some time previous. It was strongly suspected that the charge

may have been bored down by an auger from Cotter Crater. There were no surface effects as a result of the blow although later that night a large German working party was heard in Cotter Crater but due to the darkness it was impossible to observe.[14]

In between these moments of extreme excitement and fear underground work continued on a daily basis on the number 6, 11 and 16 workings. The number 6 workings had a deeper level that was now being developed. A number of shafts now fed this system, and it was also connected to the Cambridge Road dugouts. The deepest gallery 6YA was 110 feet deep. This gallery snaked its way northeastwards towards the

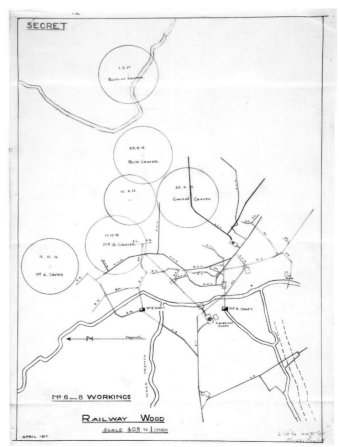

Railway Wood Nos 6 and 8 workings, April 1917. (TNA)

German lines. By the month's end it was 102 feet long. Shaft 6ZA, now down to 90 feet had a gallery driven off the shaft, 6ZB that was 101 feet long by the end of the month. A third new shaft, 6Y was in the process of being sunk during the month.

The work in the number 11 galleries during April took place on the 77 feet level of the system. Galleries were further linked and driven and by the month's end 331 feet of earth had been cut by the tunnellers in this working alone, including a dugout and a stepped incline to the surface.

A lot of repair work, as mentioned before, took place in the number 16 workings as a result of enemy mine and camouflet blows during the month. Most of the work took place at the 55 feet level of the working with a little in shallower galleries. A total of 514 feet of earth was cut during the month. The two branches left and right off 16WG that were badly affected during the month, were completely repaired. Two dugouts,

at the top and bottom of an incline were readied for use during the month.

Work continued on the various strong points allocated for construction to the company. At Lancashire Farm system continued during April with the men detailed to that project working non-stop throughout the month. Major Momber wrote in the war diary for 177, that the men worked at "... absolute maximum speed." The main drive of the working had been extended by 111 feet during April and was now 314 feet long. A second inclined stairway feeding the system was also completed. The men who had normally been working on the Canal bank dugouts were used on the Lancashire Farm project during April, apart from a couple of visits to clean and repair the system. Two more dugouts in the Hades dugout system under Wieltje were completed during the month and an inclined stairway to a Lewis machine gun post was also finished. This marked the completion of this strongpoint.

Wieltje Hades dugout, April 1917. (TNA)

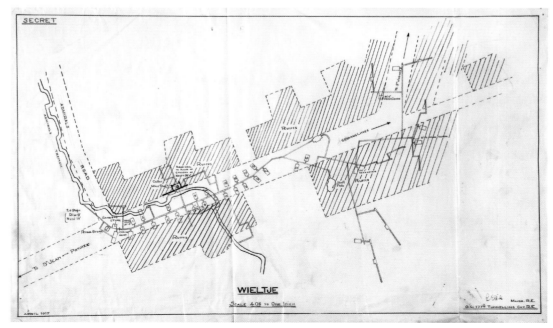

All that was left to do was to fit it with bunks and install the electric generator that would power the system. Almost at the last minute a plan had been forthcoming that would see the dugout connected not just with the front line at Wieltje but also back to Bilge trench, the support trench behind the village.

MAY 1917

The month of May 1917 would be one of the busiest months 177 Tunnelling Company experienced during WW1. There would be 16 separate blows occur under the Railway Wood sector which would culminate with 177 firing its largest mine of the war. The increased tempo in mining would see an 'all hands on deck' scenario for the company with men being taken off other projects to man the tunnels under the ridge. The company was 337 officers and men strong at the beginning of May with a further 680 officers and men attached as labour. In the first five days of the month, four underground actions would take place. On 5th May the workforce at Lancashire Farm was withdrawn to the Railway Wood sector. Lancashire Farm dugout had been handed over to 183 Tunnelling Company on 1st May. The first strike under the ridge, in May, occurred at 4.30am on the 1st of the month. A German mine, believed to be fired as a defensive measure, was fired about 10 feet from the end of gallery 6ZA. A crater, 50 feet in diameter appeared on the surface at map reference I.12.a.05.38. There was no surface or underground action following the mine blow. Two British listeners in galleries 6ZA and 6ZB were wounded slightly by timber and concussion but both men were rescued and recovered and the last 10 feet of gallery 6ZA was smashed in.

Major Momber's men struck against the Germans at 2.00am on 2nd May. A camouflet, consisting of 600 lbs in tins was fired with electric number 13 detonators from the end of 16WD (right). The reason for the camouflet was that the Germans were heard by listeners, working at a face between galleries 16WD and 16 WC (left), believed to be only 20 feet away. Authority was granted by Major Momber to take immediate defensive action. The charge was tamped with 40 feet of solid, 7 feet of air and 20 feet of solid tamping and the gallery was not damaged behind the tamping. There was no surface cratering and no gas reported in the British system. Observers on the surface witnessed a column of earth shooting up diagonally from Cotter Crater at the time of the blow. It was believed that the charge had blown through the German galleries and wrecked one of his mine entrances in Cotter Crater. This belief was also borne out of the fact that little to no damage or gas had been experienced in 177's workings, the blast taking the least line of resistance, travelled through the German system. In the time that passed between the blow and the compilation of the Mine Explosion Report by Major Momber no further sounds of German mining had been heard in that locality.

The Germans were quick to take revenge and at 5pm on 3rd May they fired yet another camouflet opposite the number 16 workings. 40 feet of gallery 16WG (left and right) was damaged by the blow and Major Momber was almost certain that the gallery from which this camouflet was fired, was driven from Cotter Crater. There were no surface effects as a result of the camouflet and gas was detected in the British workings.

137

Luckily for 177 there were no casualties as a result of the blow.

Two days later on 5th May at 4.30am the Germans blew again opposite the number 6 workings. At this time 177 was in the process of charging galleries 6ZA and 6WH with ammonal and it was later believed that their work may have been heard by the Germans. The mine left a small crater on the surface but there was no follow-up infantry action or casualties as a result of the blow. A day later, at 4.35am, the Germans blew a mine opposite the number 16 workings, its objective believed to be to destroy British workings. Distant and confused noises had been reported by listeners in gallery 16WA in the days preceding the mine blow. A crater 30 to 40 feet in diameter appeared on the surface with eyewitnesses saying that they saw no uprush of earth associated with most mine blows, instead they stated that the earth merely lifted and rolled over. Intelligence gathered by 177 led them to believe that there were no German galleries in this sector deeper than 25 to 30 feet. With this in mind, Major Momber believed that the mine was much undercharged. There were no casualties above or below ground and no gas was detected in 177's workings. There was also no infantry action following the blow. Three days later the Germans acted again blowing a camouflet that crumped in the last 12 feet of gallery 16WC. Once again 177 got away lightly with no casualties reported considering the amount of men employed in developing the number 16 workings at the time.

With the Germans now certainly mining from New Cotter Crater, the British workings in the vicinity of the crater were under great threat. For the situation to improve under the surface it also had to improve above ground. Infantry holding the trenches and posts in the vicinity of the crater needed the advantage of being able to overlook the Germans and stop them from carrying on their work in the crater. The situation underground was reaching a crisis point with many of the number 16 workings and some of the number 11 workings facing direct threat from enemy mining from this crater. It wasn't as if the Germans needed to tunnel far in order to plant camouflets that would threaten British mine workings. The location of New Cotter Crater was just a matter of metres in front of the British lines.

A conference was held on 8th May, at 165th Inf Bde HQ in the Ypres Ramparts attended by the Brigade Commander, Captain Wilkinson from 177 and the Commanding Officer of the infantry unit holding the relevant section of British front line. Major Momber had also backed up Captain Wilkinson with a letter to 55th Div HQ outlining his concern for rectifying the problem. It was agreed that 177 would fire a mine just west of New Cotter Crater that would destroy and damage the problematic German workings coming from the crater. This crater would then be seized and consolidated into the British lines giving it an advantageous position from which to overlook New Cotter Crater. After reporting back to Major Momber and after seeking verbal authorisation from the Second Army Controller of Mines, Lt Col A Stevenson CMG DSO, 177 Tunnelling Company then fired the mine from the end of gallery 16WD (left) at 9.30pm on 8th May. The mine, 1500 lbs of ammonal, fired by two sets of two electric detonators ripped through the ground forming a crater 60 feet in diameter

Aerial photograph of the Railway Wood sector dated 20th May 1917. (IWM aerial 21B302, Box 137, 1917)

and 20 feet deep with a 3 feet high lip just west of Cotter Crater. 16WD (left) at 30 feet deep, was tamped with 40 feet solid, 10 feet of air and 15 feet of solid tamping, but this did not stop over 80 feet of the 16WD gallery being lost to the mine. There was no gas reported in 177's workings and it was estimated that the radius of rupture would have been about 60 feet. A crater consolidation team under the command of 2nd Lt CH Vernon of the 1/6 Kings advanced forward and captured the crater, consolidating it above ground with the help of the 423rd Field Company RE. They were sniped and shelled with light trench mortars but no German infantry action was forthcoming and by the next morning had dug a 'T' sap from the crater back to

the British front line. The crater itself was known on future plans as No 12 crater. Major Momber was then informed by 55th Div that loopholes in the British line, now running around the eastern lip of the new crater commanded the view into New Cotter Crater. He was also informed by the CRE of the 55th Division that no further assistance was necessary from 177 in the neutralising of German positions in New Cotter Crater. The fact of the matter was that no position like the one described here existed at all. The Germans were able to continue their consolidation of New Cotter Crater and get on with the job of seeking out the British galleries. It wouldn't be long until Major Momber discovered this severe neglect of duty, but would it be too late to act?

139

On 10th May Captain Wilkinson, 177 Tunnelling Company carried out a cursory visit to the crater blown by the company on the 8th. His discovery was shocking. He wrote immediately to Major Momber back at 177 HQ near Proven his letter made it clear of the poor state of affairs:

"I have today examined the crater blown by us on the 8th inst, from the bombing post held by us on the west lip. The Germans were clearly visible working at constructing a breastwork across the crater, where it had broken into Cotter West Crater, the bags used were wet and blue. There is no doubt that the enemy are mining at this spot and that they have been allowed to consolidate that part of the crater to a great extent and in broad daylight. Our bombing post has no loopholes fitted and no entrance had been cut into the crater, although we had offered to do it when required. I consider that this post has not been completed thereby loosing command of the crater. The above condition of affairs is very serious from our point of view and would involve our blowing again at once instead of waiting until 11WG has got out as intended. I attach report from Captain A.L. James." [15]

Captain James report simply backed up what Captain Wilkinson stated to Major Momber. He had also visited the crater blown by 177 on the 8th. Captain James made a couple of interesting and very serious observations:

"...From this post one can see the enemy working hard in Cotter (New). At 12 midday today I saw at least 6 of the enemy very plainly about 40 yards off. They were apparently knocking off work for lunch. Previous to that time he had been placing wet blue sandbags on the parapet between his crater and ours. These bags had evidently very recently been filled in a wet face at a depth of more than 15 feet. A little dry earth had been thrown over some of the bags but otherwise no attempt of concealment was made."

He continued:

"...In view of obvious enemy mining activity so close to our fortifications (35 yds) I think it would be advisable to blow from 16WG as soon as possible. We are pushing this face ahead as fast as possible and if all goes well we should be able to blow on Saturday (12th)." [15]

On receipt of the news Major Momber was livid. The Germans had built, unhindered, a series of breastwork defences from the old Cotter Crater across New Cotter Crater to shield from view the work they were doing in the crater. He immediately wrote a letter to the staff at 55th Div informing them on no uncertain terms of the neglect that had taken place that now placed his miners at such danger that could have been avoided. His letter was worded very strongly:

"I simply cannot understand:
(a) Why this post was not completed, as I was informed it had been, as to command the crater.
(b) How rifle grenades, Stokes mortars etc were not used to stop the Germans from working in broad daylight."

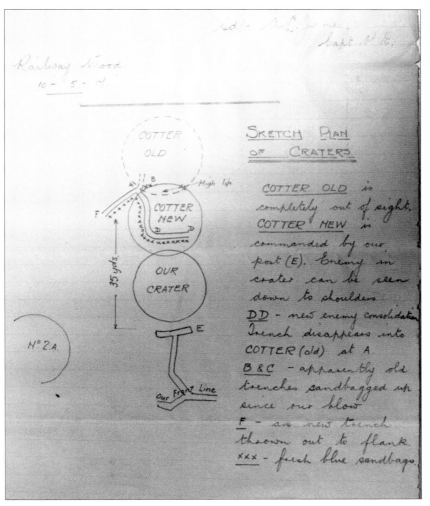

Drawing from Captain James' recce of the Cotter Craters on 10th May 1917. (TNA)

He further explained what this negligence meant to 177's operations under the ridge.

"The main gallery of 11WG had not more than an even chance of reaching its objective. Now with an almost practical certainty of the enemy blowing from his short crater galleries, the chances of ultimate success are about 4 to 1 against, with almost certainty of part of it being wrecked and men killed by these crater gallery blows, and then having to carry on repairing and driving on. 16WH and 16WD being worked hard are also in the danger zone. I beg to point out that as a company we are trying all we can to stop the enemy, but it is pretty hard on our officers and men to have to work under the above conditions of enormously increased danger and lessened chance of success, simply because of absolute neglect in the surface work and after we had offered to help."[15]

That evening at 11.30pm 177 struck twice with two charges fired simultaneously from the number 6 workings. One of the charges was a mine the other a camouflet both designed to cause maximum damage to German workings in the vicinity. The charges were wired together in series, the mine fired from the end of gallery 6ZA at 65 feet deep and the camouflet fired from the end of 6WH at 40 feet deep. The mine charge consisted of 3,700 lbs of ammonal in boxes, fired by four number 13 detonators and 1 ounce gun cotton primers. The camouflet consisted of 600 lbs of ammonal in boxes, fired by four number 13 detonators with gun cotton primers. Authority to blow these charges came from the Controller of Mines at 2nd Army HQ in conjunction with VIII Corps. The mine charge was tamped with 35 feet solid, 15 feet of air, 30 feet solid, 10 feet of air and 40 feet solid tamping! Prior to the blow sounds had been heard by listeners who continued their duty all the way up to the time of the blow. The last fifteen minutes of listening was carried out by electric listener. The estimated radius of rupture for the blow was anticipated to have been 70 feet but turned out to have been over 120 feet. The damage underground was more than had been expected. Galleries 6ZA and 6ZB were damaged for some considerable distance; a few timber sets were damaged at the face of 6WJ. The damage, coupled with the fact that when the charges blew the sound of the blow seemed to roll for a while, was put down to the belief that the charges may also have touched off a German charge planted in the vicinity of the blow. The German galleries were estimated to have been about 25 feet away. On the surface, the mine cratered into the south east lip of Gordon crater. The 600 lbs camouflet charge at

the end of gallery 6WH was tamped with 30 feet solid, 15 feet air, 30 feet solid, 10 feet of air and 10 feet solid tamping. The location of German galleries from 6WH was believed to be about 30 feet below the charge. Following the camouflet blow there was no damage done to the gallery in front of the tamping or gas found to be present in 177's workings.

Major General Jeudwine took Major Momber's points very seriously. It was obvious that great neglect had been shown by some officers in his Division in the New Cotter Crater affair and the situation needed rectifying at once. He ordered 165 Brigade to take immediate action in solving the problem:

> "The Major General directs that you will take immediate steps to deny the occupation of, and if possible destroy, the new breastwork constructed by the Germans.
>
> Your proposal for carrying this out to be sent to Divisional HQ."

In follow up orders issued the next day as to forming a post so New Cotter Crater could be overlooked, he added:

> "You will so place the responsibility that any failure to carry out your orders can definitely be fixed on an individual."

So who was responsible for the neglect? Can it be attributed to the Commanding Officer of the 1/6th Kings Lt Col McKaig, the infantry battalion holding the trenches opposite the location of the new crater? He would have had overall command of the crater consolidation party who in turn should have reported back to him that the job was done.

Plans were drawn up to carry out a raid on New Cotter Crater. The aim of the raid would be to reconnoitre the crater and destroy as much as possible. The raid would be carried out by 177 Tunnelling Company accompanied by men of the 1/6th Kings. The infantry party would provide covering fire for the tunnellers to get on with their work. This would be a chance for the tunnellers to get a brief 'eyes on' this thorn in their side. Rather than strike from below they would come in from above. The raiding party would consist of Capt B Sawers MC, 2nd Lt H Gray and eleven other ranks of 177 Tunnelling Company accompanied by Capt GD Tyson and 2nd Lt HP Robinson with 34 other ranks of the 1/6th Kings. The team from 177 Tunnelling Company would form two demolitions teams.[16] Preceding the raid, a rapid three-minute bombardment of the German lines in the vicinity would take place by Stokes mortar.

The raid was scheduled to go ahead during the night of 11th May. An advance party would go out many hours before at 3.03am following a Stokes mortar bombardment of Cotter Crater. At 3.03am, as the bombardment ceased, the party of men moved forward from the new 'T' sap under the cover rifle, Lewis gun and rifle grenade fire. The party of ten men of B Coy, 6th Kings, commanded by 2nd Lt Vernon and led by Sgt Horan moved forward to the west lip of New Cotter Crater and commenced to pull down the German barricade also placing two Stokes mortar bombs underneath it. The party was then joined by 2nd Lt Vernon who ordered a withdrawal. As they did so the party came

under fire from German grenades seriously wounding both 2nd Lt Vernon and Sgt Horan and six other members of their party.

The raid commenced at 11.03pm following the three minute, 240 rounds, bombardment of Cotter Crater. The raiders rushed forward from the 'T' sap and took up positions in Cotter West Crater, with the covering party keeping a steady rate of covering fire going on the Germans as the demolition party searched the crater. Here the men of 177 split into two groups, each led by one of the 177 officers, and discovered two inclined shafts, one in the north west side of the crater and the other in the south side. The southern incline was entered by Lt Gray who found five Germans sheltering in the incline and took them prisoner, handing them over to the infantry. Sapper Harry Holmes, not far behind Capt Sawers, missed him and continued on discovering the north-west incline. As he prepared his charge a couple Germans appeared from nowhere and attempted to seize him. Sapper Holmes called out for help and Sapper James Jones, who wasn't too far behind Holmes arrived on the scene both men shouting and fighting wildly with their fists until Holmes was freed. Alerted by their calls a member of the infantry covering party came over and promptly took one of the Germans prisoner. Only the charge laid in the southern incline exploded. Following the successful detonation of his charge, Lt Gray ordered his party to withdraw back to British lines. He came upon Sapper Arthur Gant helping a wounded infantryman and between them helped him to a position from which he was safely brought in. Captain Sawers had prepared and lit his charge after giving the order for his men to withdraw, but it had not gone off. As he himself withdrew over the north lip of the mine crater he heard a wounded infantryman calling for help from within the crater so he returned into the crater found the infantryman and carried him back to the safety of the sap head. All of the men of the 177 demolition party got back without serious injury with one man from the 1/6th Kings missing believed killed and five wounded.

The raid was deemed a success and it is worthy to note that the 177 participants of the raid all volunteered for it when asked. Major Momber wrote to the GOC 55th Div, Major General Jeudwine, just a few days later providing a list of recommendations for awards to both officers and four men of the company who took part in the raid.[17] He made especial note of the fact that many of the men were inexperienced in operations above ground and all of the raiders were volunteers. His recommendations were approved with immediate awards of a bar to Captain Sawers Military Cross, a Military Cross to Lt Gray and Military Medals to the four listed sappers.[18] Divisional award cards were given to the rest of the 177 men who took part in the raid. Major General Jeudwine wrote to Major Momber stating:

"The assistance given by Captain Sawers and Lieut Gray, Sergeant Byles and the men of your company was most valuable and greatly appreciated, and a very large share of the successful result is due to their plucky and determined work."[19]

Notes made covering the debriefing of the German prisoners captured during the raid were sent out to other tunnelling companies in the area. Captain Gregory Rich of 176 Tunnelling Company noted that the German prisoners taken during the raid belonged to the 352nd Pioneer Mining Company which was part of the 52nd Reserve Division. During their interrogation by the British, the prisoners had given a picture of how the Germans miners operated opposite 177. Their company consisted of three Lieutenants of which one was the Officer Commanding of the company. One NCO had the acting rank of officer whereas the rest of the company was made up of about 400 other ranks including about 160 attached infantry. A Lieutenant Colonel was appointed to oversee the mining companies in his sector. The men operated a shift cycle of 12-hour shifts, each followed by 36 hours rest, with four shift periods being operated before they were taken out of the line for rest. The officer on duty was in position for 48 hours visiting the workings twice during the day and twice at night. The company commander would visit his workings just once a day normally between 6am and 7am. The report also mentioned:

"The prisoners agreed that their mining policy had been purely defensive and they had often been told by their officers that they must work very hard in order not to be caught napping. They thought it was a hard struggle in order to keep pace with our work and had a great respect for our tunnellers."

The prisoners also informed their interrogators of their casualty figures caused by recent blows by 177 Tunnelling Company. The camouflet blow at 2am on 6th April, fired from the end of 16WD (left) had wrecked their galleries and killed four men and wounded eight others. The camouflet blown at 2am on 2nd May killed three men and wounded one, again wrecking their galleries and the camouflet blown at 9.30pm on 8th May had killed two men.

As the raiders carried out their brave deeds on the surface, below ground men of 177 were preparing another blow in further attempts to destroy German workings in the Cotter West Crater vicinity. This mine was estimated to form a crater between crater 2a and Cotter West Crater and would also put paid to the working that was not blown up in the surface raid. At the end of gallery 16WG, 30 feet down, 1,000 lbs of ammonal, in boxes, was laid and made ready. The familiar number 13 detonators and gun cotton primers were placed into the charge and then the gallery was tamped with 30 feet solid, 10 feet of air, 25 feet of solid and 10 feet of air. To help preserve the gallery immediately in front of the tamping, supports, known as strutting, were placed across the gallery for another 10 feet. With authority to fire the mine forthcoming from C of M, VIII Corps and 55th Division, Major Momber had the mine fired at 10pm on the night of 12th May. The mine had an estimated radius of rupture of 50 feet and caused no damage to 177's underground workings in front of the tamping. On the surface a crater 30 feet across was formed in the location estimated for the mine crater. The crater blew partially into the British crater fired four days earlier. It was 8 feet deep and had a lip 2 feet high. As soon as the mine was fired a crater consolidation party made up of men from the 1/5th Kings went over and consolidated the near lip. Saps were driven out from the right side of crater 2a and also

from the bombing post in the Vernon Crater in order to link up with the consolidation of the new crater. It was now reported that from the new crater the German positions in New Cotter Crater could be observed. This new crater would become known as Vernon Crater after the 1/6th Kings Subaltern 2nd Lt Vernon. In a handwritten note to 165th Inf Bde an unidentified officer believed to be from 177 Tunnelling Company classed the underground results of the mine on German workings as entirely satisfactory.

About a minute before the mine was fired by 177, the Germans struck firing a defensive mine at map reference I.12.c.4.7, about 80 feet east of crater 1a. There were no casualties above or below ground and no gas was reported in 177 workings. On the surface the mine formed a crater 30 to 40 feet in diameter. It was believed that the Germans may have driven this mine from the number 9 crater, however countering that belief was the information gleaned from the German miners captured on the raid of 11th May who had stated under interrogation, that no mining was taking place from number 9 crater. The interrogation of the captured German miners revealed some interesting information about the sector and revealed what names the Germans were using for the crater. New Cotter Crater, where they had been captured from was known to the Germans as 'Allenstein' and James Crater, where it was also suspected that the Germans were mining from was known as 'Angermunder'. Suspicions were confirmed when interrogators found out that there were at least three German shafts in the crater. It would now be the aim of gallery 16WC to make its silent way out to neutralise this threat.

The next mine strike took place on 17th May at 7pm, a camouflet blown by the Germans opposite gallery 11WH, slightly east of crater number 2. The blow caused no damage to 177's workings save a few lumps of earth falling from the roof and, apart from one man in the gallery being badly shaken up, there were no casualties resulting from the blow. It was believed that the camouflet was blown as a defensive measure but what was not known was from where. It was presumed that the German may now have a gallery running off the gallery that blew Blakeley Crater, but it was also believed that they did not know for sure of the existence of 11WH. There was no report of damage on the surface.

Another German camouflet and mine were fired on 19th May; the camouflet was fired at 10.15am damaging 13 feet of gallery 16WC. There was no report of gas in 177's workings, casualties or any damage reported on the surface. The location of the blow was estimated to be at map reference I12c 30.83 and believed to have been fired as a result of the sounds of repair work in 16WC (left) being picked up by German listeners. It was also believed that the camouflet charge may have sat in location for a while before the blow, from an incline put down from James Crater. The second blow of the day occurred at 11.05pm when the Germans fired the mine. Blown as a defensive, undercharged mine it formed a crater 40 to 50 feet in diameter in the southern lip of Cotter Crater at map reference I.12.c.30.88. No casualties or damage above or below ground was reported as a result of the blow and it was widely believed that the mine had been fired from one of the galleries discovered during the New Cotter Crater raid of 11th January.

It was also thought that the Germans may have picked up sounds emanating from Galleries 16WN and 16WD. If they had, they blew too soon as both of these galleries escaped undamaged. Infantry on the surface reported seeing a large flame shoot skywards but reported very little earth falling.

At 5pm on 20th May a bombardment by 6 inch howitzers and trench mortars commenced on James Crater. The large 6 inch howitzers fired 86 shells and the trench mortars a further 34 rounds at the crater. Observation by Forward Observing Officer was carried out from a trench just 50 yards away from the crater and reported back later that at least 50 of the 6 inch rounds struck home. The majority of the trench mortar rounds were also deemed effective. The bombardment of the crater also helped to change the shape of the lip of it. Large amounts of wooden beams, props and revetting was seen thrown into the air. This was just another example of an attempt to destroy and harass the German workings in the Cotter/New Cotter Crater area. At that moment, 177's only hope in really neutralising this problem lay in blowing a substantial overcharged mine under the vicinity of the two craters. They needed to get a gallery out eastwards towards the two craters and use all their guile and tact to keep its location secret from German listeners. Only one gallery, currently being worked on, was capable of delivering a charge to the location required, to do the job. That gallery was 11WG. If anything was to happen to the gallery it would ruin months of hard labour and seriously set back larger plans for the area. At a time when most eyes in the British Second Army were focusing on the Messines Ridge, 177's plan to neutralise a position probably no bigger than a tennis field may have paled into insignificance. But that was their role, they were there to support whatever division was on the surface and it would not be long before the stagnation that had existed in the Railway Wood sector and elsewhere within the Ypres Salient came to an end. The British Army would soon be on the move in an offensive; forever remembered for mud and stagnation, but an offensive which would drive the German Army back eastwards off the Passchendaele Ridge. For 177, 11WG had to work; by 28th May, at 180 feet long and the end of the gallery 66 feet deep, it had reached its location an estimated 50 feet from German galleries, and was ready to be charged. It had to be kept safe and work progressed in an almost unhealthy silence. The work was not just restricted to 11WG. This mine charge would be big and would probably damage other 177 workings in the vicinity. It was decided to place strutting in many of the galleries in an attempt to restrict damage to their workings. The tunnellers, focused on the task in hand, also realised that they needed to lure the German miners into their haven of galleries around the Cotter Crater area, ensuring both maximum damage and casualties. A small camouflet would do the trick. On 24th May an attached infantryman to 177 Tunnelling Company was killed in action.

The camouflet was fired at 10pm on 28th May from gallery 16WN, estimated to be just a few feet under the North West rim of New Cotter Crater and within 25 feet of German underground workings. The gallery was tamped with 40 feet of solid, 10 feet of air and 20 feet of solid tamping. The charge consisting of 500 lbs of blastine was fired with No 13 detonators and 1 ounce gun cotton primers. Although there was no gas or damage reported underground, the resultant blow did some damage to the British consolidation work in number 12 crater by collapsing the sap head. As the Germans on the surface moved in to repair their damaged galleries and surface breastwork, the final touches were being made in gallery 11WG.

At 10pm on 29th May, after authority granted from Controller of Mines 2nd Army, VIII Corps and 55th Division, 177 Tunnelling Company fired their largest mine of the war. The charge, 15,000 lbs of ammonal; 5,000 lbs in waterproof bags and 10,000 lbs in boxes was fired from a chamber at the end of 11WG. The explosion ripped through the ground heaving it into the air and lighting up the area as a great jet of burning gas escaped into the air. Cotter Crater, New Cotter Crater and No 12 crater were obliterated simply heaved skywards and buried by the falling debris. A crater 150 feet in diameter and 60 feet deep appeared on the surface. A crater consolidation party from 1/5 South Lancashire Regt moved quickly and by 10.45pm started consolidating the nearside western lip of the crater. Working parties continued ceaselessly throughout the night and got the position wired in on both flanks. By dawn on 30th May, trenches from the northern and southern extremities of the crater now connected to the British front line. The positions were deemed good and safe. The Germans took very little action as the men worked, firing two or three trench mortars and firing a few bursts of machine gun fire. As the first vestiges of daylight appeared it became obvious quickly that

147

A German soldier's view of Bellewaerde Lake in the summer of 1915. It wasn't until the explosion of the largest mine fired by 177 Tunnelling Company in May 1917 and the consolidation of the lip of the crater in their lines that the British were able to utilise the slight gain in height looking eastwards and see the lake. (Photo courtesy of Phillipe Oosterlinck)

the western lip was much higher than the eastern affording the British positions an enviable view over the German lines and also Bellewaarde Lake. The crater stood lip to lip with both craters 2a and Blakeley, a high mound of earth now stood on the junction of both the latter. Flames burnt in the German lines for several hours after the blow. The mine was listed as a common mine and very successful. Two further dull detonations were heard 20 to 30 seconds after the mine explosion and were believed to be gas pockets igniting in the German galleries. The Mine Explosion Report was completed within a few hours of the blow and did not list any major damage underground to 177's galleries. The reason for this was the amount of strutting

that had been put in place which needed to be removed before any inspections could take place. Galleries 11WK, 11WA, 11K, 11K dugout and incline, 11R, 11WD and 16WB were all strutted prior to the blow. A cursory glance showed that older workings off gallery 11K, some 110 feet from the blow were slightly damaged. Gas was also reported in 11F shaft, with the further effect of it found two days later whilst clearing the tamping and strutting when a rush of it overcame a gas sentry just after he managed to shout a warning to his comrades to get out of the workings. He was overcome but was rescued by 51500 Private Charles Jull, 9th Royal Fusiliers and 38476 Private James Hatton, 15th Royal Welsh Fusiliers.[20] Sadly no records survive today to tell us what effect was felt in the German workings. For those in the immediate vicinity it must have been horrendous. Death would have come quick to some, but others would have had a slow, lingering death trapped beneath the earth in their shattered galleries. One can only hope gas did its evil work quickly.[21]

In between the cat and mouse actions that occurred during the month, normal work on the galleries and strongpoints continued where possible. In the number 6 workings under the tip of Railway Wood gallery 6YA at 110 feet deep, work was carried out for the whole month, being

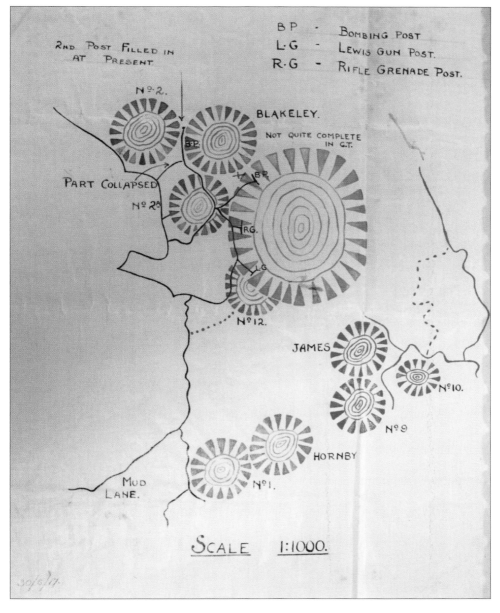

A plan made just after Momber Crater was formed by 177's largest mine blow of the war on 29th May 1917. Note how the infantry have utilised the western lip of the crater. The plan also shows how the mine finally destroyed the Cotter Craters. (TNA. WO95/2902)

304 feet long by the month's end running north east to near the tip of the German Salient opposite Railway Wood. Its partner in crime, 6YB, ran east and was 75 feet long by the end of May. Both of these galleries were the deepest operated by 177 during their time under the Railway Wood sector. They were fed from the shaft 6Y that connected both the number 6 workings and the Cambridge Road dugouts system. The main effort in the number 11 workings during the month was gallery 11WG as discussed previously. Galleries 11WH and 11WK were also worked on both galleries being driven a further 12 feet. These three galleries were at the 77 feet level of the number 11 workings. The extensive number 16 workings were also worked on regularly throughout the month. A lot of the work was general repairs to galleries but some of the offensive galleries and the laterals connecting them at both 30 and 45 feet levels were also worked on. In total, just over 1,000 feet of earth was cut in these workings throughout the month. Mud Lane communication trench which ran westwards back from the front line in the vicinity of the number 16 workings had a battalion HQ dugout constructed along it during May. Located at the end of gallery 16E and also accessible from an inclined stairway off Mud Lane was 16A; this 12-roomed dugout would provide the necessary cover for the Battalion holding the line in this part of the line. Previously all Battalion Headquarters for those holding the Railway Wood sector had been located in the Cambridge Road dugouts. These dugouts were now also being readied to have extensions built to house a Brigade Headquarters and Dressing Station.

At the Hades strongpoint in Wieltje work was harassed at the beginning of the month by shellfire but the men managed to get a bed plate set into concrete in the dugout on which its powerhouse would be located. This eventually would provide power and pumping for the dugout. The shaft of the Wieltje dugout was also bratticed 20 feet down.[22] On 5th May, the garrison of 177 men involved in the construction were withdrawn, as they were at Lancashire Farm, to help with the work at the Railway Wood sector. Work on the Hades dugout was handed over to 254 Tunnelling Company on 18th May.

JUNE 1917

June would prove to be the Tunnellers 'finest hour' of the war. It would be a month that would be filled with triumph and tragedy. The British Army now had 32 tunnelling companies working along the Western Front. In the Salient, 18 months of planning and fine tuning was coming to an end. Norton Griffiths' plan of an earthquake under the Germans was about to be realised. It was to be part of a plan to break the German's hold of key strategic positions of importance. In all upwards of eight tunnelling companies and about 50,000 attached infantry had spent the last 18 months devising and building a huge mining scheme that would shake the Germans off the Messines Ridge. The scheme had been constructed in the conditions of the utmost secrecy. Twenty-five massive mines now lay under German positions starting from the infamous Hill 60, just a couple of miles south of Ypres. The scheme snaked its way southward, through stain that was once the village of St Eloi and then wrapped itself around the foot of the Messines Ridge, passing in front of the ruins of the village of Wytschaete and then in front of the town after whom the forthcoming offensive would be named, Messines. The line of mines then followed a line south east of Messines coming across the north face of Plugstreet Wood and then running down the eastern side of the wood. It was at the south east corner of the wood that the underground scheme came to an end. In all 25 mines, totalling a massive 933,200 lbs of explosive was ready to go off under the German lines. At 3.10am on 7th June the plungers went down and switches were pulled, 19 of those mines made up of 781,300 lbs of ammonal, 42,100 lbs of blastine and 19,800 lbs of gun cotton totalling 843,200 lbs exploded over a period of about 30 seconds. The effect was devastating. The smallest mine was one of three to blow at Hollandscheschuur Farm 14,700 lbs and the largest, the biggest fired by the RE Tunnellers in WWI, was at St Eloi, The Queen Victoria mine totalling 95,600 lbs.[23] At that moment the explosion of the 19 mines was the largest planned, manmade explosion in history. On the back of the debris thrown up by the mines a huge bombardment crashed onto the German lines and 12 British, Australian and New Zealand divisions attacked the ridge. In less than 12 hours the ridge was taken and held. It now gave the British control over important strategic ground and went a long way to straightening the line south of Ypres. The operation had been a great success, in fact the most successful offensive of the Great War. It became known as a precursor for an even bigger offensive to be launched just over six weeks later that would become known as the Third Battle of Ypres or the

Battle for Passchendaele. The success of the Messines offensive would unfortunately not be mirrored during this next offensive.

177 Tunnelling Company was not involved in the mining effort of the Messines operation, but throughout June they would feel the fallout of the operation as German miners facing them started reacting to the slightest suspicions in an attempt not to end up in the sorry state of their comrades further south on the Messines Ridge. They were busy operating under their own sector of ground rather than worry about what was going on elsewhere. Whilst June may have been triumphant for the tunnellers in general, it certainly wasn't for the men of 177. On 3rd June at 3.30am the Germans blew a camouflet opposite the number 6 workings at a depth of between 70 and 80 feet. It was believed to be a defensive measure and caused slight damage to about 59 feet of gallery 6YA. There were no surface effects or casualties reported as a result of the camouflet blow. The damage to 6YA was repaired quickly up to the face and then construction began on a charge chamber for a massive camouflet 177 would unleash on the Germans. Tragedy struck the company on the 3rd when three men were killed and three injured. The dead men were 23-year-old 132729 Sapper Joseph Jacob Cadman of Atherstone, Warwickshire, 30-year-old 102450 Sapper Patrick Creegan of Wilton Park, Co Durham and 43-year-old 102425 Sapper Ernest Hull of Esh Winning, Co Durham.[24] Sadly there is nothing in the war diary of 177 or any of the other units in Railway Wood sector to say how these men were killed. However, whilst researching information to compile the book, the author was sent an email by

151

Val Hutchings, the granddaughter of 202114 LCpl Hubert Cherrett of the 1/4th South Lancashire. She transcribed a letter written by men of the 1/4th South Lancs which described her grandfather's involvement in a shelling incident which killed and wounded members of 177 Tunnelling Company:

"Sir, I beg to bring to your notice the bravery and gallant conduct of No 202114 Lance-Corporal Cherrett H.

At 10am 4.6.17 during a heavy bombardment of YPRES a party of 177 Tunnelling Company was caught by a number of shells at the railway crossing near bridge 10. Several men were killed and wounded.

LCpl Cherrett, hearing cries of 'help' left his dugout and ran to the railway under heavy shellfire and carried Sapper Probean, 177 Tunnelling Company, on his back to safety a distance of about 50 yards.

LCpl Cherrett himself became a casualty through his bravery, being gassed and crushed by falling debris as he entered his dugout.

Yours obediently Sir."

Name Intelligible (CSM)

Bridge 10 mentioned in the letter is just west of Ypres on the old road to Poperinge where the road and railway pass over the Yser Canal. The author firmly believes that the incident described here is the incident in which Sappers Cadman, Creegan and Hull were killed. There is an error in the date mentioned in the letter. A check of 177's monthly return for its men and attached infantry shows no fatalities or wounded for 4th June but three fatalities and three wounded for 3rd June. LCpl Cherrett's brave action that morning cost him his life, he sadly died of his wounds on 4th June.

During June the Railway Wood dugouts scheme had a Battalion and Brigade HQ added to the system. In addition to them a Dressing Station for the Royal Army Medical Corps was also added. The Brigade HQ was named 'Archie' and during the month a gallery, off which were three dugouts, was completed. The Battalion HQ was named 'Gladys' and a gallery, three dugouts and inclined stairways were completed during the month and finally, the Dressing Station, 'Horace', had a gallery and five dugouts completed during the month. An exit from the system onto Cambridge Road was also completed. The harassing fire put down by the Germans went a long way to prevent the disposal of clay-filled sandbags and also hindered the delivery of timber and other material coming up to the dugout from 177's advance dump near Hellfire Corner. On some nights, due to the heavy shelling, there was practically no movement up to the dugout. The shelling also caused many repairs to be made to the dugouts' inclined stairways and entrances.

Work was also carried out on 'Muriel', another Battalion HQ, entered via Mud Lane communication trench. The second battalion HQ along that trench was 'Maud' whose dugouts were completed in June.

177 were also given a new working tasked to the company during June. It was a set of tunnelled dugouts that would be located off Beek trench. As Mud Lane trench ran south westwards off the front line it skirted the northern edge of Y Wood and then crossed Cambridge Road about 330 metres north of Birr Crossroads. Once across Cambridge

Road it continued southeast for about 185 metres until it met with the junction with River trench which ran off to the left southwards. Beek trench started here, running in the direction of Mud Lane and commenced a gradual right turn northwards until it joined with West Lane, which ran alongside the Ypres to Roulers railway line. Four attempts were made by the men working on the project, to step down from Beek trench in order to dig the dugouts but due to the nature of the ground it was found impossible. Arrangements were then made to try sinking a steel tubbed shaft and a location was chosen 100 feet south of where they had been working before. A traverse was cut in order to start a 10 feet by 10 feet chamber from which to sink the shaft from.

On 4th June the Germans blew a mine about 80 feet north of Blakeley Crater. There were no trenches in the near vicinity belonging to either side and it was presumed to have been a defensive move by the Germans, perhaps picking up sounds believed to be those of 177's miners in the area. The mine caused no damage to the British lines or workings below ground and left a small crater on the surface which was reconnoitred by British infantry.

177 were now concentrating on helping to prepare the ground on which the infantry would move forward in the forthcoming offensive that would take place at the end of July. Their role would be to negate any problems facing troops from enemy miners underground. With the big bang of Messines occurring on 7th June, it would not take long for word to get around German mining companies that they had been undermined. Was this tactic of going deep restricted only to the area covered by the Messines offensive? They wouldn't know and the only option to them would be to start camoufleting on receipt of reports of suspicious noises. Another option open to Army commanders on the ground would be to withdraw a few hundred metres thereby ruining many months hard work by opposing tunnellers. But giving up ground was not what the Germans wanted to do in the Salient; thereby 177 had to make sure that the frontage under which it operated was safe. On 9th June at 2am, from the end of the deepest working under the Railway Wood sector, gallery 6YA, 110 feet deep, 177 Tunnelling Company fired its largest camouflet charge of the war – 9,000 lbs of ammonal fired by number 13 electric detonators using gun cotton primers. 6YA was tamped with 100 feet of solid, 15 feet of air and then 30 feet of solid tamping. The aim of the camouflet was to destroy German workings in the vicinity to buy a few weeks of safety for the northern flank of the Railway Wood sector. Although the blast broke through the surface it did not crater. Underground there was some minor damage to 177's workings for up to 20 feet outside the tamping. 9,000 lbs is a huge amount of explosive to use for a camouflet charge. The effect of this must have ripped through the German galleries opposite the number 6 workings causing untold damage and casualties to anyone in their system at the time.

By 11th June, gallery 16WC was in a position where a charge could be fired to damage German workings emanating from James Crater. A 2,000 lb charge of ammonal in boxes was laid at the end of the gallery, 35 feet deep and then the gallery tamped with 50 feet of solid, 10 feet of air and

153

70 feet of solid tamping. Authority to fire the mine came from the 55th Division, and on 12th June at 11pm that night the plunger went down and the last mine fired by 177 in the war detonated. There was no damage or gas reported in 177's workings outside the tamping. With German galleries estimated to be only 20 to 30 feet away the damage to them was untold. On the surface a crater, 90 feet in diameter and 25 to 30 feet deep formed. A crater consolidation party made up of men from V and X Companies of the 1/10th Kings Liverpool Regiment (The Liverpool Scottish) made their way forwards and captured the near lip of the crater. Under the command of Captain LG Wall and 2nd Lieutenant A Gledsdale, the party worked hard to consolidate the near lip into the British line suffering only one casualty in the process. They observed that the lip of the crater was low on the western side and high on the southern side where it now joined with Hornby Crater. With new positions in place and under observation the Germans would find it near impossible to use James Crater.

It wouldn't take the Germans long to react, but it was the frequency to which they reacted which initially surprised some. On 13th June the Germans fired five camouflet charges. The first two blows came at 3am occurring to the north of the tip of Railway Wood at map reference I.11.b.9.6 in the area of the number 6 workings. Just eight minutes later the third blow occurred on the southern extremity of the crater field within the Railway Wood sector. The last two blows occurred just seven minutes later in the James and Hornby Crater area, the fifth blow caused a very small crater. It became obvious that the Germans were panicking, aware of what had happened to their comrades further south just a few days before, they were now blowing maximum camouflets from their listening posts underground to try and ruin as much of the British workings as possible so that the same would not happen to them. The blows caused no damage to any of 177's workings and just a slight effect of gas was felt in galleries 11G and 16WE. The next day, 14th June, the same happened again. Five camouflets were blown by the Germans. The first blow occurred at 2.05am just behind Gordon Crater in the area of the number 6 workings, it is not recorded whereabouts the second, third and fourth blows were located but they happened at 2.10am, 2.14am and 2.22 am. The last blow occurred at 2.43am and was recorded as occurring at map reference I12c Central. The mine explosion report compiled by Major Momber stated that the probable reason for the blows was defensive. He also wrote: "He is obviously nervous" describing the German tunnellers and also drawing the conclusion in the remarks column that:

> "Part of the results of the Messines Ridge mine success is shown by this obvious attempt at cutting any mines we might have under his lines."

Not that anyone would have known it at that point, but the last of the camouflets to be fired by the Germans that morning heralded the end of the offensive mining war under the Railway Wood sector. Work would continue for a few months more maintaining the many galleries that existed under the sector with most of the work focusing on the Railway Wood dugouts scheme. The

14th June also saw the departure of the 55th Division from the Railway Wood sector. Coming into the sector were the men of the 23rd Infantry Brigade of Major General Sir William Heneker's 8th Division, the men of the 2nd Northamptonshire Regiment relieving The Liverpool Scottish by 4am on 15th June. The 8th Division were part of the British 5th Army and it was for a short time that 177 Tunnelling Company came under its control.

On 18th June Major Momber was seriously wounded. Where he was and what he was doing when he was wounded are uncertain as unfortunately no record has been found. Nothing in the war diary of 177 Tunnelling Company or the relevant divisional, brigade or regimental war diary tells us what happened to him. From his officers' record held at The National Archives we can see that he was admitted to No. 2 (Canadian) Casualty Clearing Station located at Remy sidings, a couple of miles south west of Poperinge. Also in his file is a telegram sent by Messrs Cox and Sons to Major Momber's father in Biarritz, France which erroneously states he was admitted to No. 1 Red Cross Hospital in Le Touquet on 29th June, but it does state that he was admitted with:

> "... gunshot wound left hand and head severe."

A letter from Major Maurice Wilkinson of 177 to his sister Isabella stated:

> "Major Momber my C.O. was killed last week – hit in the spine and only lived 2 days – and I am commanding the Coy and so very busy – poor chap, I can hardly realise that he has gone. He was such a gay fine young fellow and doing so well in his profession. He was a regular, only 29 and had got a DSO and MC this war."

Unfortunately, Major Momber never recovered from his wounds and died on 20th June 1917. His death certificate, also in his file, states that he died in Number 2 (Canadian) Casualty Clearing Station, Belgium on 20th June 1917 from wounds received in action.[25] 177 Tunnelling Company had lost their Officer Commanding. To many he would have been a good friend, certainly well respected by men not just in 177 but also by those under his previous command in 176 Tunnelling Company. He had been badly wounded by trench mortar whilst in command of 176 and had spent some time recovering from his wounds both in the UK and in Biarritz, France with his parents. During his recovery he had asked for a position at GHQ in mines staff, but was instead sent to command 177. The loss of this brave tunnelling officer would have been felt by many.

177 Tunnelling Company lost another of its men on 20th June. 102368 Sapper Robert Moseby of Great Lumley, Co Durham died of wounds.[26] Again, nothing is known about the circumstances of his wounding. Was he perhaps with Major Momber at the time, or wounded in the same action? The monthly manning sheet attached to 177 Tunnelling Company war diary shows that 23 other ranks were wounded throughout the month but none of them on 18th June. Seven attached infantry were killed throughout the month.

Taking over as OC of 177 Tunnelling

Company on 20th June was 40-year-old Major Maurice Hewson Wilkinson MC. Born in Gateshead, Co Durham, he was a mining engineer working in Peking, China when war broke out, returning and getting a commission in the South Wales Borders. He arrived in France on 1st July 1915 and after a short time he transferred to the Royal Engineers, joining 177 Tunnelling Company on 14th February 1916. He now had the reigns of the company at hand as preparations moved forward for the opening of the Third Battle of Ypres.

With planning underway, throughout the rest of the month work continued on the Railway Wood scheme and other Battalion Headquarters. At Mud Lane, Muriel and Maud were completed and the Battalion and Brigade Headquarters and Dressing Station in the Railway Wood dugouts, Gladys, Archie and Horace were also finished. The steel 6 foot 6 inch steel shaft at Beek trench was sunk and work continued on the tunnelled dugouts scheme. During the month the company took over two dugouts under construction from the 2nd Canadian Tunnelling Company. The first was a dugout known as 'Railway Cutting' located along the Ypres–Roulers railway line just south west of Hellfire Corner. This was to be a fairly shallow dugout with just 5 feet of cover. The second dugout known as 'Halfway House' at map reference I.17.c.5.8 was located very close to the ruins of a building of the same name. It would end up being able to accommodate close to a thousand men along with a battalion and Brigade Headquarters. 177 only worked on Halfway House until 29th June when work was handed over to 171 Tunnelling Company.

1 Crater 1a, slightly south east of Hornby Crater.
2 102808 Spr Thomas Bird is buried in Plot 2, Row B, Grave 15 in Poperinge New Military Cemetery.
3 Pte Thomas Davies body was never recovered and he is now remembered in the RE Grave Cemetery on the. Unfortunately I have been unable to identify who the second fatality was in the number 6 workings that day.
4 See 55th Division HQ war diary and appendices WO95/2901 for February 1917 for exchange of request and approval to the naming of the craters. Future requests and approvals appear in later months of the war diary.
5 Both 2nd Lt Shield's and Pte Frederick Bigley's bodies were never recovered. They are both commemorated on the Menin Gate. 2nd Lt Macintosh's MC citation reads: For initiative and great determination on patrol. At Railway Wood on the 1st/2nd March this officer was in charge of the reserve party in our own trenches. As soon as he learnt that the officer and one man of a patrol had failed to return he took out a party to look for them. He conducted four parties in all and was out searching for nearly four hours. The following night he was sent to make a special reconnaissance of the crater blown on night 1st/2nd March. The patrol was ordered early, and was held up by an enemy listening post. As it was a very bright night he was compelled to return. He volunteered to go out again and did so at 3am making an excellent and daring reconnaissance.
Sgt Gaffney's MM citation read: Was senior NCO of a fighting patrol which attempted to enter an enemy sap near railway Wood on night 1st/2nd March 1917. He set a fine example of courage and leadership and made an excellent reconnaissance. After returning from the patrol, although suffering from a slight sprain, he accompanied two search parties sent to look for a missing officer and man. He has shown great gallantry on many occasions and is a fine soldier.
6 2nd Lt George Herbert Coleman's citation read: "For Conspicuous gallantry. On the night of March 4th/5th, 1917 near Railway Wood when the enemy blew a mine in front of our trenches and seized the crater, this officer displayed great coolness and ability in organising and leading

two separate bombing attacks, which, however were not successful. Without any regard for his personal safety, 2nd Lt Coleman remained to the last superintending the withdrawal of his party and then, although bombed by the enemy and exposed to heavy rifle and machinegun fire, he succeeded in carrying a wounded man from the lip of the crater back to our lines. On a former occasion on 25th February 1917, when the enemy blew a mine in no man's land this officer showed great initiative and bravery by reconnoitring the crater, although almost daylight."

7 Spr Sidney Firth's name is engraved on the cross of sacrifice of RE Grave Cemetery.

8 Pte Edward Nicholls was awarded the Military Medal for his prompt actions following the mine blow. His citation reads: About 6.45pm on the 9th March 1917, the enemy exploded a mine near Railway Wood. This Private was in charge of a Lewis Gun Team about 50 yards from the crater. He got his gun into action, flanking the crater, before the earth had ceased falling. When the enemy attempted to get into the open he drove them back. He kept his gun in action until wounded. (8 to 11 Information courtesy of private collection of Mr Simon Jones)

9 2nd Lt Ronald MacDonald was awarded the Military Cross. His citation reads: For conspicuous gallantry and devotion to duty, on 9th March 1917, when the enemy exploded a mine in front of our trenches near Railway Wood. This officer on his own initiative immediately collected a party of men, who were in the front line, and led them out to the crater to prevent the enemy from occupying it. Later when the Officer Commanding the crater consolidation party was wounded, 2nd Lt MacDonald took command of this party, which he superintended for 10 hours with great energy and resource. On two occasions when the consolidation party was bombed, he led counter attacks which drove off and silenced the enemy.

10 240365 Cpl (A/Sgt) Thomas Huartson of the consolidation party was awarded the Distinguished Conduct Medal for his actions that night. His citation reads:.....This NCO was in command of a section of the consolidation party, which immediately left the trenches at the pre-arranged place. Finding that the crater

could not be reached from this position, and the Officer Commanding the consolidation party had been wounded, Sergeant Huartson assumed command, withdrew the party to our trenches, and after a hurried reorganisation, led it out from a more suitable point in the line. He then posted the necessary covering parties and started the consolidation of the crater which he directed with the greatest courage and energy until wounded.

11 241424 L/Cpl (A/Cpl) Harold Dickinson, 243994 L/Cpl Joseph Ashcroft and 240231 Sjt John Kilbride were awarded the Military Medal.

12 18795 Cpl Daniel Evans and 19105 Private Richard Roberts names are commemorated on the cross of sacrifice at RE Grave Cemetery.

13 358513 Pte Edward Poultons body was never recovered from the gallery. He is commemorated cross of sacrifice in the RE Grave Cemetery. The body of his comrade 358564 Private Robert Henry Blair was recovered and he lies in Plot 6, Row H, Grave 2 of Vlamertinge Military Cemetery.

14 WO95/2901. 55th Divisional Intelligence summary for 25th to 26th April 1917. Found in appendices of war diary for April 1917.

15 This amazing exchange of letters and plans can be found in the 55th Division HQ war diary appendices for May 1917.

16 The demolition teams from 177 Tunnelling Company were; Captain Basil Sawers, 2nd Lieutenant Henry Gray, 139138 Sergeant Herbert Byles, 132902 Sapper Arthur Gant, 175851 Sapper Frederick Morrell, 104901 Sapper James Jones, 121669 Sapper Harry Holmes, 132819 Sapper Joseph Cockerham, 158179 Sapper William Colterall, 104891 Sapper Samuel Johns, 155838 Sapper William Greenway, 158181 Sapper Benjamin Lowndes and 102816 Sapper Alfred Jones.

17 Private papers, courtesy Simon Jones.

18 The citations for the medals are as follows:

Temp Lt (Acting Captain) Basil Lindsay Sawers MC and Bar: For conspicuous gallantry at Railway Wood on May 11th 1917. When it was ascertained that the enemy must be driving mine shafts in Cotter Crater this officer volunteered to take a party of miners over to destroy these shafts. He organised and led two parties and having ascertained there were two shafts (inclined), that one had been evacuated, and that one of his parties had evacuated prisoners captured by them, he gave orders that one of these inclined shafts should be destroyed. He himself obtained a charge from one of the men for the second shaft, and gave the signal for the party to withdraw. He went back and lit his charge and was coming back last from the "N" side of the crater when he heard a wounded infantryman calling for help. He went out again and carried him in on his back through the crater and up into our sap head. He made certain all his men had returned with the exception of one officer and a Sapper, who were bringing another wounded infantryman in. He went out again to their assistance and helped to bring the man in. His courage, coolness and leadership made his parties work a complete success.

Temp 2nd Lieut. Henry Gray MC: For conspicuous gallantry at railway Wood on may 11th, 1917. This officer volunteered to take charge of one of two parties going over with a raid to destroy mine shafts in an enemy crater. He discovered an enemy inclined shaft in which five German miners were sheltering. He captured these and handed them over to an infantry guard. He then laid his charge and went across the crater to report to his senior officer. Acting on the latter's orders he returned and lit his charge which successfully exploded. He then saw his party safely off, and in doing so he found a Sapper helping a wounded infantryman. Between them they carried this man back to our lip when with further assistance he was safely brought in. This officer throughout the operation displayed great coolness and courage. It is the fifth raid in which he has taken part. He has done excellent work as a mining officer.

132902 Sapper Arthur Gant MM: For conspicuous gallantry at railway Wood on may 11th, 1917. Although a specially enlisted tunneller, untrained in above ground operations, this sapper volunteered to go over with a raiding party to destroy enemy shafts. He carried his charge till it was taken over by an officer to place in an inclined shaft. He then went in search of any wounded. He brought one man back to our sap head and then went out again, till he found an officer assisting another man in. Both trips were done after the withdrawal signal had been given, and the covering party had withdrawn, and he himself had been wounded. For two years this sapper has done consistent good work, always volunteering for any dangerous work underground and assisting in rescue work on several occasions. He has always set a fine example of fearless devotion to duty to his comrades.

175851 Sapper Frederick Morrell MM: For conspicuous gallantry and devotion to duty at Railway Wood on 11/5/17. As an untrained tunneller he volunteered to go over with a raid to blow up enemy shafts in a crater. He acted as orderly to the officer in charge, assisted him in blowing a charge after the remainder of his party had withdrawn, and later went out again to help to bring in a wounded infantryman. His assistance was invaluable to his officer. For several months his work has been consistently good and reliable.

104901 Sapper James Jones MM: For conspicuous gallantry at Railway Wood on 11/5/17. This Sapper missed his officer when the latter entered the enemy mine shaft. He went on with his charge and discovered another mine shaft. Another Sapper was preparing to blow it up when the latter was seized by German miners. He shouted for help and fought with his fists to rescue his comrade, till an infantryman with his rifle came to their rescue. Between them they secured a prisoner.

121669 Sapper Harry Holmes MM: For conspicuous gallantry at Railway Wood on 11/5/17. He volunteered to take part in the above raid. He was with Sapper Jones when they lost their officer and went ahead. As soon as they had found the mine shaft he placed his charge and was about to light it when he was seized by Germans. He fought with his fists till help came. The signal for withdrawal was given but he again went forward to try and destroy the shaft. He could not find his charge so ultimately withdrew, being the last of the party, unarmed, and with no covering party.

19 Private papers, courtesy Simon Jones.

20 Private papers, Simon Jones. Privates Charles Jull and James Hatton were both immediately awarded the military medal for their actions. Their citations are:

51500 Private Charles Henry Jull MM: For conspicuous gallantry and coolness at Railway Wood, near Ypres on May 31st, 1917. As a result of a mine blown by the 177th Tunnelling Company, there was gas in the galleries. A trained NCO with rescue apparatus and canary was posted inside the gas doors as sentry to warn men working near in case of danger from gas. Through a rush of gas this NCO was overcome. One of the men working at the gas dam gave the alarm and all men, acting on these orders cleared to the surface. Private Jull, the last man, hearing a man in distress went for assistance and he and Private Hatton returned and rescued the gas sentry. The latter was only brought back to consciousness after 30 minutes artificial respiration, and but for the promptness and courage of Private Jull and Private Hatton would undoubtedly have lost his life. Private Jull was himself gassed and had to be taken to hospital.

38476 Private James Hatton MM: For conspicuous gallantry and coolness at Railway Wood near Ypres on may 31st, 1917. As a result of a mine blown by the 177 Tunnelling Company, there was gas in the galleries. This man assisted private Jull in affecting the rescue of the gas sentry and was himself slightly gassed.

21 There were reported cases of Germans heard trapped in galleries and dugouts following mine explosions. An interesting yet awful account is mentioned briefly by Captain HR Dixon RE, Assistant inspector of Mines at GHQ, in his visit diary when on visiting the Queen Victoria Crater at St Eloi hours after the mine blows that heralded the start of the Messines Ridge offensive, he was told of infantry hearing the sounds of imprisoned Germans underground trying to escape from their collapsed workings. Author's private collection.

22 Brattice was a fire resistant fabric used in workings to channel air where it was needed. It could be used to help clear galleries of gas used in conjunction with a brazier.

23 The Work of the Royal Engineers in the European War, 1914-19 Military Mining, Institute of Royal Engineers, Chatham, 1922. – Plate XVIII

24 All three Sappers are buried in Vlamertinghe Cemetery. Sapper Creegan is buried in Plot 6, Row N, Grave 6 and Sappers Cadman and Hull are buried in Plot 7, Row E Graves 22 and 23 respectively of Vlamertinghe Cemetery.

25 Major Edward Marie Felix Momber was buried in Lijssenthoek Military Cemetery Plot, 13 Row A, Grave 19.

26 102368 Sapper Robert Moseby is buried in Plot 2, Row D, Grave 65 of Medingham Cemtery near Proven.

CHAPTER SIX

JULY 1917

The month began with 177 Tunnelling Company 336 men strong with 251 attached infantry working as labour. Up in the Railway Wood sector the Germans kept up the rate of shellfire which severely hampered work on the various workings under the care of 177. The shelling would hinder the transport of materials from the advanced dump near Hellfire Corner up to the Railway Wood sector. A shortage of timber in general didn't help the situation either. With major preparations in place for the 5th and 2nd Armies to launch the coming offensive, timber would have been required for a multitude of tasks both at the front and behind the lines. In the offensive galleries under the sector, general repair work took place keeping the system up and running. One particular incident occurred in gallery 6G, 27 feet deep, when an armour piercing shell penetrated the ground exploded, causing particularly bad damage to the gallery necessitating a lot of repair work so electrical cables could once more be run through the gallery.

The dugouts at Beek trench and at Halfway House accessible off Ritz trench were also both completed throughout the month, as was a Battalion Headquarters dugout at Birr Cross Roads.

The coming offensive would be an attempt by the Allies to break through the German lines driving them back. The long term aims for the forthcoming offensive wasn't to stop on the Passchendaele Ridge but to continue north driving the German out of the Belgian coastal ports from where they were sailing U-Boats, causing untold damage on the high seas. Commander of the British Expeditionary Force, Field Marshal Sir Douglas Haig had long planned an offensive in the Ypres Salient, plans of which had been put on hold in 1916 due to a number of factors. The German offensive launched in the Verdun sector drove home a coalition between the French and British armies that saw the joint Franco/British effort on the Somme take place in 1916 with the Arras/Nivelle offensive in April 1917. With the failure of the Nivelle Offensive that in turn had led to mutiny in parts of the French Army, Haig was now free to pursue his own strategy in his preferred battleground – The Salient. With General Sir Herbert Plumer's Second Army launching the prelude to the Third Battle of Ypres at Messines the month before, and achieving great success, valuable time was lost, with a poor command decision when it was decided that the 5th Army would carry out the next phase of the battle some six weeks after Messines. General Sir Hubert Gough had recently taken command of the Fifth Army; he was the youngest of the army commanders and was always keen to try and impress. In some circles he was known as the 'Young Thruster' in other's 'Bloody Gough'. Those lost six weeks were spent in transferring his army to the Salient and then preparing it for the battle. It was a serious mistake in taking the battle away from General Plumer, known as a meticulous planner; he knew every corner of the Salient, unlike Gough. The six weeks also gave the Germans the chance they needed to beef up their defences. The Germans brought in Lt Col Fritz Von Lossberg, the foremost German expert on defensive warfare and then set about beefing up the existing four lines of German defences in the Salient with the construction of a strategic line of defence with all lines intermingled and hundreds of concrete bunkers manned by machine gun teams. The Fifth Army's objectives, using nine divisions on the first day, would be to advance 4,000 to 5,000 yards starting from Houthoulst Forest in the north of the Salient down to the Zillebeke area in the southeast. It was an ambitious plan that unfortunately failed to pay sufficient attention to key German positions on the Gheluvelt Plateau. As the divisions prepared for their battles, on 16th July a massive preparatory bombardment began in which over 1,100 British and French heavy artillery guns and over 1,900 field guns began firing in the order of 4½ million shells at the German front and lines of communication. Parts of the Salient, especially the Railway Wood sector already looked like the face of the moon due to heavy shelling. In reading the various divisional, brigade and infantry war diaries in the course of putting this history together, I have come upon many references to planned trench raids or patrols having to be cancelled due to the nature of the ground. One can only imagine with an extra 4½ million shells falling in the top half of the Salient what this must have done to the ground, albeit with fairly good summer weather at the time.

The tunnellers also had an important part to play in the preparation for the Battle of Paschendaele. Since Messines there had been a decrease in German offensive mining in the Salient, apart from the panic blows under the Railway Wood sector on 13th and 14th June. German miners were on edge and had had the wind knocked out of them. This had a knock-on effect for their surface troops holding their lines. Any suspicion of the British mining opposite their fronts and the nightmares of Messines returned. For the British tunnelling companies time was limited and a lot of work needed to be done. With little possibility of a German mining offensive, many miners were withdrawn from the offensive and defensive galleries, save a few listening shifts, and employed on more general tunnelling work. Dugouts for brigade and battalion HQs, dressing stations, infantry subways, observation posts, machine gun positions, troop accommodation and deep cable trenches all needed constructing and completing in time ready for the offensive. All this was carried out while still under the harassment of German artillery fire of which HE, shrapnel and gas hindered the progress of both men and material. Making sure that infantry and HQ dugouts were ready for use on time became the tunnellers' top priority. A lot had been learnt by the British tunneller over the last year especially on the Somme where they discovered deep German dugouts with far more overhead protection than the fairly shallow British affairs. This type of work would not be strange to 177 Tunnelling Company as they were the first tunnelling company in the Salient to dig tunnelled dugouts when they started with the Ramparts in Ypres. With Messines still fresh in the memory of the German soldier, intelligence reports gleaned by raiding and reconnaissance parties in the Boesinghe

161

sector, contained information that sent shockwaves through local commanders on the ground. Patrols and aerial photographs revealed what looked like shafts just behind the British front line. Not wanting to experience the hell of being blown sky high or buried alive under tons of earth as their comrades had been the month before, the Germans pulled back here, 500 yards in places. The fact of the matter was, there were no mines. It was the tunnellers' hard at work on dugouts that the German reconnaissance patrols had discovered. Captain W. Grant-Grieve wrote after the war:

"It was difficult to drive the Germans out of their trenches, as the Allies found to their cost, but it was not very often throughout the whole of the war that we were able to frighten them out. On these few occasion the governing factor was the fear of mines – surely a significant feature." [1]

As the fighting troops of the 8th Division practised behind the lines and the men of 177 helped prepare under the lines, zero hour was set for 3.50am on 31st July. Their frontage would run from the south side of the Ypres – Roulers railway line running south to Zouave Wood. It would be the men of the 23rd Infantry Brigade who would attack over the Railway Wood sector. Once through the German lines they were to advance to the Blue line which ran across the Bellewaerde Ridge and then onto the Black line which ran across the Westhoek Ridge. 24th Infantry Brigade would be on their right side with 25th Infantry Brigade to the rear in support. The 8th Division had the widest front to attack out of all the Divisions going over on the 31st. They would be attacking using a frontal assault on a strong and easily defendable position. Two battalions per attacking brigade would move forward and capture the Blue line. They would then be leapfrogged by the remaining two battalions per brigade, who would advance and capture the Black Line.

With the Railway Wood and Birr Cross road dugouts now the main priority of 177 Tunnelling Company, work continued feverishly to make sure that they were ready for occupation. Both dugouts offered brigade and battalion HQs and valuable troop accommodation. In the case of the Railway Wood system it was a sprawling system of galleries and dugouts and to ease confusion street name boards were put up in the dugouts with signposts guiding their occupant to his relevant location.

With the start of the offensive looming it became apparent that time to equip the dugouts with their double width, triple high bunk beds would not happen. Priority was given to equipping the various brigade and battalion HQs with wooden tables and benches, a task given to the already overstretched Royal Engineer field companies belonging to the 8th Division. The dugout floors had already been concreted by 177 as they worked and extended the dugouts. Some of the bunk beds were already in situ. Those soldiers using the dugouts in the days prior to the offensive would just have to make do with what space they could find. It was of small comfort to realise that at least they had mediocre shell cover over their heads. A warning order issued by the Commander of Royal Engineers, 8th Division on 22nd July[2] stated that both the Railway Wood, Ritz and

Halfway House dugouts were to be clear of all tunnelling personnel by the evening of 25th July. Just a small team of tunnellers employed to pump, maintain and light the dugouts were to remain with them. 177 had done their job and done it well at the Railway Wood dugouts and elsewhere, an 8th Division Operational Order issued earlier in the month described what was available to them when they were to move up to the front on the eve of the coming offensive:

- Brigade HQ at Railway Wood
- Double Battalion HQ at Railway Wood
- Accommodation for 600 men at Railway Wood
- Dressing Station for 20 stretchers at Railway Wood
- Tunnelled Accommodation for 1000 men near Halfway House
- Brigade HQ at I.11.d.5.5

- Dressing Station for 30 stretchers at Birr Cross Roads
- Accommodation for 150 men south west of Hellfire Corner

On the eve of the battle German shelling of the Railway Wood sector was surprisingly less than normal. The attacking brigades had reached their assembly positions over difficult ground and at 3.50am went over the top, under the cover of a machine gun barrage and an artillery creeping barrage, moving forward 100 yards every four minutes. 23rd Infantry Brigade attacked with the 2nd West Yorks on the right and the 2nd Devons on the left. They stormed over the ground making good headway, capturing the Blue Line and were then leapfrogged by the 2nd Scottish Rifles and the 2nd Middlesex who advanced onto the Black Line with what is described in their Divisional History as "... **an unqualified**

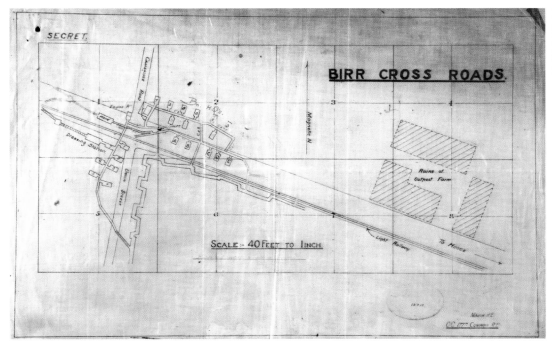

Birr Cross Roads dugout on handover to the infantry in July 1917. (TNA)

success." The 8th Division captured all its objectives that day apart from the far right of the 24th Infantry Brigade.

In what was the furthest move from the Railway Wood sector since the line had become static there in May 1915, it didn't mean that the dugouts constructed under Railway Wood would become redundant. It would take many weeks for the infantry to advance further forward. Divisions would come up through this sector for many more weeks utilising all the dugouts. It was only the offensive and defensive galleries that would now remain redundant. Their job under the sector was over, 177 Tunnelling Company had succeeded in defeating the German mine threat under the Railway Wood sector. Their effort coupled with the success at Messines had meant the troops going over the top from the sector on 31st July could form up and use the front lines without the threat of enemy mining. Success had not come cheaply for 177 Tunnelling Company. They lost four members of the company in July. The first to be killed was 157781 Sapper William Bagley of Bishop Auckland, Co Durham on 4th July.[3] On 22nd July 86601 Cpl George Woolley of Bagthorpe, Notts, aged 42,[4] was killed in a collapse of a dugout due to shellfire whilst trying to rescue a comrade. The circumstances of his death were laid out in a letter to George's widow by 177's Adjutant at the time Lt Gardner:

"Dear Mrs Woolley, You will be surprised to see a letter from a stranger, and I will at once explain the reason. In these times we have to be prepared for so many things and for all sorts of news and deeply regret to say I have sad news to tell you. Things have been active here lately and yesterday morning early was particularly so. Your husband was in what was considered to be a very safe dugout, when some gas shells burst near the stairway entrance and caused a great deal of confusion and many men were overpowered. Your husband at once went to try and help the others who were rendered helpless and in doing so lost his own life. I can do no more than offer you my sincere sympathy in your loss, which I fear will be a great shock and grief to you. I furthermore have, unfortunately, to tell you that it has been impossible to recover his body and bury him in a cemetery. You see after the gas shells had burst some other shells dropped and wrecked the whole place and the men were buried in the fall of ground. They worked hard to get the men out but all of their efforts proved failures. I am sorry of I have told you all this too bluntly, but I am terribly busy.
Yours very truly,
    B.L. Gardner, Lt, Adjt."[5]

Lt Gardner's blunt apology at the end of the letter goes to show the pressure the company must have been under in getting preparations for the forthcoming offensive completed. His apology will have come as little relief to George's widow Martha who was left to bring up six children.

The other two were killed on 31st July, one of whom was Major Maurice Wilkinson MC, the OC of the company.[6] He had held the reins of the company for just 41 days, finalising the preparations for the great offensive and was killed by shellfire as he moved up to the front that morning. Also killed that day was 40-year-old 102957 Sapper Stephen Judson from Walsall, Staffordshire.[7] Again, sadly, I have not been able to find out exactly how these men were killed, *Soldiers Died in the Great War* (SDGW) lists them as being killed in action. Throughout the month the company also lost two of its attached infantry, killed in action. In response to Major Wilkinson's death, Captain Basil Sawers MC and Bar took over as OC of the company temporarily.

As the infantry advanced forward on the opening day of the offensive so parties of men from 177 went forward to explore German workings. A very short report, lacking in great detail, can be found in the war diary of the Chief Engineer of II Corps, Brigadier General C. Godby, in the appendices attached to the July 1917 section of the war diary. It tells of a couple of investigation parties made up of officers and men from 177 Tunnelling Company that move forward to explore old German workings. One of the parties, ten men led by Captain James, started their exploration from Bliss Crater. They found only small dugouts until they reached Blakeley Crater. Here they found a small dugout system, full of mining tools, in which was a vertical shaft full of water. The party later met German bombers and Captain James and two of the party were wounded by grenades. The report mentions that his party was reduced to six men. With three man wounded, that would have left seven men. What of the other man? Could it be that the other man was Sapper Judson?

Was it also possible that Major Wilkinson was killed doing something similar? With the infantry advance successfully moving over the German front this would have

Grave of Major Maurice Wilkinson, Poperinghe New Military Cemetery. He was 177 Tunnelling Company's Third Officer Commanding and was killed in action on the first day of the Third Battle of Ypres. (Author's collection)

been a perfect opportunity for those who had been in the sector for a long time to eventually see their opponents' positions.

The company also helped out their Royal Engineer colleagues in the Tramway Units. These units, one per corps, were responsible for the laying of narrow gauge tramway to supply the troops at the front. More importantly, they also provided a line along which was maintained a steady flow of ammunition for the large calibre heavy artillery, vital for smashing the German positions. A section of each tunnelling company involved in the battle assisted a Royal Engineer Tramway Unit in laying and maintaining heavy battery feeder lines.

AUGUST 1917

August saw the company continue its maintenance of the Railway Wood, Birr Cross

Roads and Halfway House dugouts and also undertake reconnaissance for German bunkers in support of the infantry, these taskings continuing until the 12th of the month. On 4th August a new OC joined the company; 27-year-old Major Laurence Carr Hill was posted in from the Controller of Mines office at GHQ where he had been Assistant Controller of Mines. Before the war he had qualified as a mining engineer and worked on the staff at the Rio Tinto Company in Spain. He returned to England after the war broke out and was commissioned into the Royal Engineers arriving on the Western Front with 78th Field Company RE on 24th October 1914. With the formation of the tunnelling companies he joined 174 Tunnelling Company in May 1915 until taking up his position as Assistant Controller of Mines, 3rd Army, on 19th April 1917. With the change of command within the company came some other minor changes. From August 1917 onwards in the war diary of the company we see individual mention of sections, something which lacked before. Their diary is very good at describing what work was done to specific workings and dugouts and includes many colour plans, but prior to Major Hill taking the reins of the company the war diary fails to detail who did what work.

August would also see 177 starting another one of the roles allocated to tunnelling companies – road repair. It had briefly carried out repairs to roads earlier in the war prior to concentrating its efforts on offensive/defensive mining and dugout construction. On 12th August 1 and 2 Sections were now taken off their dugout repair and maintenance task given the tasking of carrying out repairs on Cambridge Road. This work would be part of a huge task of road repair and construction to allow for the logistical element of the army to move up behind the fighting troops engaged in the current offensive. As the army crept slowly forward its supply chain, artillery and engineer support needed roads building and repairing in order to keep a fluid flow of support and supply going.

The weather now also hindered those on the battlefield. Although July's weather had been fairly good, the threat of rain had appeared just before the offensive began. Just a day into the battle the heavens opened and it poured down. The effect the rain had on the churned up battlefield can only be really appreciated by those who were there. The region, with its high water table and impervious blue clay strata, had seen irrigation channels dug by the local farmers centuries before to aid with the drainage of rainwater off their fields. Allied and German bombardments had now completely smashed that shallow infrastructure and the water had nowhere to run off to. The soft, clayey ground soon became a quagmire through which men and animals fought, slowly advanced, drowned and died. The work of maintenance and construction of roads was critical in keeping these ever flowing arteries of the British Army open. It was during this phase of road repair and construction that Lt Dalgas the Danish officer in charge of Number 3 section was awarded the Italian *Medaglia D'Argento* for bravery under shellfire.

On 15th August the men of Number 4 Section started on the construction of Slab Switch, a 50-yard section of trench located at Birr Cross Roads. On 17th August 3 Section was sent to a rest camp at Equihen near Bolougne for some hard earned rest and recuperation. Slab Switch was completed on the 18th and then on 22nd August 26-year-old 112753 Sapper Josiah Nancarrow, of Camborne, Cornwall was killed in action.[8] He was more than likely working with either 1 or 2 Sections on the Cambridge Road repair work. On 24th August 2 Section was taken off its tasking of road repair and told to undertake an extension to the Railway Wood dugouts and the repair of various entrances to the system which were still under heavy use by troops in reserve and support to that further east at the front. Four days later on the 28th, the company lost another of its attached infantry, killed in action. On 29th August 1 Section replaced 2 Section on the Railway Wood dugouts, with 2 Section retiring back to company headquarters at Proven. Posted into the company that day was Lt Robert Murray who came over from 175 Tunnelling Company.

SEPTEMBER 1917

The month began with 177 Tunnelling Company 318 officers and men strong with 217 attached officers and men. The month would see a complete change for the company as a whole. On 1st September, after two weeks at rest camp near Bolougne, 3 Section rejoined the company, with 2 Section heading off to Bolougne for a hard earned rest the next day. An order also arrived on 2nd September that saw the company transferred back to the Second Army, which was now further south on the Messines Ridge. This meant all change for 177. Its time in the Railway Wood sector had come to an end after a period of two years and two months. It was the longest serving unit ever to stay in the Railway Wood sector. It had seen many divisions come and go and worked hard in the support of those men. It had not been easy for the company. To date they had lost 68 officers and men killed, including two OCs, with plenty more injured.[9] This may not seem like a heavy loss for a unit over a two year period when compared with other WWI combat arm statistics, but their loss will have certainly have been felt by 177. When they left the Railway Wood sector most of the men probably did so glad to be away from the horror of the Salient; to most it was a rotten stinking mess of a place. Those that had spent some time there really got to know the sector and had lost comrades there. They probably departed with the memories of their comrades at heart, perhaps a tinge of sadness at leaving them behind. When they finally left the Railway Wood sector the men could do so knowing that they had played a critical, integral and successful part in the sector's history. Their experiences in countering and defeating the German mine threat was foremost in many of their minds. None more so than Agner Dalgas, now a captain, who prior to the company's move further south erected a memorial to the men of 177 and its attached infantry who had been killed and remained in their tunnels below the sector. With their withdrawal from the Railway Wood sector, 177 also said goodbye to its permanently attached infantry. These men, many of them also miners, had worked as hard as the tunnellers under the sector in the workings and dugouts and bringing supplies up from the advanced dumps. Ninety-eight of them were withdrawn on 1st September, 101 men on the 4th and 12 on the 8th. Only one officer and five men remained attached to the company when it left Railway Wood.

177 moved back under the familiar umbrella of VIII Corps who now held the line from midway between the towns of Wytschaete[10] and Messines with a line running south to the River Lys. They were to take over the construction and maintenance of dugouts, mine workings and roads in the corps area of responsibility. On 4th September, 3 Section moved south to take over this responsibility from the 3rd Tunnelling Company, Canadian Engineers. The mine workings and dugouts in the Railway Wood sector were then handed over to Major Henry Hudspeths, 171 Tunnelling Company. On 5th September, 177 Tunnelling Company moved to Garden Camp, about a mile south east of the town on Bailleul. The camp was located alongside the road that ran from Bailleul to Armentières and was surrounded by a number of other camps used for troop accommodation and served by a number of Railway Operating Division sidings connected to the national railway line. The headquarters of the 177 arrived and set up camp a day later on the 6th.

As well as taking over workings and dugouts in the VIII Corps area of responsibility, 177 also took over the construction and maintenance of dugouts and roads in the IX Corps area of responsibility which ran northward from midway between Wytschaete and Messines to the Ypres Comines Canal. This takeover was carried out on the 8th by 1 and 4 Sections of 177, who relieved the 1st Australian Tunnelling Company. On 13th September, 2 Section returned from its break at rest camp and replaced 1 and 4 Sections on the work that they were doing as they headed off for a period of rest and recuperation the next day to a rest camp at Marquise on the French coast.

The month also saw casualties within the company as a result of non-combat incidents, when on 21st September 2nd Lieutenants Geoffrey Eager and Robert More were admitted to hospital following a motorbike accident. Whilst at the camp at Marquise they had been escorting a convoy of the men to baths at Wissant when a hen ran out and collided with the front wheel of their motorbike. The resultant crash threw Lt More off the motorbike and badly injured his right knee, so badly, that he was evacuated to the UK and remained in hospital until 1919.

On the 24th the company finally took over all dugouts and workings from 250 Tunnelling Company and 2nd Tunnelling Company, Canadian Engineers in the Wytschaete – St Eloi area. One of the mine workings of interest that was taken over by the company earlier in the month was a group of four mines under the German lines close to the southeast corner of Plugstreet Wood. The German position here was known on the trench maps as 'The Birdcage' and was originally started by the British in 1914; the Germans had taken the position and turned it to their best advantage, naming it 'The Ducksbill'. It was a very well defended position; the large amount of barbed wire used in its defence is what gave it its British name. 174 Tunnelling Company had begun underground operations on The Birdcage firing two mines on the 6th and 28th of June 1915.[11] 171 Tunnelling Company had taken over the workings around Plugstreet Wood not long after and they were the ones who started deep mining at The Birdcage as part of the planned Messines offensive scheme of mines. By January 1916 three shafts, M1, M2 and M3 were feeding the system. Shafts M1 and M3 were begun just off the British front line, trench 121, with M2 being sunk in a second line trench about 50 metres behind the front. Galleries were driven off shafts M1 and M3, now just below 80 feet deep, and out towards The Birdcage. Shaft M2 was discontinued but a replacement, M4, was constructed to the rear of M1 and M3 and a 'Y' gallery linked all three shafts. The galleries were 4 feet high and 2 feet 3 inches wide. As with all offensive mining operations a series of defensive galleries were also constructed in order to protect the offensive galleries from discovery and destruction. By the end of the summer of 1916, four mines lay under The Birdcage. The gallery from shaft M1 ran in a south easterly direction until it was under the rear of The Birdcage, here at 65 feet deep lay mine number 2. It was charged with 32,000 lbs of ammonal. About halfway along the gallery was a right branch running south. Just a few feet down the branch lay mine number 3, charged with 26,000 lbs at 80 feet deep. At the end of this branch gallery lay mine number 1 at 65 feet deep charged with 34,000 lbs of ammonal. The gallery from shaft M3 ran an eastward course under No Man's Land branching into a 'Y' gallery just under the German front line. The right branch ran southeast for about 60 feet and then came upon the chamber containing mine number

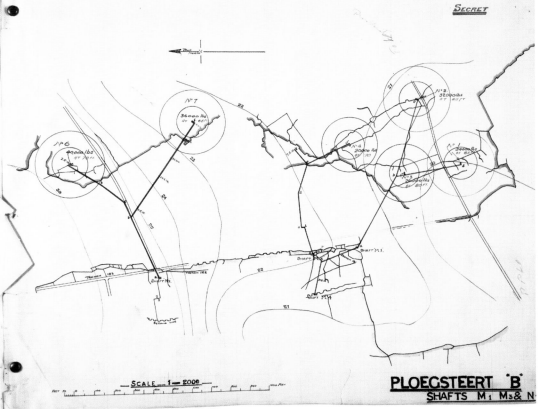

The Birdcage mines. Not used in the Messines offensive of June 1917, these mines came under the care of 177 Tunnelling Company when they moved south to the Messines area in September 1917. In July 1955 during a storm, mine number 2 exploded, thankfully causing no casualties. The remaining three mines are still in situ. (TNA. WO153/909)

169

4, charged with 20,000 lbs of ammonal at 70 feet deep. The left branch remained unfinished and was probably going to contain a fifth mine. Work on the system was taken over by 3rd Tunnelling Company, Canadian Engineers in November 1916 who carried out the careful maintenance of the system in preparation for the Messines offensive. On 27th May they received news that the mines under The Birdcage were not going to be used in the opening stage of the offensive and that it was doubtful they would be used at all.[12] One of the main reasons for not using them was the subject of crater consolidation. It was estimated that the German garrison in reserve behind The Birdcage could probably reach and hold the craters before the attacking Australian troops would in this sector. There was a possibility that the mines could be utilised if the offensive did not go to plan. The galleries, already charged, wired and tamped were now further strutted to protect them from the shockwave of the two blows from the Factory Farm and Trench 127, a few hundred metres to the north that would be fired on 7th June 1917. Following the detonations of the mines on 7th June 1917, there was a substantial amount of damage done to the mine galleries by the mine blows further north although the armoured firing leads remained undamaged. The system was continually pumped by the Canadians and continued by 177 after their arrival during September.

OCTOBER 1917

On 1st October 1917, orders were received from VIII Corps stating that 177 Tunnelling Company had to vacate Garden Camp in order to move to a new location. Their new company location was to be at Betterole Camp which was located about 600 metres north of the village of Neuve Eglise on the road to Kemmel. The problem with the move was that there were no huts available for the HQ of the company or the men so all would need to be built from scratch. On 2nd October both 1 and 4 Sections returned from their break at rest camp and got back to work. On the 4th every available man started construction of wooden huts at the new camp location and then on the 8th of the month the company HQ vacated Garden Camp and moved into temporary billets in Bailleul. On the 15th, under orders from VIII Corps, 4 Section started construction on a dugout along the Verne Road at map reference O21 central. The Verne Road ran from Torroken Corner, about 1 kilometre south east of Wytschaete and ran slightly northeast through the hamlet of Oostaverne, with the location of the dugout being just under 2 kilometres behind the front line which, after the success of the Messines offensive, was now further east across the Ridge. Unfortunately there is no mention of what type of dugout the Verne Road dugout was to be, it was only worked on until the 21st of the month before orders arrived via 30th Division for work to halt. On 17th October the company Headquarters moved to their new huts at Betterole Camp. On 22nd October, 2 Section took over the maintenance of dugouts from 3 Section as they moved onto road repair in the VIII and IX Corps areas. The next day both 1 and 4 Sections, with a party of 60 attached infantry, took over the construction of a dugout, sheet 28SW, at map reference O.10.d.2.8 that had been started by 250th Tunnelling Company just a few weeks before. The dugout was to be a 250-man system incorporating a Battalion

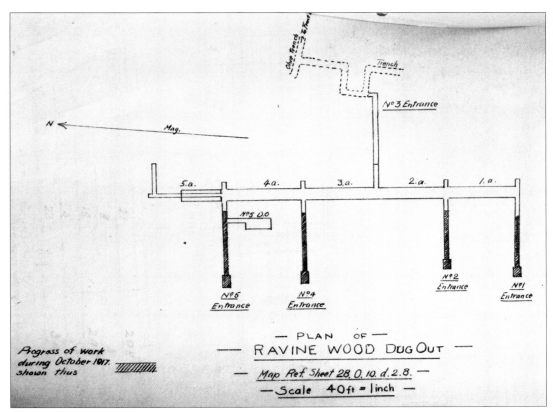

Ravine Wood dugout plan for October 1917. (TNA)

Headquarters, infantry accommodation, dressing station and an Observation Position. The dugout would be named after its location, Ravine Wood, which was situated about 1.4 kilometres southwest of the village of Hollebeke. A ravine varying in depth from 9 to 12 feet deep ran parallel with the eastern face of the wood from the north and exited through the southeast corner of the wood. The dugout was worked on for the remainder of the month with another 30 attached infantry joining the party on the 31st.

NOVEMBER 1917

As November arrived the company continued its work on dugout construction and road repair. The chief work of the tunneller under the Salient, and its environs, at this stage of the war was the construction of dugouts to accommodate troops who had gained ground in the Second and Fifth Army areas following Messines and the slow, painful gains of the Passchendaele offensive. It was hard enough taking the ground off an enemy who for most part refused to budge, but it could be even harder holding the ground in face of German counterattacks and coming offensives. With the hellish destruction wrought upon the ground by both sides by artillery, accommodation on the surface, in the forward zones, was difficult to find and most of all dangerous. The tunnellers would spend the coming winter digging hundreds of dugouts to aid the situation. Both 1 and 4 Sections continued their work on the Ravine Wood dugout whilst 2 Section focused on the maintenance and repair of existing dugouts and The Birdcage mine system at Plugstreet. A dugout of worthy of note that fell into their care was the Catacombs dugout constructed the year before by 2 Section of the 1st Australian Tunnelling Company. Sometimes referred to as the Wallangarra dugout, it ranks as one of the largest dugouts constructed by the allied tunnelling units. It could accommodate around 1,500 men. It was literally carved into the side of Hill 63 which sat about 2 miles south of Messines alongside the Messines to Plugstreet road and offered great observation across the Messines Ridge. The dugout was 442 feet long, 82 feet wide and 6 feet 8 inches high. It was fitted with 18 rows of double tiered bunks accommodating some 1,200 men. At least a further 200 to 300 men could be accommodated in steel-framed dugouts located near the three entrances to the system.[13] 3 Section continued on its repair

of forward roads in the Wytschaete area. On 12th November, 2 Section carried out the sinking of a trial shaft at map reference U.2.d.2.5 just off an old disused German communication trench, Ulcer Street, south-west of Messines. On 18th November 177 once again said farewell to VIII Corps as they moved further north being replaced by 1st ANZAC. The 5th Australian Division moving into the area 177 were responsible for. On 23rd November, 3 Section was taken off its road repair tasking as it made preparations to start the construction of a new dugout. A site about 400 yards south of How Farm at map reference O.27.b.10.15 was chosen and construction started the next day. On 25th November the work on the trial shaft off Ulcer trench was stopped. The company also had a batch of 170 permanently attached infantry attached to them for ration and discipline purposes. On 25th November the area that 177 was responsible for shrunk slightly when all

Ravine Wood dugout. (Courtesy Great War Digital)

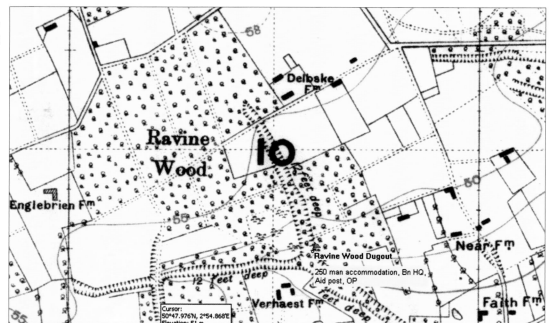

dugouts and mine workings south of the River Douve were handed over to 184 Tunnelling Company.[14] On the 26th of the month Major Hill wrote to the Commander Australian Engineers, 5th Australian Division outlaying his proposals for the various dugouts 177 were working on in the Corps area and also outlining those that had been proposed. The information given to the CRE also included what the various dugouts would consist of and made interesting reading. Approval for his plans came just a few days later on the 30th. The information was entered into the CRE, 5th Australian Divisions war diary and consisted of:

"The following tunnelling programme submitted to Divisional Headquarters on the 26th has been approved and 177 Tunnelling Company notified accordingly. The following deep dugouts should be constructed. They are arranged in the order in which they are to be worked on:

1. Ravine Wood (O.10.D.2.5) for Battalion HQ, Company HQ, 200 Other Ranks and Advanced Dressing Station.
2. How Farm (O.25.b.1.1) For Company HQ and 200 Other Ranks.
3. Verne Road (O.21.c) For Company HQ and 200 Other Ranks
4. Bethleem Farm (U.3.a.9.3) Company HQ and 200 Other Ranks
5. Fanny's Farm (O.33.a.7.5) Company HQ and 200 Other Ranks
6. O.22.a For one Company and 200 Other Ranks
7. Brigade HQ Wytschaete (O.19central)

Nos 1, 2 and 3 sites have been verified by boring. Nos 5, 6 and 7 are in hand and OC 177 Tunnelling Company thinks they are suitable. It is proposed to abandon the Gabion Farm site (U.9.d.2.5) for the present in favour of more forward work. Sgd VAH Sturdee, Lt Col, AE"

177 Tunnelling Company received an interesting set of orders towards the end of November in that they were ordered to abandon the unfired mines of Messines, the four mines under The Birdcage, the mine under the Petit Douve Farm and the second mine under Peckham Farm. Although there is no mention of this order or its subsequent carrying out in 177's war diary there is a surviving summary of the receipt of this order in the weekly mine summaries sent to GHQ during November 1917. The summary further states that: **"The leads to these mines will be carefully disconnected and the galleries and shafts closed up."** Unfortunately there is no further information in either their war diary or the GHQ mine summaries to say that this order was successfully carried out. One wonders whether it was, especially following the detonation of one of the Birdcage mines in July 1955!

DECEMBER 1917

December saw 177 continue its work on dugouts across the Wytschaete/Messines front. Boring teams, from the AEMMBC, continued work throughout the month in their search for ground suitable for dugout construction. On the 1st a few men of 4 Section commenced their work on the planned dugout at Verne Road; they would first construct a penthouse under which the head of the shaft would be located. The next day, 2 Section started construction on Messines South dugout. Both 1 and 4 Sections continued their work on the Ravine Wood dugout until the 9th December when 4 Section was tasked to start construction on a dugout for an artillery Battery Headquarters at map reference O.19.b.3.2.

By 12th of December the shaft at How Farm, started the previous month was down to 50 feet; considerable difficulties with poor running ground were experienced as the shaft went through the 14 to 25 feet level. The tunnellers detached from 4 Section for the Verne Road dugout started the sinking of the shaft on the 1st. A site for a dugout was

Messines South dugout plan for December 1917. (TNA)

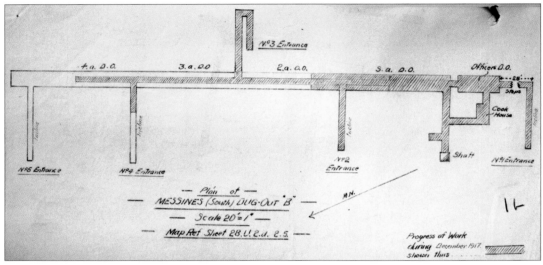

Messines South dugout. (Courtesy Great War Digital)

Far right: 114 Battery dugout plan for December 1917. (TNA)

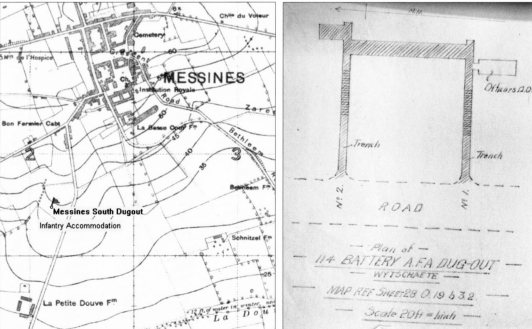

also chosen at Mahieu Farm at map reference O.21.d.4.7 when the test bore revealed the blue clay was only 8 to 12 feet below the surface in this area. On 15th December the 1st Australian Division replaced the 5th Australian Division in the sector, with 177 continuing its work. A site for a brigade HQ was located at Wytschaete at map reference O.19.d.2.7 as per Major Hills proposal. The next day, the 18th, Ravine Wood dugout was completed, the last task of the tunnellers before handing over the dugout to divisional engineer assets was to concrete the floor. The construction and fitting of bunks, tables chairs etc would be the responsibility of the Field Companies.

By the 19th, work on the Verne Road shaft was abandoned due to running into very

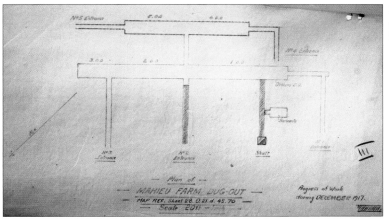

Mahieu Farm dugout plan for December 1917. (TNA)

bad running ground. Work on the Brigade HQ at Wytschaete and the dugout at Mahieu Farm commenced on the 19th and 21st of the month respectively. Work continued on How Farm but ran into difficulty when bad ground was encountered. A sudden rush of running ground lost the tunnellers 14 feet of gallery and the future of the dugout looked perilous for a short period. But the tunnellers were at the depth they needed to be with the important work of sinking a shaft done

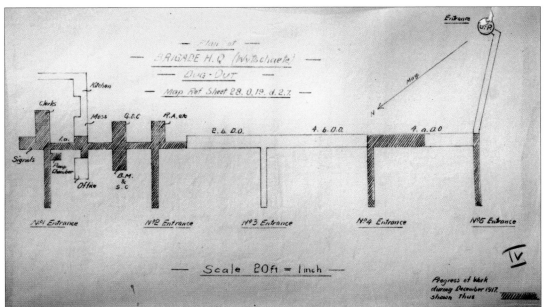

Brigade Headquarters dugout at Wytschaete plan for December 1917. (TNA)

175

Wytschaete,
Lancashire House.
(Courtesy Great
War Digital)

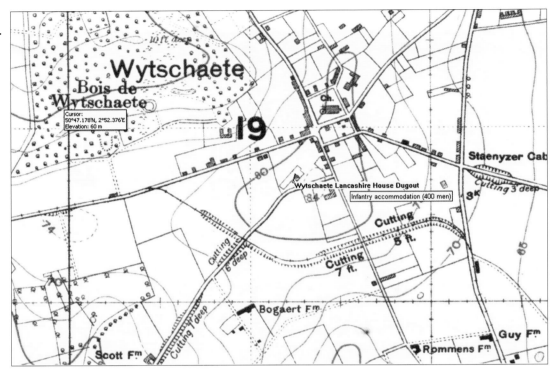

so the direction of the gallery was altered until good ground was encountered and the construction of the dugout continued, albeit losing one of its entrances.

On Christmas Day 177 played 184 Tunnelling Company in a game of football resulting in a score of 2 – to 177! With the end of 1917, 177 Tunnelling Company had been at war for 2 and a half years. At the end of the month it was 348 officers and men strong with 270 attached infantry assisting the company.

How Farm dugout
plan for December
1917. (TNA)

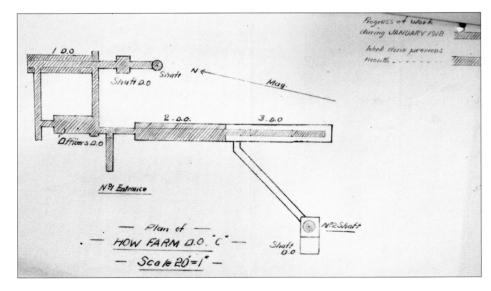

1 Tunnellers – The story of the Tunnelling Companies, Royal Engineers, during the World War. Captain W. Grant – Grieve and Bernard Newman, 1936. Reprinted by The Naval and Military Press. Page 254.

2 Appendix to July 1917 of the war diary of CRE 8th Div held at the Royal Engineers Library, Chatham.

3 Sapper William Bagley is buried in New Irish Farm Cemetery, Plot 27, Row D, Grave 16.

4 Corporal George Woolley is commemorated on the cross of sacrifice at Royal Engineer Grave Cemetery.

5 Lt Gardeners letter was published in the Eastwood and Kimberley Advertiser, Friday 10th August 1917.

6 Major Maurice Wilkinson is buried in Poperinge new Military Cemetery, Plot 2, Row G, Grave 43

7 Sapper Stephen Judson is buried in Menin Road South Cemetery, Plot 1, Row C, Grave 10.

8 Sapper Josiah Nancarrow is now commemorated on the Tyne Cott memorial to the missing, Panel 8.

9 This figure includes all attached infantry fatal casualties. It does not include those attached infantry who may have later died of wounds and were not recorded by 177.

10 Known to the British Soldier as "White sheet".

11 174 Tunnelling Company war diary. WO95-404

12 3rd Tunnelling Company, Canadian Engineers war diary. Online at the library and collections of Canada.

13 The dugout was officially opened on the 1st November 1916 by the Second Army Commander, General Sir Herbert Plumer, GCB, KCMG, GCVO, ADC. Also in attendance were five Corps Commanders, fourteen Divisional Commanders and a score of Brigadier Generals, such was the significance of this massive dugout.

14 This included the Birdcage. Although an order to untamp and de charge the birdcage mines was given in early 1918, this never happened. The area fell back into the hands of the German in their push during April 1918. Whether they explored the mines is not known, the system, or at least its deeper levels, were probably full of water by the time they arrived. The four mines sat until the 17th June 1955 when one exploded during a thunderstorm. It is highly probable that lightning struck the armoured firing leads of mine number 2. Fortunately no one was killed or injured by the blast, it occurred in a farmer's field. The other 3 mines of the Birdcage still lie underground.

Aerial photo of Railway Wood sector from 1918 long after mine warfare finished. The surviving craters have been named and dated. (Author's collection)

177

CHAPTER SEVEN

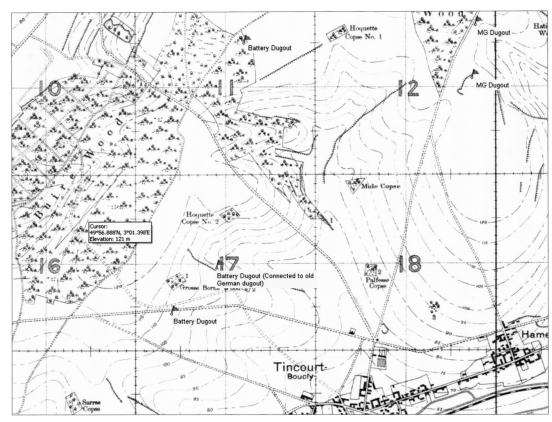

JANUARY 1918

Since the formation of 177 Tunnelling Company in June 1915, the unit had remained fairly static in terms of where it had been located. With its HQ located near Proven, the main bulk of the unit had been involved in underground operations in the Railway Wood sector. In the early days of its campaign, sections had moved around on various tasks, although no further south than the Wytschaete area. Following the launching of the Third Battle of Ypres the company's job in the Railway Wood sector was over and it had moved south to the Messines sector taking over the construction of deep underground dugouts to be used as headquarters, dressing stations and, most importantly, troop accommodation for the many thousands of allied troops now holding the Messines Ridge. Their change in location had also seen the company HQ move from Proven to Betterole Camp near to Neuve Eglise, on the Franco Belgian border. Their change had also seen them involved in new taskings as tunnellers, a brief time spent on road repair. If the company was used to little movement over the last two and a half years then 1918 would change that perception.

Fluidity was returning to the Western Front, the British Army in the field was no comparison to the BEF of 1914 or 1915. The whole face of warfare and technology had changed dramatically and 177 were going to have to adapt to those changes. Germany's perception on its long-term war aims had changed as well. It no longer realised that it could win the war, but at the same time did not want to give up its hard earned gains. With the USA now in the war and many thousands of American soldiers arriving on the Western Front, Germany would need to deal a blow to the allies before those inexperienced, fresh, troops could take effect. The British Army at the beginning of 1918 was worn to the bone. Casualties over the last two years had been horrific for minor gains of ground. Units were operating well under strength, meaning there were divisions in the line carrying out taskings with manpower well under strength. The army and its men were war weary. Change would come to the army in early 1918 with the complete restructuring of infantry divisions, brought about by the manpower shortage and also political decisions at home not to send replacement troops to the front as fast as army commanders needed them. This was brought about by the reaction of those in power to the losses experienced in 1916/17. The same could be said for its French allies. After the disastrous Nivelle offensive of 1917 mutiny had occurred within the French Army, it was now a force with very low morale indeed. But war was to continue in 1918, with suspicions rising that the Germans would launch an offensive to try and improve their lot.

On 4th January two sites were chosen for two new dugouts, the first at Earl's Farm located to the north of L'Enfer Wood just west of the Messines to Wytschaete road. The second was in the locality of the 5 km marker stone along the Messines to Wulverghem road. The Earl Farm dugout was to be a brigade HQ and 5 km dugout to be an artillery battery HQ dugout. Both 1 and 2 Sections started work on the two dugouts respectively on 5th January. The battery HQ dugout that 177 had been working on near Wytschaete was finished on the 6th and handed over to local units to finish off. The winter weather, snow, rain and flooding caused delays to the various dugouts under construction by the company throughout the month.

On 18th January the Brigade HQ at Wytschaete started by 1 Section thirty days previously, was completed and handed over. The dugout at map reference Sheet 28 SW O.19.d.2.7 ran in a north easterly direction. At the bottom of the shaft a gallery ran north westerly for just over 20 feet. This connected to a longer and initially wider gallery running northeast along which, in the wider section, would be the NCO's and other ranks' bunk beds. Running off the left side of the wider section of the gallery were three stepped galleries connecting to the surface. Once past the bunked area the gallery narrowed to the standard 6 feet high, 3 feet wide dimensions. Along this section of the gallery were dugouts located left and right providing offices and accommodation vital for the running of a brigade. A fourth stepped incline also ran off the left side of the gallery for use by the brigade commander and his officers.

Work had continued on the Messines South dugout until 18th January when work stopped due to a shortage of steel shoes. These were vital in the construction

Brigade
Headquarters
dugout
Wytschaete plan
for January 1918.
(TNA)

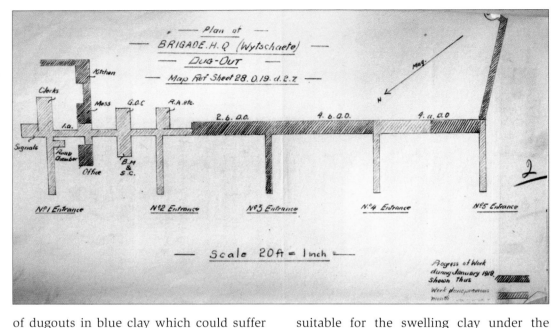

of dugouts in blue clay which could suffer from the tremendous pressures placed on them by the blue clay geology. Tunnelling companies working in the sand and clay of northern France and Belgium had developed types of dugouts to suit the geology they were working in. Once tried and tested the plans were submitted to GHQ to be of aid to future companies working in their area. 171 Tunnelling Company had invented the 'Type D' dugout that was widely used in the blue clay of Flanders. The use of steel girders interspaced with wooden lagging between them produced a strong constructed dugout

suitable for the swelling clay under the Messines Ridge. The shoes mentioned in the diary of 177 refer to a design unique to the tunnelling companies. They were used to connect vertical sections of steel, as part of the wall frame of the dugout, to a horizontal steel joist used as part of the roofing. Sections of railway line, steel girder and reinforced steel joists could be used for the dugout frame. Another one of the benefits in utilising this type of dugout construction is that timber of any size could be used for the lagging which could prove beneficial during timber shortages experienced on the front. The shoes that were made from cast iron sometimes broke under the heavy pressure of swelling clay. It was the 3rd Canadian Tunnelling Company working in this area prior to the Messines offensive that experienced this and produced a heavier steel shoe capable of withstanding the enormous pressures exerted on it.[1] It was a supply of these that 177 needed in order to continue with the Messines South dugout.

Steel shoe,
designed by
3rd Canadian
Tunnelling
Company and
used to hold a
metal framed
type 'D' dugout
together. It
was capable of
withstanding
enormous
pressure.
(Author's
collection)

180

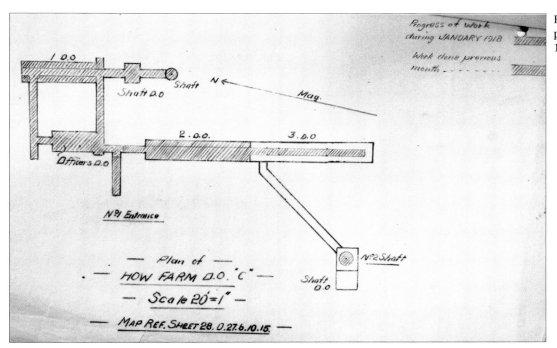

How Farm dugout plan for January 1918. (TNA)

By 19th January preparations were underway to construct a second shaft for the How Farm dugout and an adit was dug into the slope of the Messines ridge to aid with draining the Earl Farm dugout.

FEBRUARY 1918

On 1st February, as the 5th Australian Division took over the sector, 177 Tunnelling Company began construction on the second steel tubbed shaft at the How Farm dugout. The weather at the beginning of the month was fine and frosty, but the company was experiencing a shortage of timber for its dugouts construction. A lesser used wooden planked road at the back of Messines was lifted and the wood – 10 feet long sections of 9 inch by 4 inch softwood – was taken back to the 5th Australian Division's workshop at Lindhoek where it was cut into the required sections for the tunnellers. 177 Tunnelling Company received word via the CRE of the 5th Australian Division, Lt Col Vernon Sturdee DSO, that dugouts were required to be dug at both divisional and Brigade Headquarters locations and on the 3rd of the month started boring at the 5th Australian Division's Headquarters location in Dranoutre. At the end of the first week of February the second shaft at How Farm was now down to 28 feet and in good ground; work on all of their dugouts in the Wytschaete/Messines sector was going well. But for 177, their time in Belgium and the Ypres Salient was coming to an end. On the 12th they received news that the company was to be transferred to the 5th Army holding the line further south, and Major Hill travelled down to Villers-Brettoneux to meet the Controller of Mines of the 5th Army to be briefed on what the company's new role would be. Two days later Captain Kennard and Lt Clark took an advanced party in two trucks down to 180 Tunnelling Company's

Headquarters at Hamelet, a village one mile south east of Corbie on the Somme. The next day at 2pm, 177 Tunnelling Company handed over their work in Flanders to 184 Tunnelling Company. A further two lorries full of company stores under the command of Lt Morgan, moved down to join the advance party. Major Hill departed Flanders for Hamelet on 17th February, the rest of the company were to be moved by train and entrained at Bailleul at midday, finally moving off at 6pm. The next day Major Hill reported to the Chief Engineer of VII Corps, Brigadier General R.D. Petrie RE to get a picture of what was happening in the Corps area. It became apparent that the 5th Army was in defensive mode and constructing a series of defensive dugouts along a series of lines starting from its front and working to the rear. 177 would initially be constructing machine gun dugouts along what was known as the Green Line from Tincourt through Templeux and Nurlu to Manancourt and anti-bombing dugouts

further back towards Corps Headquarters at Templeux les Fosse. With the offensives of 1917 wearing the BEF to the bone, coupled with Lloyd George's refusal to commit badly needed troops to the front, the BEF needed re-structuring before it could take to the offensive again. To do this it needed to make sure it held well defended positions, especially as intelligence was starting to seep through that the Germans were possibly preparing to go on the offensive.

The rest of the company arrived at Tincourt at 1pm that day marching to camp at Longavesnes. The next day the OC, accompanied by his Section Commanders, visited the locations chosen for the sites of dugouts along the Green Line. Eleven dugouts, each containing four machine guns and twenty dugouts each containing two machine guns were to be constructed. One section was to be employed in the construction of anti-bombing dugouts back at Corps HQ. On the 20th three of the sections marched out to their camp

Battery and machine gun dugout plans for February 1918. (TNA)

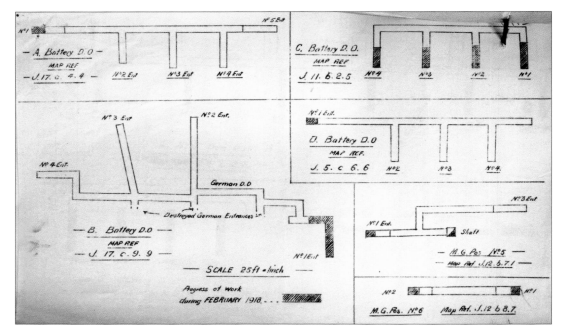

locations and began erecting them as 2 Section started work just east of Corps HQ on a dugout at map reference J.4.b.3.8.

On the 21st of the month work began in earnest on the construction of eleven machine gun dugouts along the Green Line. On 24th February the northern part of the line worked on by 4 Section was to be altered and their work stopped. They then moved back to Corps HQ to join 3 Section on

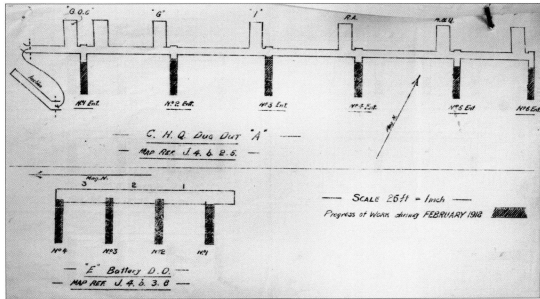

GHQ and Battery dugout plans for February 1918. (TNA)

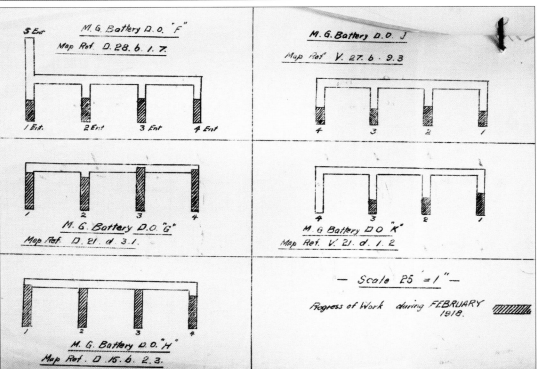

Machine gun dugout plans for February 1918. (TNA)

anti-bombing dugouts, with four underway by the end of the month.

On 25th February 177 Tunnelling Company moved its headquarters to Hamel, sheet 62CNE at map reference K.19.a.1.9.

MARCH 1918

March would see the launching of the first phase of the German spring offensive – Operation Michael. It was all part of a grander plan, dubbed Kaiserschlacht (Kaiser's Battle), overseen by General Ludendorf. With the collapse of Russia at the end of 1917 he was now able to transfer a large number of German divisions to the Western Front. The Germans were concerned as with every month more troops belonging to the American Expeditionary Force arrived on the front bolstering allied numbers. The Germans were to set about negating this numerical advantage. The spring offensive would consist of four major assaults: Michael, Georgette, Gneisenau and Blücher-Yorck. Operation Michael, the largest of these offensives, was intended to strike the BEF along the Somme front with the intention of cutting them off from their French allies to the south. Once through the British lines the attacking German divisions would turn northwest and head for the Channel. Facing the onslaught of Operation Michael would be the British 3rd and 5th Armies. The 3rd Army held a front of 28 miles with 14 divisions and the 5th Army a front of 42 miles with 12 infantry and 3 Cavalry Divisions. The front lines across both armies were incomplete, the result of the British advance after the German retirement to the Hindenburg Line in 1917. For the most part of the front the positions held by the infantry consisted of a series of redoubts, the Blue Line, in what was known as the Forward Zone. Behind the Forward Zone was the Red Line known as the Battle Zone. Behind the Battle Zone lay the incomplete Brown Line. The last bastion of defence was the Green line, along which was employed 177 Tunnelling Company

Work on the construction of the dugouts along the Green Line continued into March. By the end of the first week of the month four new machine gun dugouts and an anti-bombing shelter had been started. By 6th March 177 Tunnelling Company had extracted some 31,700 feet of Somme earth and chalk in its construction of dugouts. The second week of March saw dugouts completed at map references J.11.b.2.5, D.28.b.1.7, D.21.d.3.1, J.5.d.3.3 and J.10.b.9.6. seven new machine gun and one anti-bombing shelter dugouts were also begun. The company dug out a further 42,000 cubic feet of earth and chalk in the second week and on 13th March they explored an old phosphate plant with its underground workings at map reference D.15.a to assess the suitability of utilising the caves for troop accommodation. Their recce of this plant showed that the workings were good up to 300 yards away from the shaft at a depth of about 100 feet. The third week of the month saw the tunnellers start another nine machine gun dugouts and finish off dugouts at map references J.17.c 9.9, K.13.c.4.4, D.16.b.2.8, D.10.c.8.3, D.10.c.7.7, D.4.c.5.1, D.4.c.5.6, J.2.d.9.3 and J.6.b.3.3.

The early hours of 21st March 1918 saw fog across most of the front. At 4.40am the German bombardment of the British lines, preceding their assault, began. The first 120 minutes of the bombardment struck British positions in the first and second lines of defence with a mix of high explosive, lethal and lachrymatory gases. The bombardment continued to move from the front to the rear searching out targets to soften before the advancing infantry. At 9.35am, for five minutes before zero hour, all German howitzers, field guns and trench mortars pummelled the British first and second lines of defence in a hurricane bombardment of high explosive. The first German soldiers to attack, stormtroopers, crept into No Man's Land as far forward as they dared to the British lines in the final minutes of their covering barrage. The stormtroopers would advance through the British lines, bypassing strongpoints with the objective of disrupting lines of communication and engaging reinforcements moving up to the front. Following waves of German soldiers would deal with the strongpoints.

The German bombardment caused 7,500 British casualties. As the Germans advanced, Byng's 3rd Army fought tooth and nail to hold onto the Flesquières Salient, while further south Gough's 5th Army was in retreat. As the 5th fell back Field Marshall Haig became concerned that a gap may open between the 3rd and 5th Armies and ordered Byng to make sure his right flank maintained communication with the 5th Army even if it meant falling back as well.

177 Tunnelling Company continued their work on the Green Line until noon on 22nd March. The noise of the opening bombardment and witnessing of the infantry falling back to the Green Line prompted Major Hill to act. The infantry consisted of troops from 9th, 16th and 22nd Divisions, many of whom were completely unaware of the multitude of machine gun dugouts available to them so 177 spent the day giving assistance to the troops informing them of their existence. Three Sections of 177 and the company HQ gathered at Pussu that day spending the night there. Captain Montague Wright spent the day assisting the 21st Battalion of the Machine Gun Corps and acted as a guide for the supplying of ammunition to machine gun dugouts in front of Templeux during the night. At 6am the next morning Major Hill ordered company HQ and the three sections to fall back to Clery Sur Somme which was reached by 10am. In Clery he received orders from the Chief Engineer of VII Corps, via CRE 39th Division, to prepare for demolition bridges at Clery Sur Somme and Halle.

Three demolition parties were organised by the company. The first, under the command of Captain L Kennard, was to prepare the bridges at Halle on sheet 62C. NW at map references I.19.A and H.24.B. The second party, under the command of Captain Dalgas, was to prepare four bridges from Clery through Ommiecourt Les Clery in grid references H.12.B and H.17.A. The third party under the command of Captain Wright was to prepare a trestle bridge at map reference H.11 central. Explosives for the demolition of the bridges were obtained from the Royal Engineer Field Companies of 21st and 36th Divisions and work began on the task at 1pm that afternoon. At 6.30pm that evening as men of the 17th Entrenching Battalion crossed the bridges at Halle they brought with them the alarming news that they were in contact with the Germans who were hot on their heels. At 7pm a party of Germans was observed 200 yards east of the village, so Captain Kennard fired his charges destroying the bridges. As troops fell back a truck mounted anti-aircraft gun partially fell through the centre of the trestle bridge looked after by Captain Wright and his men. This truck was blown setting the bridge alight. Four spans of the bridge were demolished but it was still feasible for infantry moving in single file to cross the wreckage of the bridge. Luckily the crossing was commanded by a high bank on which a strongpoint was hurriedly prepared. The four bridges between Clery and Gommiecourt were being crossed by the remnants of the 9th Division. After the last man had crossed the bridges were blown whilst under heavy German machine gun fire. The last of these bridges was a heavy girder bridge that crossed the canal. It was cut close to its north pier and dropped into the canal and a set of the lock gates also destroyed to stop infantry from crossing over.

The remainder of 177 withdrew to Maricourt arriving there at 5pm. Here it was joined by 4 Section of the company which had withdrawn from Magancourt via Bouchavesnes. Major Hill joined the company at 11pm with orders received thirty minutes before to move to Corbie and then ordered to fall further back to Bray Sur Somme which was reached at 2am on 24th March. Here, Lt Cartwright and a demolition party were left to destroy the pumping station as the rest of the company fell back towards Corbie reaching the Prisoner Of War cage three miles east of the town at 3am on the 25th. The pumping station at Bray was blown at 6.15am that morning. The company then received word from the Chief Engineer of VII Corps that it was to fall back to Baizieux which it reached at 12.30pm that day, the men going into billets. The company was then given orders to improve the old French trenches in the vicinity and

200 men from the company got straight into work repairing old strongpoints on the French trench lines between Ribemont and Baizieux. This work was continued until the end of the month.

The retreat was very tiring for all who took part. Even though 177 Tunnelling Company got away relatively lightly in terms of casualties in comparison to other units, it had lost almost of its stores and motorbikes, although the rest of its motor transport was complete. The men had withdrawn with their personal kit but half of the officer's kit was lost.

The German advance was a devastating blow for the allies. Huge numbers of men had been killed, wounded and taken prisoner in the days following the start of the offensive. But the offensive had departed from its original goals in favour of exploiting more localised success and Ludendorff was keen to get it back on track. On 28th March an attack, dubbed Operation Mars, was launched against Byng's 3rd Army but met with little success. That same day General Gough was removed from his position of command of the 5th Army and replaced by General Sir Henry Rawlinson. Many people look at Gough's actions in 1917 at Bullecourt and then Passchendaele with some disdain. His handling of the retreat of the 5th Army, considering the circumstances, was handled very well, yet he was still removed.

APRIL 1918

The monthly manpower sheets for March and April 1918 in the war diary of 177 Tunnelling Company shows that none of the company were killed or wounded in the retreat, yet a report typed by Major Hill to the Controller of Mines, 4th Army[2] on the 11 April 1918 states that one man was killed, two wounded and one missing from the period of 21st March to 3rd April. On 1st April 1918, 37-year-old Sapper Willoughby Hayton, a miner from Barnsley, Yorkshire, died of his wounds at a field hospital in Rouen, on the French coast.[3] The next day 20-year-old 34999 Pte Ben Walker of the 7th East Yorks attached to 177 Tunnelling Company was killed.[4] 177 spent the first few days of April continuing their work on strongpoints and trenches between Ribemont and Baizieux. The village had come under regular German shelling and the section's accommodation was moved to a wood 1 mile west of the village. On 6th April the 4th Army relieved the 3rd Army with VII Corps now replaced by the Australian Corps. Major Hill suspected that 177 would move with the 3rd Army. His suspicions were confirmed when he was told to move the company to the 3rd Army area on 11th April. The company began its move north at 6am the next morning marching to Bac Du Nord, a crossroads about 5 miles south west of Arras. The company was to come under the command of the VI Corps located at Bailleuval. An advance party was sent on and erected shelters with the rest of the company arriving at 1pm on the 13th. The next day 177 set about digging trenches between the town of Beaumetz Les Loges and Bac du Nord. The trenches they were digging were part of a greater system of defence known as the Red Line. On the 15th two sections of 177 Tunnelling Company were ordered to start constructing road mines. These were in effect a denial weapon. Placed at critical points along a route such as crossroads and junctions to stop or hinder the advance of the enemy. Mines were

started at sheet 51C.SE, map references: R.23.a.1.8, R.26.d.6.5, R.25.d.7.3, R.31.d.7.6, Q.23.d.9.5, Q.34.d.7.6, W.4.a.6.8, Q.33.c.4.1, Q.29.b.3.4, R.8.c.8.3 and W.15.c.8.3.

On 19th April men from 119 and 146 Labour Company were placed under the direction of 177 and set to work on the Red Line. Lt Solomon and twenty men were sent to Doullens to work on the citadel under the command of the CRE Rear Zone Division and the next day a further ten men under the command of Lt Murray were sent to Berles au Bois, 9 miles south west of Arras, to work on the extension of two existing cave systems under the guidance of 174 Tunnelling Company. On the 21st Captain Basil Sawers returned to the company from his time at the 3rd Army Controller of Mines Office. On the 28th of the month the road mines, started on the 15th, were charged and made ready.

MAY 1918

On 2nd May 4 Section moved into a camp in Berles au Bois to work on the two sets of caves under the village. They were primarily involved in working on the entrances to the systems located on map references W.15.d.1.2. (No 1) and W.21.b.03.54 (No 2). The section also worked on a road mine at W.15.c.8.3. located at a cross roads in the north of the village. The rest of the company was to work on Machine Gun Dugouts on the Red Line under the umbrella of VI Corps. On 3rd May 1 Section moved out to a camp near Pommiers, a village about 1.5 miles south east of Berles au Bois. The next day, 4 Section moved out to a camp in Bailleuval, 1.5 miles north of Berles au Bois and all of the road mines worked on by the company were handed over to 174

Plan of No 1 cave Berles au Bois for May 1918. (TNA)

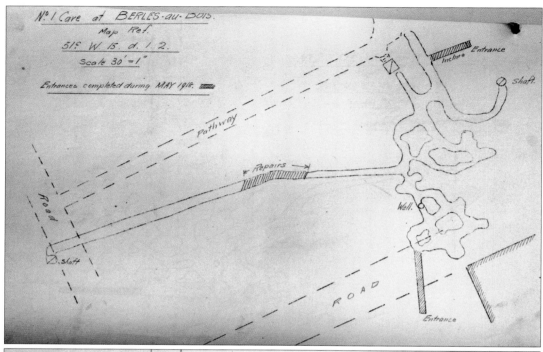

Plan of No 2 cave Berles au Bois for May 1918. (TNA)

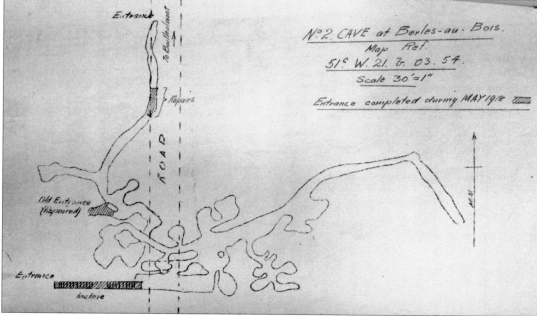

Tunnelling Company. With Lt Solomon and his section to remain in Doullens the rest of the company got to work on the Red Line. On the 7th Major Hill received orders from the Chief Engineer of VI Corps, Brigadier General R.N. Harvey,[5] that made Major Hill, OC No 3 Sector of the Red Line, which stretched from Bac du Nord to Berles au Bois. His garrison, which consisted of 177 and 181 Tunnelling Companies, 232 Army Troops Company RE and No 2 Siege Company Royal Monmouthshire Royal Engineers, was to man the Red Line in the event of an attack by the Germans. On 8th May ten new machine gun dugouts were started by 177 and on the 10th the headquarters of the company moved to Bac du Sud, about a mile north west of Bailleuval at map reference Q.32.a.7.2. It was about this time that a Pioneer Platoon of American Military Engineers were attached to 177 for instruction. It was part of a wider programme in which the fledgling American Expeditionary Force, now arriving in droves but inexperienced, were being sent to the British and French armies for training.

By 15th May dugouts were under way, on sheet 57D.NE, at map references D.18. a5.9, E.13.a.0.3, E.8.c.5.5, E.1.c.8.3, and on sheet 51C.SE at map references W.26.b.1.7, W.27.a.0.3, W.20.b.2.4, W.9.c.7.2, W.10.c.6.0, W.10.c.0.7, W.10.b.2.8, W.11.b.0.8, Q.35. c4.6, Q.35.a.3.4, Q.29.d.3.1, Q.29.d.4.9, Q.24.d.2.1, R.19.a.0.9, R.13.d.6.5, R.9.c.5.7, R.15.b.0.8 and Q.24.d.7.6. Another tragedy struck the company on 15th May when 102015 Sapper Benjamin Fellows died in hospital.[6] His age is unknown by the Commonwealth War Graves Commission and just what he died of is also unknown, although the casualty evacuation chain had by now started to see cases of men and women sick with influenza in what became known as the Spanish Flu pandemic, so there is a possibility he died as a result of this.

By the end of the week 16,000 feet of earth had been dug out by the tunnellers. On 17th May, Major Hill met with the Controller of Mines, 3rd Army, Lt Col P. Bliss, first OC of 177 Tunnelling Company, who informed him that all priority was to be given to finishing the work in the caves, before starting work on infantry dugouts. The caves existed long before the dugouts; the tunnellers just had to add to them, connect them together and construct

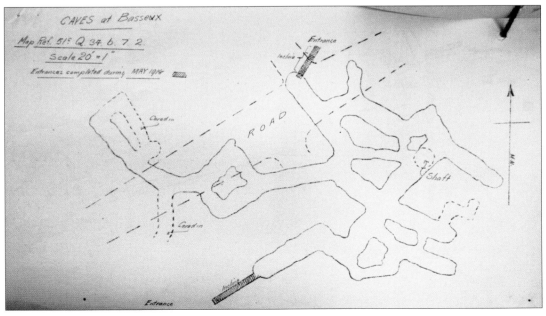

Plan of caves at Basseux for May 1918. (TNA)

entrance and exits to them. The next day Major Hill went to inspect the caves at Pommières, Humbercamp, La-Cauchie, and La Herliere. Whilst on his rounds, 1 Section started work driving out the entrances of the Pommières caves.

On 22nd May five new dugouts were also started at sheet 57D.NE map references W.12.d.3.5, E.1.c.7.5, E.7.a.5.5 and at sheet 51C.SE, map references W.26.c.5.5 and W.11.c.8.5. The 29th May saw the departure of the US Pioneer Platoon back to the AEF and the completion of one of the dugouts being worked on and the starting of another at map reference W.14.d.4.4.

A new piece of equipment, used to

Machine gun dugout plans Part 1 for May 1918. (TNA)

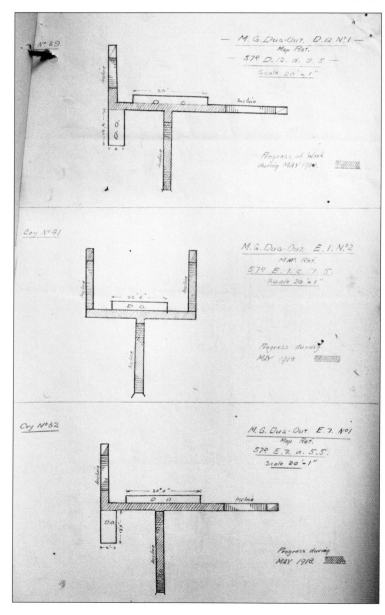

rapidly blow out a shaft, was trialled at St Leger Les Authie on 29th May. Major Hill went along to watch the trial. The 'Wombat' bored a hole in which was placed metal pipes charged with between 2½ to 3 lbs of blastine per feet. When fired it left a shaft between 4 to 5 feet in diameter, which, once cleared out, was lined with corrugated iron

tubing 3 feet 6 inches in diameter. The time taken to complete a shaft was 19 hours. On the last day of the month the Controller of Mines allotted the company the work to construct 9 Brigade HQ dugouts. For the time being the main focus of 177's work was to be on the brigade HQ and machine gun dugouts.

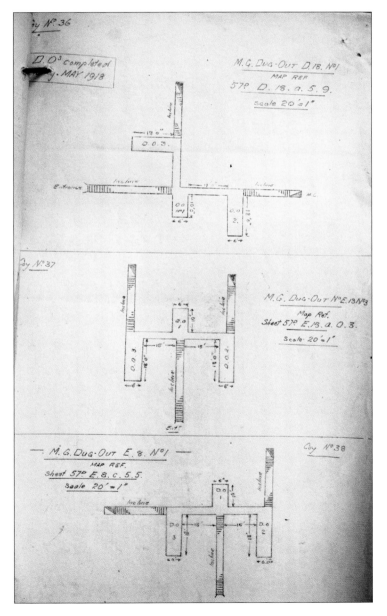

Machine gun dugout plans Part 2 for May 1918. (TNA)

Machine gun
dugout plans
Part 3 for May
1918. (TNA)

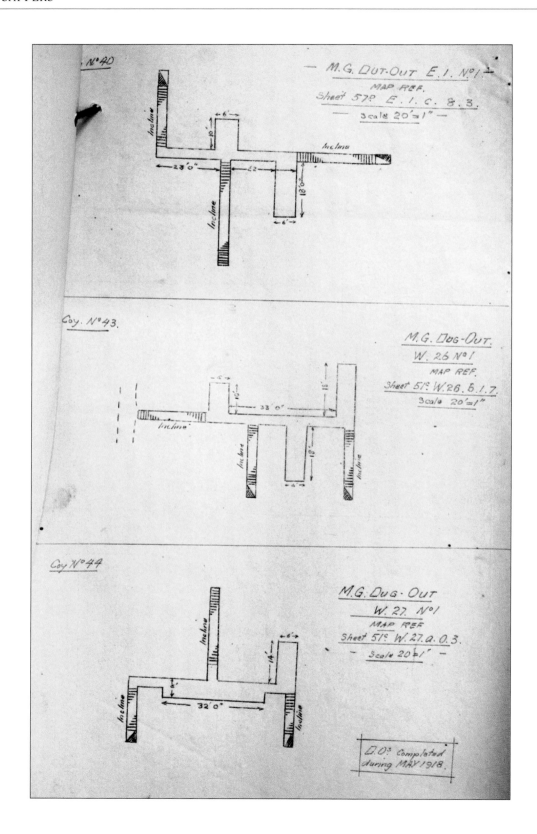

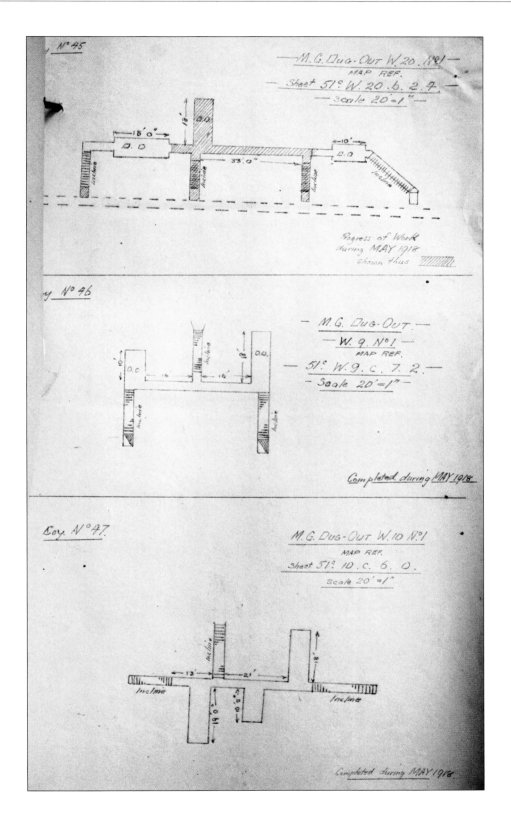

Machine gun dugout plans Part 4 for May 1918. (TNA)

Machine gun
dugout plans
Part 5 for May
1918. (TNA)

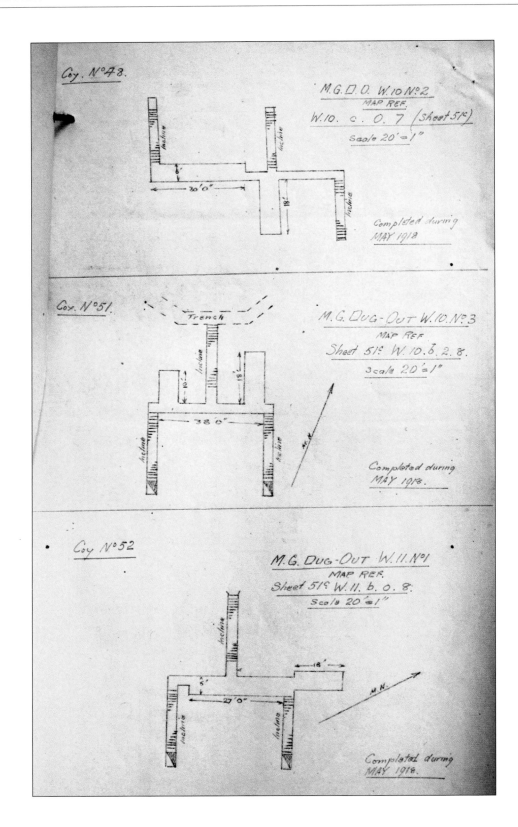

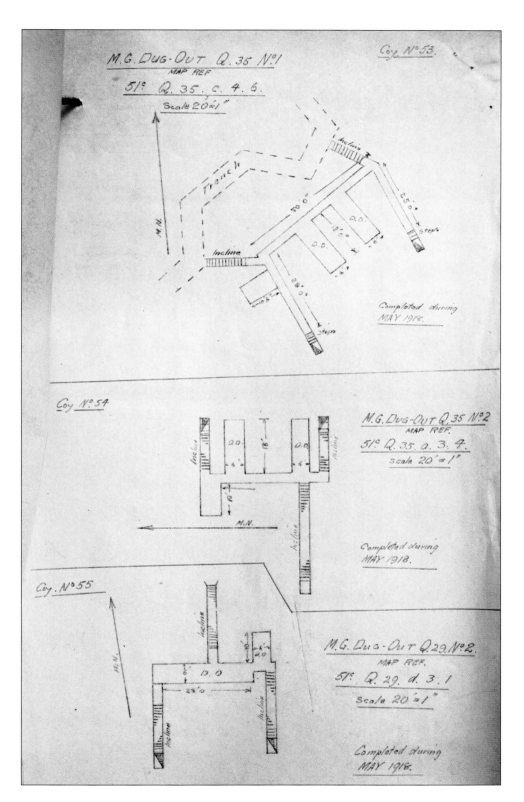

Machine gun dugout plans Part 6 for May 1918. (TNA)

Machine gun
dugout plans
Part 7 for May
1918. (TNA)

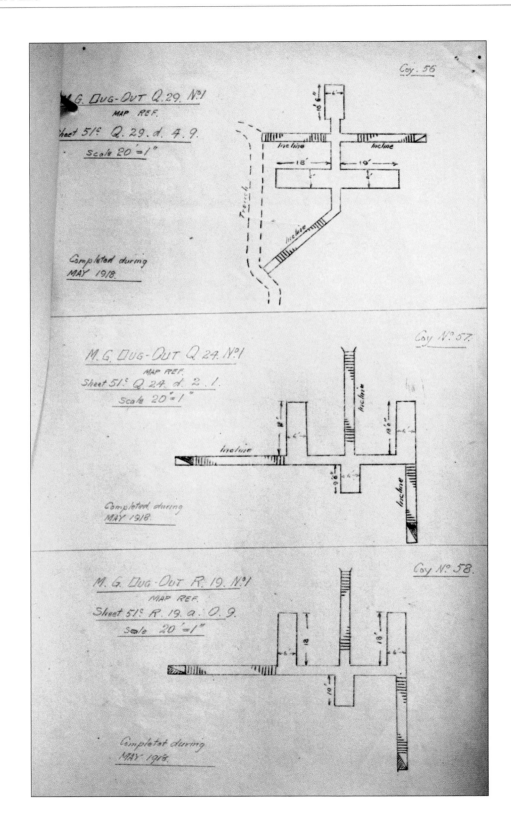

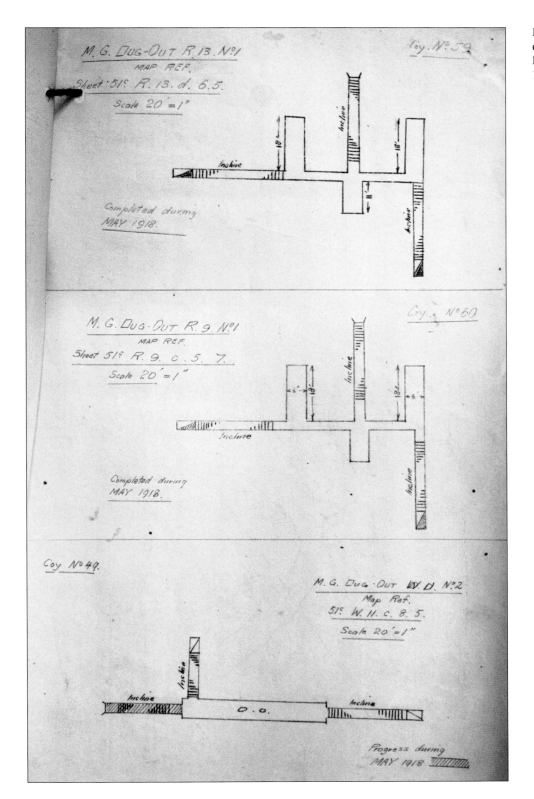

Machine gun dugout plans Part 8 for May 1918. (TNA)

JUNE 1918

On 1st June, 2 Section were detailed to start on four of the nine Brigade HQ dugouts with 3 Section working on the remaining. 2 Section would be working in the southern area of 177's area of responsibility and a site was selected for them at Bazque Farm about 1 mile south of Laherlière, with the section moving in on 4th June. On 5th June, 4 Section moved to Toutencourt and started work on dugouts in the vicinity of Lealvillers. During the week three dugouts in the sheet 57D area and sixteen dugouts in the sheet 51C area were completed. Two new dugouts were started at, sheet 51C.SE, map references Q.5.b.0.2 and Q.9.a.5.7. By 11th June all of the Brigade HQ dugouts had been sited and started by the company. The end of the week saw a further two dugouts in the sheet 51C area finished and four new ones started at map references V.21.d.0.8, Q.19.c.0.4, W.7.a.4.9 and V.12.a.9.1. In the sheet 57D area six new dugouts were started at map references D.8.b.3.7, D.8.b.2.1, U.8.c.3.0, U.8.d.8.8, O.33.d.8.0 and O.34.a.7.4. The extraction of earth for the week for 177 Tunnelling Company was about 20,000 cubic feet of earth.

On 14th June, as per a request by the Controller of Mines, Captain Kennard was sent to 181 Tunnelling Company and replaced by Captain Walter Beasley DSO from the same company. Captain Beasley had served as a Sergeant with the West African Tarquah Volunteer Corps from 1910 until 1915. He was commissioned into the Royal Engineers in early 1916 serving with 181 where he was awarded his DSO for overseeing a mining operation on 8th and 9th March 1916 by which a large part of a German gallery had been destroyed. He carried out a search of the German system until overcome by foul gas. On the 15th of the month an entry is placed in 177 Tunnelling Company's war diary that influenza is now prevalent within the ranks of 3 Section. On the 18th and 19th of June two more officers left 177 Tunnelling Company when Lt R.B. Murray and Capt Montague Wright transferred to the fledgling Royal Air Force. By the 19th a further seven dugouts had been finished and a cave system was discovered under the village of La Cauchie. A detachment of 3 Section started work on the caves at Souastre and by the week's end the company had extracted some 43,000 cubic feet of earth. On 22nd June Captain Basil Sawers moved to Toutencourt were he took command of 4 Section, prior to his departure from 177 at the end of June when he transferred over to the Canadian Engineers.

By 26th June three more dugouts in the sheet 57D area had been completed and three started at map references U.15.b.8.8, O.28.d.9.1 and O.22.d.8.6. The section deployed at Doullens under Lt Solomon started a machine gun dugout at map reference A.10.b.5.2. By the end of the month five entrances to the Laherlière cave system had been completed and two entrances started and the La Cauchie cave system.

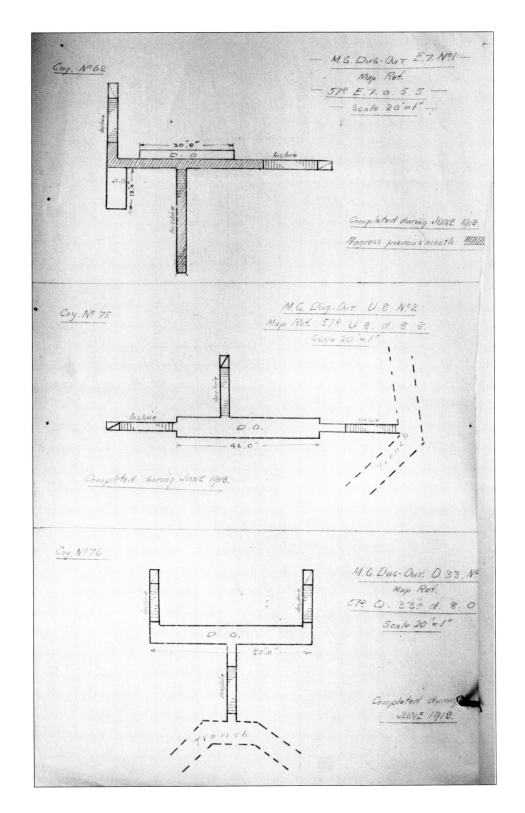

Machine gun dugout plans Part 1 for June 1918. (TNA)

Machine gun
dugout plans
Part 2 for June
1918. (TNA)

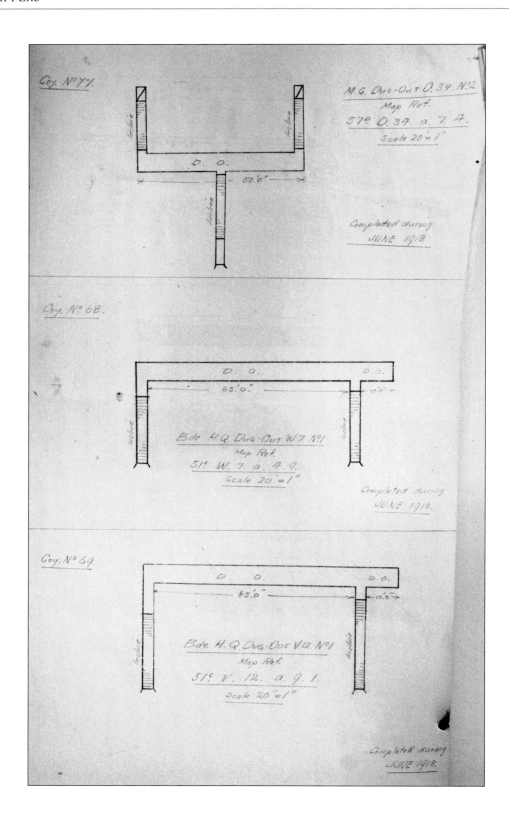

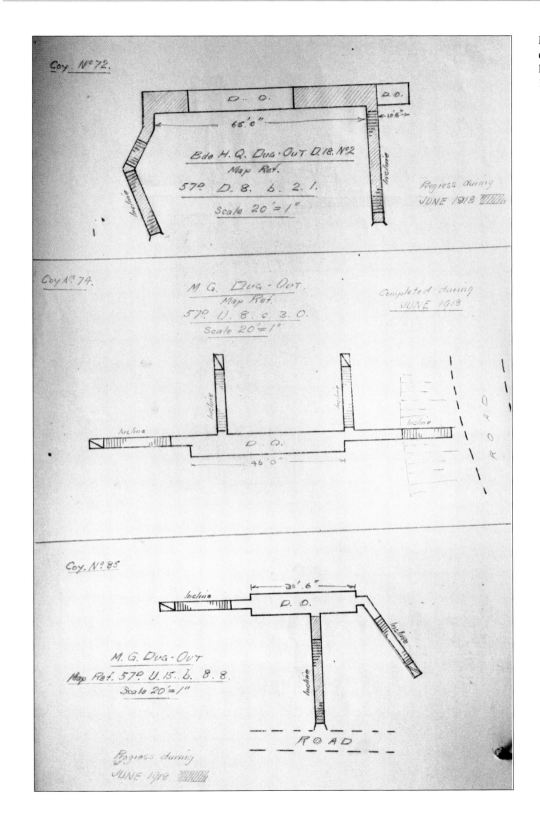

Machine gun dugout plans Part 3 for June 1918. (TNA)

Machine gun
dugout plans
Part 4 for June
1918. (TNA)

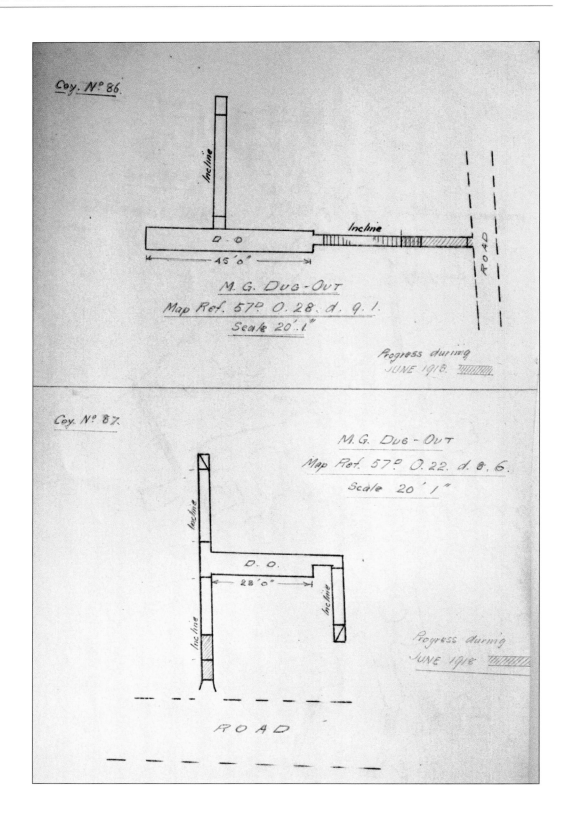

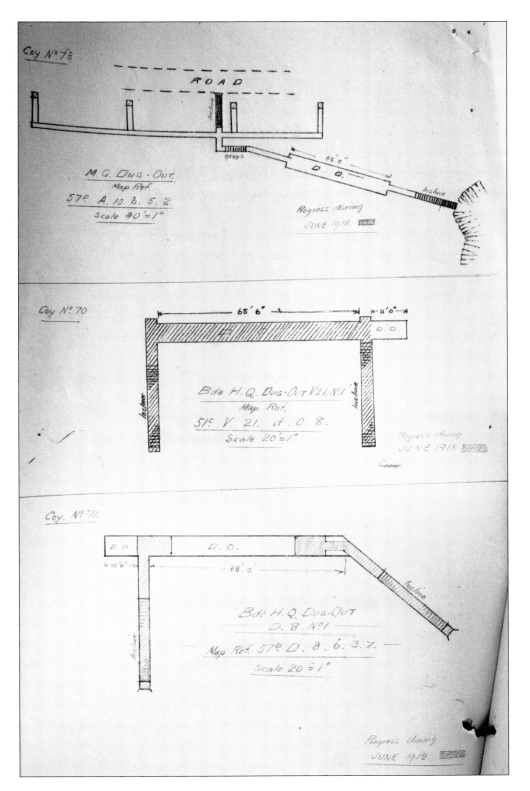

Machine gun dugout plans Part 5 for June 1918. (TNA)

Plans for cave at Laherlière for June 1918. (TNA)

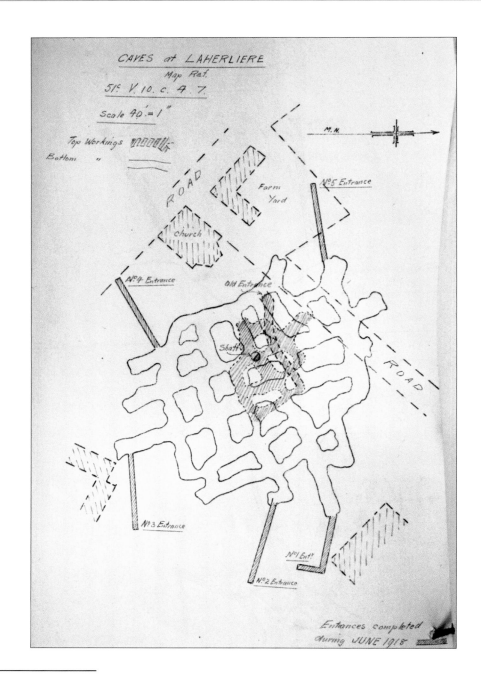

1 Mining Notes 103, Author's private collection.
2 WO158/153 GHQ Mining Reports, By Army and Company.
3 Sapper Hayton is buried in Plot 9, Row I, Grave 10a of St Sever Extension, Rouen.
4 Pte Walker is buried in Plot 5, Row H, Grave 4 of Beacon Cemetery.
5 Brigadier General RN Harvey was the first man to hold the position of Inspector of Mines at GHQ.
6 Sapper Benjamin Fellows is buried in Block Q, Plot 2, Row H, Grave 18 of St Sever Extension, Rouen.

CHAPTER EIGHT

JULY 1918

With the onset of July 1918, 177 Tunnelling Company was 328 officers and men strong. Major Hill spent 1st July on a reconnaissance of the villages of Bailleulmont and Bailleuval looking for cave systems that had been mentioned by the mayor of La Cauchie. The next day he was in Arras, accompanied by Captains Dalgas and Johnson, visiting the many cave systems that had been worked on by British and New Zealand tunnellers prior to the battle of Arras in April the year before. In the first week of the month a dugout in the sheet 57D area was completed and three more were started at map references O.35.a.4.2, U.4.a.5.8 and U.11.c.8.5. In the Pommier cave system two of the three entrances were completed and a lot of work was being done in timbering the caves to make them suitable for habitation. The caves at Laherlière and St Amand Road were finished in the first week of July. Work continued on the caves at Humbercamp, La Cauchie, Souastre and Berles au Bois with the tunnellers driving through entrances and timbering the cave systems. On 5th July Major Hill visited Bienvillers with Captain Dalgas who now had orders to start work on subways leading from the cave system under the village to strongpoints on the Red Line. Later in the day he visited Captain Beasley who was to do the same from the caves at Berles au Bois. Number 3 section made a start on the subways at Bienvillers on 8th July as 1 Section moved camp to Berles au Bois.

By 10th July three dugouts in the sheet 51C area were completed and one started at map reference W.26.d.5.2. The Pommières cave system was also completed along with both caves at Souastre and Humbercamp Number 1 cave. Work commenced on Humbercamp Number 2, La Cauchie Number 1 caves and 2 subways at Bienvillers and Berles au Bois. The next day the Controller of Mines 3rd Army, Major Hyland RE, mentioned to

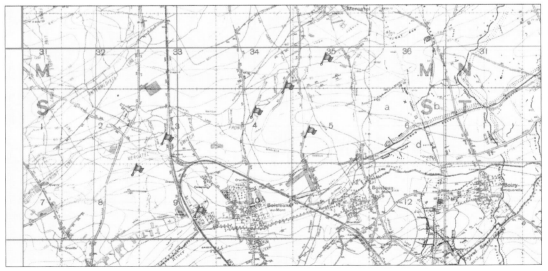

Selection of dugouts constructed by 177 in July 1918 prior to the Advance to Victory. (Courtesy Great War Digital)

205

Major Hill that he was going to swap the workings being done by 177 Tunnelling Company with those being done further forward by 181 Tunnelling Company. On 12th of July, Major Hill visited some of the workings being worked on by 181 Tunnelling company in front of Adinfer and Boisleux au Mont. In preparation for the change of work 4 Section handed over their work to 178 Tunnelling Company and returned to the company HQ location. The next day forward billets for 1 and 4 Sections were selected and sited near Ransart. 2 and 3 Sections were to take over 181 Tunnelling company's billets in

Battalion Headquarters and machine gun dugout plans for July 1918. (TNA)

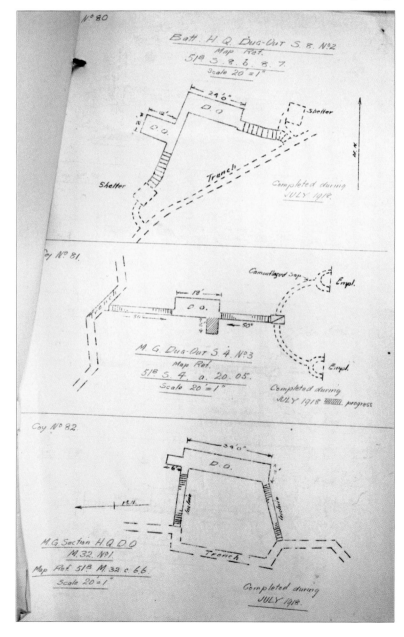

Wailly about 5½ miles north east of Berles au Bois. Lt Solomon and his detachment of men returned from Doullens and he took over command of 4 Section.

On 14th July, 2nd Lt A. Warwick reported for duty with the company, with both 1 and 4 Sections moving to their new billets the next day. As they made the move Major Hill visited the 3rd Canadian Divisions area of responsibility with Captain Johnson. He did the same in the Guards Division area accompanied by Captains Beasley and Solomon on 17th July as the company started to take over some of the workings

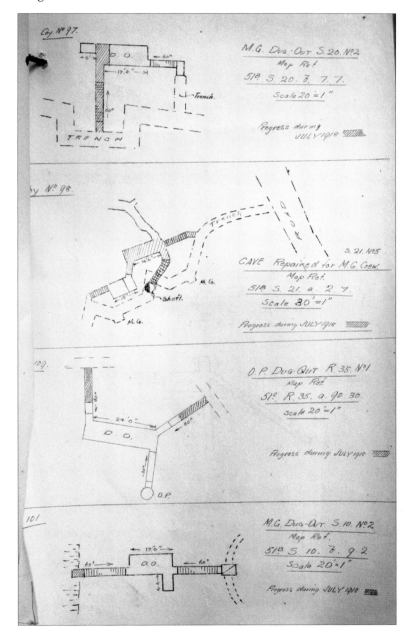

Machine gun dugout plans Part 1 for July 1918. (TNA)

handed over to them by 181 Tunnelling Company. Dugouts were worked on at sheet 51C.SE, map reference X.15.d.95.70 and sheet 51B.SW map references S.8.b.8.7, S.40.a.20.05, M.32.c.6.4, M.33.b.57.80 and M.37.d.65.05. Three new dugouts were started at map references S.4.a.9.2, S.5.c3.7 and M.35.c.7.6.

On 23rd July Major Hill visited the CREs of the Guard's Division, Lt Col E.F.W. Lees RE and the 3rd Canadian Division, Lt Col H. Hertzberg CE, to discuss with him them

Machine gun dugout plans Part 2 for July 1918. (TNA)

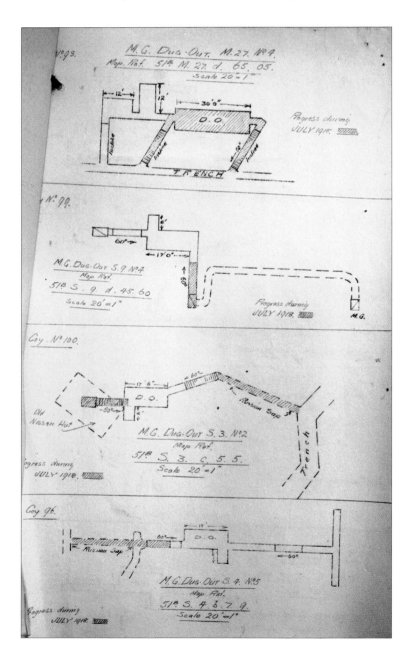

the programme of works in their divisional areas, visiting the 3rd Canadian Division's area the next day. The end of the third week of July also saw the completion of four dugouts and the starting of five more on sheet 51B.SW at map references S.9.d.45.60, S.3.c.5.5, S.4.b.7.9, S.20.b.7.7 and S.21.a.2.7.

The final week of July saw the 59th Division relieving the 3rd Canadian Division on the 25th and by 31st July two more dugouts were completed in the sheet 51B.

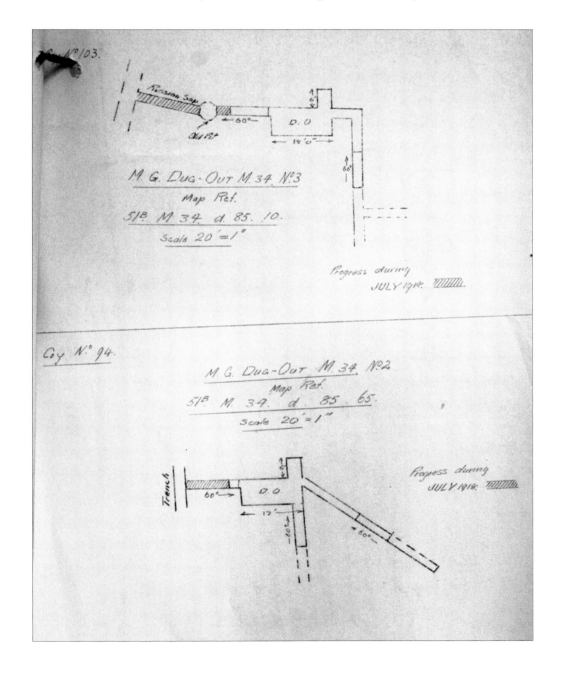

Machine gun dugout plans Part 3 for July 1918. (TNA)

SW area with three started at map references S.10.b.9.2, S.4.b.75.65 and M.34.d.85.65, a further dugout was started in the sheet 51C. SE area at map reference R.35.a.9.3.

Further south preparations were underway to launch a major attack against the Germans east of Amiens to take back the land lost during the German spring offensive. This action would herald the start of what would become the last one hundred days of the war, the Advance to Victory. It would start east of Amiens on 8th August

Machine gun dugout plans Part 4 for July 1918. (TNA)

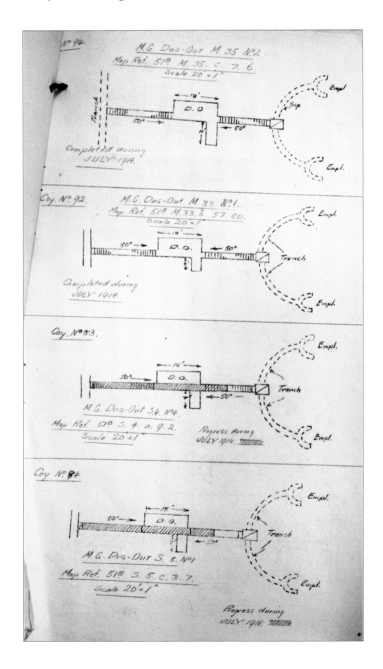

and then encompass more and more allied armies as further phases drove the Germans back to the Hindenburg Line.

Late September would then see the allied armies breaking the Hindenburg Line and having the Germans on the run. Unbeknownst to the officers and men of 177, they were about to play a pivotal role in this final but costly action that would bring an end to the war.

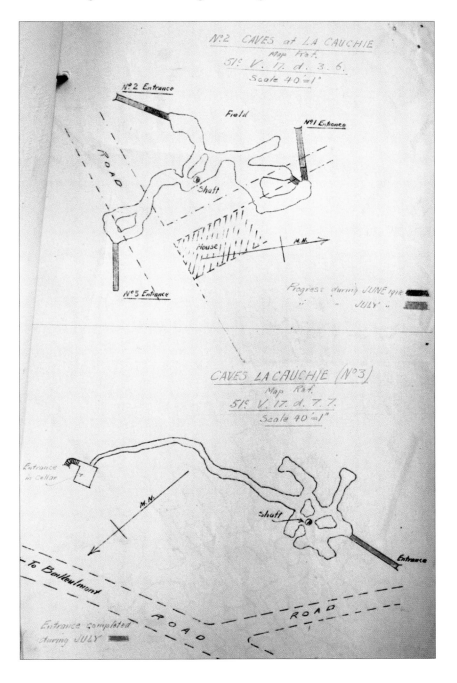

Plans of No 2 and No 3 caves at La Cauchie for July 1918. (TNA)

Plans of No 1
and No 2 caves at
Souastre for July
1918. (TNA)

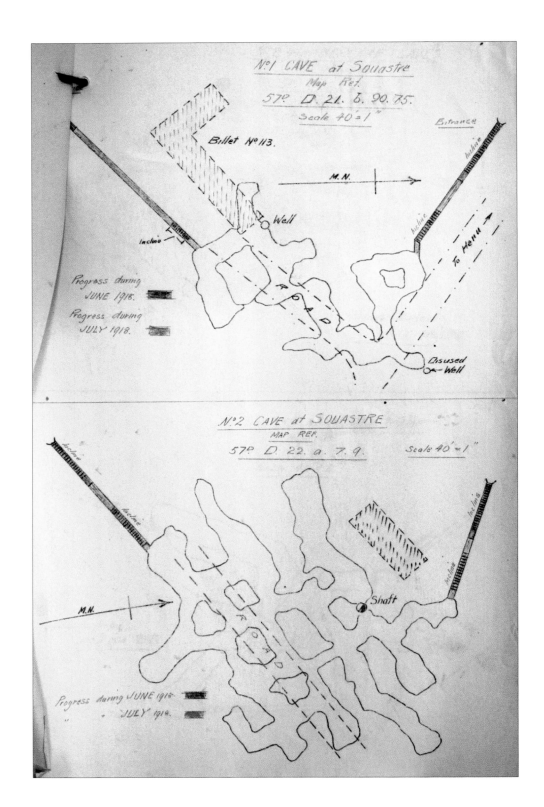

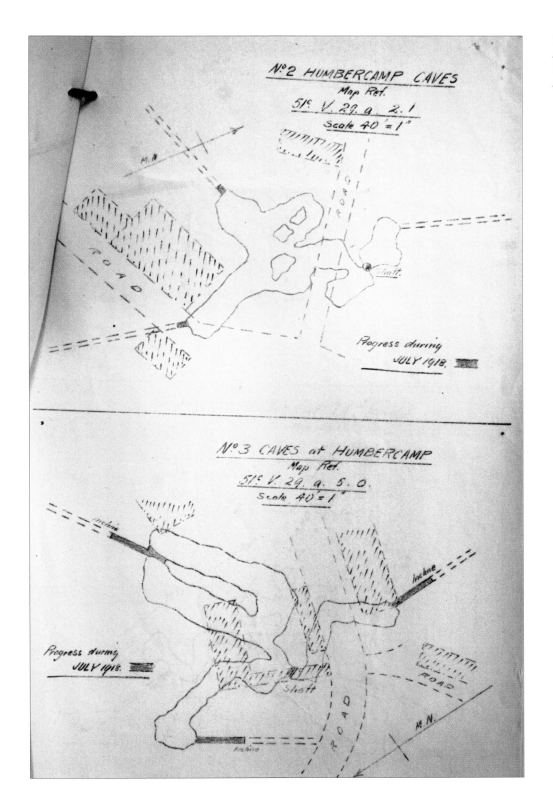

Plans of No 2
and No 3 caves at
Humbercamp for
July 1918. (TNA)

AUGUST 1918

For the first two weeks of August the company continued on its dugout work as preparations for a move eastwards across the 3rd Army front gathered pace. Two dugouts were completed in the sheet 51C, SE area, with one completed in the 51B, SW area and three started at map references S.19.b.5.4, S.21.b.1.4 and S.3.c.1.9. The second week saw another five dugouts in the 51B.SW area and one started at map reference S.14.d.2.8. During this period it became apparent that 177 had been using its own method of dugout construction and not that standard to VI Corps. On one of his weekly inspections of work in progress, the Chief Engineer of VI Corps, Brigadier General Harvey, expressed his displeasure to Major Hill. On 14th August the Chief Engineer once again visited Major Hill informing him that he thought discipline within the company was slack.

On 20th August, while most of the company was being instructed in infantry tactics and drills, Major Hill met with the Chief Engineer of VI Corps to discuss what the company's role would be once the advance got under way. If the forthcoming advance was to be as rapid as that seen further south in the recent two weeks, the tunnellers' role in digging dugouts would be negated. Their work underground would still be needed though as they would be required to use their skills in searching and clearing German dugouts. Brigadier General Harvey informed Major Hill that the company was initially to be employed on forward road clearance and repair. Attached to 177 for this task would be two sections of men from 174 Tunnelling Company and men from 565 and 232 Army Troops Companies.

Three detachments of men commanded by Lts Alexander, Buckworth and Warwick were sent to the Guard's Division area in preparation for the advance where they were to be involved in the reconnaissance and clearance of German dugouts. At 1am on 21st August Major Hill received the news that he and the rest of the 3rd Army had been waiting for. The advance was to begin at 4.55am that morning. 2, 3 and 4 Sections were to be on their allocated roads by 5am. The morning started with a heavy mist and by 9am reconnaissance parties had reached Moyenneville. By 7pm that evening thirty-five German dugouts had been investigated.

By 22nd August the Ayette to Courcelles road, one allocated to 177, was in poor condition due to heavy use, but the tunnellers did their best to maintain the road and keep traffic flowing with a shortage of scrapers and brooms. One of the main problems faced by units engaged in road clearance, was that in the lead up to the start of the push forward, the many road embankments common to the area had had dugouts dug into the sides of the embankments by non-tunnelling units employed on dugout construction. Much of the earth extracted from these dugouts remained on the roads causing traffic problems now the roads were under heavy use.

The next day, the 56th (London) and 52nd (Lowland) Divisions moved up and relieved the 59th Division. They then attacked to the north of the Guards' Divisional area. Two parties from 3 Section were attached to the 56th Division to reconnoitre captured dugouts in their area. 174 Tunnelling Company took over the road works on the Ayette to Courcelles road. Major Hill spent the day on the road visiting Boiry

Becquerelle and Hamelincourt, receiving information from 3rd Army, via the Chief Engineer, XVII Corps, Brigadier General W. Waghorne, that 177 Tunnelling Company were to now work under him. The corps had moved in to the left of VI Corps and 177 were to be involved in road works on the Mercatel to Boiry Becquerelle Road. Later in the afternoon of the 25th, Major Hill moved the company HQ to Ficheux. The next day the Canadian Corps attacked across their front, east of the city of Arras, and managed to retake the important hill top town of Monchy le Preux. Captured the year before with great loss of life, during the Arras offensive, it had fallen back into German hands, now finally wrestled out of their grasp it was in allied hands once again. The ground east of Arras held by the Germans consisted of the northern part of the Hindenburg Line. As you move east of Arras you travel over a number of north-south running ridges that the Germans held, their defences consisting of networks of trenches, bunkers and dugouts, many kilometres thick and many connected by underground tunnels. The Hindenburg Line had been seen by the Germans as an impregnable fortress. The Canadian Corps were now poised to start their push through those defences. 177 continued to supply reconnaissance parties to the 52nd and the 56th Divisions employed in the clearing of German underground positions. By 28th August 177 had also taken on the Henin to Croissilles Road. They also had 130 men of the 115th Labour Company attached to help in their work. Over the previous week 177 had successfully cleared and reconnoitred 238 German dugouts. As the British Army moved forward, so too did the ever important logistics and supply chain. New wells needed drilling to find a water supply for the army and the men found themselves employed in this task as well. They commenced the sinking of two wells on sheet 51B, map references S.15.a.0.5 and S.20.a.5.5. An old well in the ruins of Boisleux at map reference S.9.d.9.4 was cleared and put into use.

The last week of August saw the company busy at work on roads behind the River Cojeul. The company Headquarters moved on the 29th to sheet 51B, map reference S.6.d.5.8 on the main Arras to Bapaume Road. Reconnaissance was carried out of the Bullecourt to Hendecourt Road.

SEPTEMBER 1918

The beginning of the month saw the company working on roads behind the Cojeul River, by the 2nd of the month the works had incorporated roads between the Cojeul and Sensée rivers. On 3rd September the company moved into a former German Pioneer park west of Bullecourt at sheet 51B map reference U.20.d.5.5 and got to work on roads between Bullecourt and Croissilles. With the war now moving eastwards more rapidly than before it wouldn't be long until the company moved again and when it did on the 4th, it moved to the village of Hendecourt. 177 commenced repair works on the Hendecourt to Riencourt Road and throughout the rest of the week deepened three wells at sheet 51B map references T.2.a.8.5, T.24.c.2.9 and U.2.c.2.6. Dugout clearance parties from 177, employed in the dangerous tasking of searching former enemy dugouts for booby traps, searched and cleared 241 German dugouts, fortunately finding no traps.

The night of the 5th and day of the 6th saw the Germans shelling 177's camp and it was evacuated with the company moving to Moulin Sans Souci just east of Riencourt. The Riencourt to Queant road was in a terribly bad shape, not having been repaired since March 1917, so the company was put to work repairing the road. 2 Section, under the command of Captain Johnson, was given the unenviable task of setting out to locate and clear a former British anti-tank minefield sown months before. Road repairs and minefield clearance continued for a few days, the section of the Hendecourt to Riencourt road that ran through the Canadian Corps area was in a very bad way with several feet of earth sitting on top of the road metal. With heavy rain now falling, the road became impassable and, adding to the strain of the work being done by 177, was the fact that the Canadian Corps were not putting any of their own engineers on the job. On 10th September Major Hill met the Chief Engineer of XVII Corps to discuss the problem. The road was an important arterial route and needed to be cleared so the whole of 177 Tunnelling Company were out working on the task along with men from 115 Labour Company.

By the end of the week three more wells at sheet 51B map references U.2.c.2.6, T.2.a.8.5 and U.30.b.2.9 had been cleared and deepened in order to boost the important supply of water to army troops. Six British minefields were also cleared, although it was discovered that one of them was already being cleared by the Germans. They were located at Sheet 57C map squares W13c and d, C18b, C12a and c and C6a and c. A total number of 1,448 mines had been cleared. Dugout clearance parties had further searched another 358 dugouts, all luckily clear of booby traps.

On 13th September work commenced on deepening two more wells at sheet 57C map references C.11.d.0.5 and sheet 51B map reference T.28.c.85.65. The next day saw the departure of Lt Alexander as he left the company for England on his transfer to the RAF. The company finally finished working on the Hendecourt to Riencourt road on the 15th and by the 18th of the month a further 258 former German dugouts had been searched. On 19th September 177 lost another member of the company when Sgt George Ball MM died of a cerebral embolism at home in Bristol. He had fallen ill during May 1918 and had been evacuated to the UK.[1]

A reconnaissance was carried out in Louverval for well sites and then on 21st September the company moved to Noreuil and commenced work repairing the Noreuil to Queant road. The following day the company was set the task of constructing trench shelters for Corps heavy artillery near Queant at sheet 57C map reference D.7.b.7.1.

As the allies prepared to push further eastwards orders were received from the Chief Engineer of XVII Corps that a section of one officer and ten men were to be attached to the 52nd, 57th and 63rd Divisions and used for dugout and road reconnaissance duties for the forthcoming push east. By 25th September twelve shelters for the Corps heavy artillery were completed. Lt Howl and fifteen men from the company were sent to the Royal Engineer Park at Poyelles in order to start the movement of bridge girders up to Louverval in readiness for the forthcoming push.

On 26th September the three reconnaissance parties moved up to their respective divisions. Lt Daggar went to the 63rd Div, Lt Cartwright to the 57th Div and Lt Buckworth to the 52nd Div. All parties were moved up to the forward zone and were in place ready to go that evening.

The next phase of the allied advance began at 5.20am on 27th September. Canadian and British troops found themselves having to get across the Canal du Nord, a major French arterial waterway which in places, where the allies were advancing, was unfinished and not yet full of water. The worry in the minds of the allies was that the crossing places would become choke points and fall vulnerable to German artillery who would concentrate on the goose necks. Both the Canal du Nord and Bourlon Wood sitting just west of Cambrai were two main obstacles that sat between the ground gained by the allies and the city itself. The tasking of taking Bourlon Wood fell to the Canadian Corps who would have to traverse

the Canal prior to attacking the wood. 177 Tunnelling Company set off at 5.30am that morning arriving at Moeuvres at 9.15am where they set about the immediate task of filling in a 27 feet diameter, 12 feet deep crater which was located on a road diversion over the Canal du Nord at sheet 57C map reference E.15.c.1.3. By 10pm that night the crater had been filled and 80 feet of slab road had been laid. The gamble had worked and the Canadians found themselves safely crossing the dry canal bed. General Currie, commander of the Canadian Corps, had taken a huge risk by funnelling his assault force through this narrow defile, but it had worked in the favour of the allies.

The next day 177 found themselves working east of the canal on roads opposite the Moevres to Cambrai road. Lt Veale and a squad of men set about removing a steel sleeper barricade erected by the Germans at a factory on the main road at sheet 57C map reference E.29.a.7.8. They also had the precarious task of clearing land mines in the

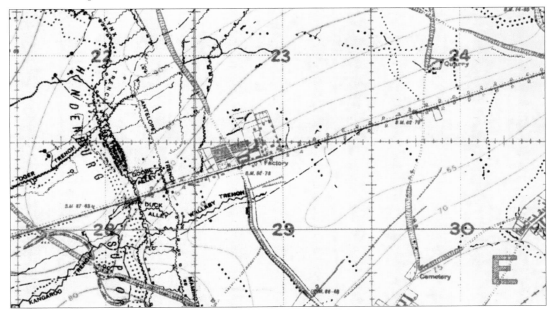

Factory where Lt Veale and men from 177 cleared German booby traps on the advance to Cambrai, September 1918. (Courtesy Great War Digital)

217

vicinity of the factory. The area in which the company was working was far from safe. They were still harassed by German artillery and six men were wounded as they worked on the road. The company was earmarked for assisting the Canadian Corps entry to the city of Cambrai. It would carry out reconnaissance of major roads, road junctions and rail bridges searching for any delayed action mines and booby traps left behind as the Germans withdrew.

By 30th September the company had moved to Fontaine just west of Cambrai. The Canadian Corps was now poised and ready across the junction of the Cambrai to Bapaume and Cambrai to Arras roads. The 63rd Division was located on the outskirts of Proville. A reconnaissance was carried out by Captain Dalgas of a towpath bridge located over the River Escaut by the lock at map reference F.29.d.7.1. The bridge was searched for mines and booby traps with none being found.

OCTOBER 1918

177 Tunnelling Company was 17 officers and 318 other ranks strong at the beginning of October. They started the month working on roads heading towards Cambrai. 3 Section got to work reopening a well located at a bombed out factory in Fontaine and commenced the sinking of another at sheet 57C map reference F.16.c.7.1. During the night of 4th October 36-year-old Sapper John Howells DCM from Swansea and Sapper George Muirhead from Ayrshire 2 were both killed by shellfire at 177's base camp as it came under heavy German bombardment. The company continued their work for the rest of the week on the roads around Fontaine with most of their

effort being spent on the main Cambrai to Bapaume road. It remained on short notice in readiness to move as soon as Cambrai was taken. The shelling of their camp continued every night unabated. But they didn't have to wait for long. At 1am on 9th October the Canadian Corps attacked north of Cambrai. Major Hill, accompanied by Captain Dalgas and Lt Soloman, visited the company outposts near Proville early that morning. News of the German retirement from Cambrai took a while to filter through but by 8am that morning elements of 177 entered the city of Cambrai by the main east west road. The streets were packed with Canadian soldiers. There was no time for celebration as it was unknown if the retiring Germans had left any unwelcome surprises for the soldiers. 1 Section arrived at 9am that morning and set about working on the west side of the city. The remaining three sections arrived via Proville at 11am that morning. Company HQ moved to a mill on the southwest of the city alongside the river Escaut. The many underground catacombs, dating from medieval times that existed under the Place des Armes, Citadel and Château de Selles were thoroughly searched by the company. Intensive house to house searches also took place as German booby traps were sought out by the men. On 11th October a 175 kilogram explosive charge was discovered by search teams under a bridge over the St Quentin canal alongside Boulevard Jean Bart at 57B map references A.4.c.4.3.

177's search work continued for the next few days and further explosive charges were found under railway bridges at sheet 57B map references A.4.d.07.85 and A.4.d.37.17, in the north of the city. On the

Locations of booby trapped canal and railway bridges cleared by 177 during the liberation of Cambrai, October 1918. (Courtesy Great War Digital)

16th the company, less 3 Section, moved to Avesnes les Aubert, a village, a few miles northeast of Cambrai where it established its company HQ in the south of the village. 3 Section remained in Cambrai to survey and reopen the caves around the Place des Armes. The remainder of the company spent the next day and a half working on roads in the vicinity the villages of Avesnes, St Vaast and St Aubert. At midday on the 19th orders were received for the company to prepare to construct a heavy bridge over the River Selle at the village of Montrecourt at sheet 51A map reference P33.d.6.4. The bridge was to be constructed the next day, so Major Hill and Captain Johnson went forward to carry out a reconnaissance of the bridge site, establishing that the Germans had pulled out of the village earlier that day although they still kept it under regular shell fire. The gap which they were required to bridge was 38 feet across and 11 feet deep. At 3.30 am on 20th October the company marched off for Montrecourt arriving there at 5.30am. Arriving at the same time was a convoy consisting of five lorries and

two trailers with the required bridging equipment. Once they were unloaded, 2 Section was detailed to construct the bridge with the remaining sections getting to work on the roads leading up to the bridge. Two 20 feet spans of 8 RSJs were put on a double central trestle and the bridge put in place and opened for traffic by 2.45pm that day. The Germans continued their frequent shelling of the bridge and Lt Buckworth and two other ranks were wounded during the building phase. Work on finishing off the bridge continued through the night and into the next day and, in the process of laying protective decking on the bridge, 26-year-old Driver George Nicol of the Army Service Corps (MT) attached to the 177 Tunnelling company was killed by shellfire and three men wounded.[3]

A couple of days later on the 23rd orders were received for 177 to construct another bridge. The next bridge was to be built at the village of Vendegies, over the River Ecaillon about 3 miles to the northeast of Montrecourt. The bridge construction was planned to take place on 24th October after infantry had taken the village and driven the Germans out. Eight lorries and all of 177 Tunnelling Company less company HQ was moved up to the village of Saulzoir. At 5am the next morning, Major Hill and Captain Soloman tried to reconnoitre the bridge site. But the village had not been cleared of the Germans, in fact they had driven the allies out of the village and the reconnaissance team could only get within 500 yards of the site selected for the bridge. Captain Soloman's 4 Section remained on standby with the lorries in readiness to move into Vendegies when ready. The other sections of the company were put to work on road repairs on the Saulzoir to Vendegies road and the company HQ moved up to Saulzoir. During the night of the 24th and early hours of the morning of 25th October, the Germans eventually pulled out of Vendegies. Major Hill and Captain Soloman were able to go forward and reconnoitre the bridge site at sheet 51A map reference Q.14.a.5.0 about 5.45am that morning. A gap of 33 feet wide, 8 feet from the water level needed bridging, the men and bridging materials arriving at 6.30am that morning. A double central trestle bridge with a skew of 30 degrees was ready and traffic flowing over it by 12.45pm that afternoon. The bridge was finally completed at 2.30pm. Another bridging site was identified just half a mile west of the bridge at Vendegies. This new site at the village of Sommaing required a bridge to span a gap of 27 feet. Captain Beasley's 1 Section was given the task in hand and told to use local salvaged material to make the bridge. His section completed the task the next day using three floor beams 27 feet long with shore trestles to complete the task. The rest of 177 was busy working on roads in the neighbourhood.

On the 29th of the month more orders were received to bridge another gap, this time over the River Rhonelle near the village of Maresches at sheet 51A grid map reference K.30.d.6.6 just over 3 miles to the northeast of Vendegies. The bridging operation was to take place on the next day, the 30th. Major Hill and Lt McCracken, one of the 3 Section officers carried out a reconnaissance of the area to be bridged, approaching the site through the village of Sepmeries and via Les Marais Farm just north of the village. On the map a small track was shown to be running from the farm northwards to the Rhonelle River. This road was found to be nonexistent. The operation to bridge the gap was delayed for a couple of days due to the difficulty in driving the Germans out of Maresches.

NOVEMBER 1918

A further reconnaissance of the new bridging site took place at 7am on 1st November but was hampered due to the weight of gas shells landing in the area around the bridge site. 3 Section arrived on site at 9am, the bridging equipment 30 minutes later. The village of Sepmeries and the bridging site came under harassing shellfire for the rest of the day. Things got a little hot for 3 Section when at 11am the Germans drove back the allied outpost line, in a counterattack using tanks, until they were level with the bridge site. 3 Section continued the construction of the bridge as the German counterattack was furiously driven off by infantry from the 19th (Western) Division, literally yards away from where they were working. Sadly during the foray LCpl Ernest Neville from Wigan, Lancashire was killed and one sapper wounded by machine gun fire. But

3 Section still got the bridge constructed and put into place by 3.30pm and finished by 5.00pm that evening. They were not to know it just yet but LCpl Neville was the last member of 177 to be killed in the war.4 The next day was spent working on road repair in the rain, but on the 3rd orders were received that a section of 177 would be attached to the 19th (Western) Division for a forthcoming push. 2 Section was allocated the task; their job to search for booby traps and mines and to reconnoitre any abandoned German dugouts. 4 Section was allocated the task of building a bridge at the village of Wargnies le Grand, Sheet 51, map reference G.14.d.9.2, once the village had been cleared of Germans and was in British hands. On the 4th the company moved off and began working on roads. The OC and Lt Simmonds i/c 4 Section carried out a reconnaissance of the area where the bridge was to be built. The town bridge had been destroyed by the retreating Germans leaving a 12 feet gap 7 feet above the water level. 4 Section moved its bridging equipment up to the village of Jenlain just west of Wargnies, waiting there as the last German pockets of resistance were fought out of Wargnies. Construction of the bridge began on the 6th at 6 am, the first traffic rolling over the bridge six hours later with the bridge completely finished by 3pm that afternoon. Other sections continued working on the roads in the area with 3 Section working on repairing culverts in the village of Bry north east of Wargnies.

177 continued in their support of the 19th Division and were directed to erect another bridge, this time in the town of Bettrechies, at sheet 51A map reference H.10.a.3.6.1. 3 Section under Capt Beasley was allocated the task and the site was reconnoitred at 8am that morning. A gap of 50 feet needed bridging across the River Hogneau which ran north/south just east of the village. The span of 50 feet was about 15 feet above the river. Supplies of bridging equipment were running low and all 177 had was one single 20 feet span. The OC spoke with the CRE of the 19th Division and was allocated another 20 feet span of bridge with two 10 feet trestles. The roads approaching Bettrechies were heavily cratered in the latest fighting and by the Germans as they continued their withdrawal. Both 1 and 4 Sections got to work in filling the craters. On the 8th, as crater repair continued, Lt Veale arrived with the bridging material. The lorries carrying the equipment were sent down to Bettrechies and unloaded at 5pm that afternoon. Company HQ moved up to the village of Flamengrie maintaining readiness to move again the next day. On the 9th the bridge at Bettrechies was passable to traffic by 10pm. The men of 1 Section had scoured the local area and made two more 10 feet trestles and a single 11 feet span from local salvaged timber. As the company HQ moved up later that night to Bettrechies orders were received for yet another bridge to be constructed. This next bridge was to go over the River Hogneau on the road that led north east from the village of Hon-Hergies just next to the ruins of a brewery. The reconnaissance party discovered a 60 foot gap 5 feet above the river. Bridging equipment was becoming scarce and orders were passed down from the Chief Engineer to Major Hill that this bridge was to be constructed from timber salved from Bettrechies. On 10th November company HQ moved up to Hon-Hergies

with 1 Section being left at Bettrechies to complete the bridge there as 3 Section made a start at Hon-Hergies. The timber needed to construct the bridge did not arrive until after dark that night.

The entry in the war diary of 177 Tunnelling Company for Monday 11th November 1918 barely mentions the armistice that came into effect at 11am that day. The diary itself states: "**Hostilities ceased at 11.00 hrs.**" We can only imagine what effect this monumental news had upon 177 whose men were as war weary and longing for home as much as the men in regiments and corps fighting alongside them. The company had been in existence for 1,283 days. One only wonders if any celebrations were held that day by the men in the company. The war diary records a very busy day as life continued close to the front, albeit the men safe from sniper and shellfire.

Although 11th November marks the end of the hostilities on the Western Front and is seen by many as the end of the war, the war itself would continue 'on paper' until peace was signed on 28th June 1919. Work had to continue for the time being as the armistice was just that, an armistice which could technically break down and fighting restart. Luckily for the men of 177 and the rest of the allied armies on the Western Front this would never happen. The biggest threat the men now faced was that of accident and unexploded ammunition. Work that day continued as normal with the bridge at Hon-Hergies passable by 11am that morning just as the armistice came into effect. The ration lorry bringing breakfast to the men of the company was ditched that morning and they received no breakfast, but one can just

hope that moral was not damaged too much as news of the armistice passed around the company!

Work on the bridge at Hon-Hergies was completed within two hours of the timber decking arriving on 13th November. The BEF was still moving forward and the roads it was moving on needed repairing following their damage by the shells of war. 177 was tasked to repair the road between the towns of Bavai to Binche. On 14th November both 1 and 4 Sections moved into Ferme de Beaurevoir close to the junction of the Bavai-Binche and Mons-Maubeuge roads with the company HQ moving into location the next day. For the next two days the company worked tirelessly on two more bridges and a number of culverts before the whole company took a day off on the 18th.

On the 21st the company HQ moved into the city of Maubeuge and the rest of the company followed suit working to clear debris off a bridge over the Sambre near the old barracks south of the town. Some of the houses in the area had been badly damaged by shellfire and now posed a safety problem to traffic using the road approaching the old town from the south, so they were pulled down until they were no longer deemed a threat to traffic. On the 25th the company took another day off playing 178 Tunnelling company at football.

DECEMBER 1918

Work on clearing debris off bridges in and around Maubeuge continued for the first week of December. The company also constructed two new bridges, one in Maubeuge and one in an outlying village north east of Maubeuge. Although day by day it now appeared the war was over, as work continued many of the men, especially those who had been with the company since its formation, cast their thoughts on those comrades who did not make it. The peak of 177's work and sacrifice during the war was certainly their time spent in the Railway Wood sector a couple of miles east of Ypres. It was to here on 8th December that Captain Agner Dalgas and a party of 177 returned in order to erect a memorial to the memory of their comrades who had been killed during 177's tenure in the Railway Wood sector. On their arrival back at the Railway Wood sector they found their memorial cross that they had erected just as they left the sector in the late summer of 1917. The cross had fallen behind German lines in the April of 1918 as they surged forward towards Ypres this time taking the complete Railway Wood sector. The cross had been blown over by the ravages of war but had survived more or less intact and it was this that Captain Dalgas and his men re-erected in December 1918. The cross was placed on a pyramidal base and enclosed by a wooden fence. Two panels stood each side of the memorial describing the sacrifice made by 177 during its time in the sector. In front of the cross was a diamond-shaped wooden board with a brass plaque mounted on it.5 The plaque had the following words engraved upon it:

> IN MEMORY OF
> THE UNDERMENTIONED OFFICER,
> NCOS AND MEN
> OF & ATTACHED TO
> 177TH TUNNELLING COMPANY RE
> KILLED AND BURIED IN ACTION
> BELOW HERE DURING
> THE MINING OPERATIONS 1915–17

The plaque then went on to list the thirteen brave men who still remained under the sector deep in their tunnels.

Work continued in and around Maubeuge with Capt Dalgas and party arriving back on 11th December. The next day 3 Section took over the construction of a heavy bridge over the moat at Maubeuge's Mons Gate.

Work continued in Maubeuge for the rest of December. The army was now faced with the problem of demobilisation. Many men had joined purely for either three years or the war's duration. Many men, who had seen it their duty to join to defend freedom and many men who had been conscripted into the army, now rightly wanted to go home. Those with jobs vital in keeping the country running were demobilised first. The jobs this priority demobilisation encompassed included men from the mines. In the last three days of December 123 men from 177 were demobilised and returned home to their families, civilians once again. Many of the men awaiting their names on demobilisation lists were sent home on leave.

---

1 102818 Sgt George Ball is buried in Arnos Vale Cemetery, Bristol.

2 147848 Sapper George Muirhead and 79886 Sapper John Thomas Howells DCM are buried in plot 1, row B, graves 11 and 12 at Anneux British Cemetery just west of Fontaine.

3 T4/241199 Driver George Hay Nicol, MT Section, Army Service Corps attached 177 Tunnelling Company is buried in Plot 3, Row A, Grave 20 of St Aubert British Cemetery.

4 155837 LCpl Ernest Neville is buried in row B grave 8 of Crucifix Cemetery, Vendegies Sur Ecaillon.

5 The memorial plaque still survives today and is on display in the Royal Engineers Museum at Chatham.

CHAPTER NINE

1919 TO TODAY

177 Tunnelling Company spent until 28th January in Maubeuge continuing its clean-up work and bridge construction. It also employed men on salvaging tasks trying to recover tons of military equipment dumped and abandoned by both the retreating German Army and the advancing British Army prior to the armistice. In between work time was spent doing sport and cleaning up. Finally on 28th January the company was ordered to move to Cambrai. A further 51 men were demobilised during the month. February was spent by the men on camp duties and wood collecting fatigues as described in the company war diary. During the month, 177 amalgamated with four other tunnelling companies also billeted in Cambrai. A further 39 men were demobilised in February, 20 of them whilst at home on leave. Boring mundane camp duties such as cleaning harnesses and barracks continued through March. During the month a further seven men were demobilised and 54 transferred to other units to either await demobilisation or to stay in the army. By the end of March the company strength was down to one officer and 19 men. In April, what remained of 177 Tunnelling Company moved to Roisel Dump were it continued to de-kit, handing in its stores. The manning sheet for the month stated that a further seven men were demobilised. The final sheet making up the official war diary for 177 is the cover sheet for May 1919. It states that the company

The original RE Grave Cemetery. Originally erected by 177 in September 1917. This photo was taken in December 1918 by Capt Dalgas MC who led the repair party. (TNA. WO32/5892)

remained at Roisel camp and continued to box up its stores. The wartime story of 177 and the many hundreds of brave men that served in and were attached to the company ends here. But this is not the end of the story of the men.

They returned to their families, many after long periods away on the Western Front. Most went back to their pre-war occupation, mining, exchanging a military uniform for civilian clothes. The war for many had been the most exciting time that they would experience in their lives. Many former 'moles' joined the Tunnelling Old Comrades Association when it was formed in the years just after the war. TOCA ran until the eve of the Second World War but then finished. Many of the men, just glad to be home, set about rebuilding their civilian lives and pushed their military experiences to a corner of their minds, maybe only revisiting the memories in the company of another comrade who had shared the same deprivation and hardships both on and below the Western Front.

What of some of the characters of 177? The first OC of the company was Major Philip Bliss, the man whose vision of how underground warfare would evolve, often clashed in the early days with John Norton Griffiths who wanted the Germans undermined ASAP. Bliss' vision of building a network of both defensive and offensive tunnels coupled with deep underground dugouts for HQ and accommodation set the benchmark for 177's work at Railway Wood. After leaving 177 he went on to become Controller of Mines, 3rd Army and was mentioned in Despatches in 1917. He finished the war as Deputy Assistant Director of Engineering Stores. Staying in the army, in 1919 he married his sweetheart

RE Grave memorial as it stands today. (Author's collection)

Monica Hunt. In 1937 he is listed as being a Colonel, Assistant Director of Fortifications and Works. He was later awarded the CBE. He retired with the rank of Brigadier in 1942 and went to live in Budleigh Salterton in Devon. He died in 1966.

Major Lawrence Hill MC who joined the 177 in August 1917 and commanded the company to the end of the war finally left 177 on the 17th January 1919. In June 1919 he was awarded a DSO and a month later was Mentioned in Despatches. He married in 1920 and continued in the mining industry working for Rio Tinto. In 1951 he became President of the Institute of Mining and Metallurgy.

Captain Agner Dalgas MC, the Danish Army officer residing in Canada when war broke out, joined the CEF and then transferred to the Royal Engineers upon being commissioned and found himself posted to 177 Tunnelling Company. Above all who served in 177, it is through this man's drive and determination that a beacon of sorts still shines in the Railway Wood sector today, forever remembering those men who still remain in the now silent, water-filled tunnels under the sector. He finished the war with an MC and the Italian Silver Medal for Valour. He was demobbed in 1920 and returned to his wife Alicia in British Columbia, Canada, where he joined the 88th Victoria Fusiliers serving with them until the unit was disbanded in 1930. In the early 1920s he became involved in the campaign to have a permanent memorial erected over the Railway Wood sector to replace the original he and his men erected in both 1917 and again in 1918. He wrote an emotive and moving letter as to why he believed 177 Tunnelling Company should be deserving of a permanent memorial at Railway Wood. His letter stated:

"With reference to Army order of 12th April 1919, part XI, I hereby give the following statement.

The photograph attached is from a sketch which was made just after the memorial was erected in December 1918. It covers an area of 18 feet by 18 feet (more or less).

The exact map reference of the memorial site I am unable to give, as I am at present not in possession of the map required, but with reference to Army map of north west Europe, scale 1:250.000, Sheet 1, part of 4, the memorial is situated in square D8 and about 400 yards south, 55 degrees east of where the road from Wieltje to Hooge crosses the Railway from Ypres to Roulers.

The historical facts are as follows. The memorial stands over the centre (more or less) of the great mining system of Railway Wood, which was started in the middle of 1915 and discontinued at Zero Hour of the big Passchendaele offensive of 31st July 1917, when mining warfare on the Western Front came to an end. As the 177 (T) Coy RE was there from start to finish, the memorial was erected by the officers and other ranks of that company, twice. First time, after the fall of Passchendaele late in 1917, when Railway Wood was far enough back of the front line to allow the erection of such a conspicuous landmark, authority being obtained from the 17th Corps thus holding the line. During the German counteroffensive in early 1918, the memorial became unfortunately a German possession, being about 400 yards inside their line and of course it was blown over.

It was erected again for the second time in December 1918

It stands there in all its simplicity to the undying memory of:

1. One officer and 15 NCOs and Sappers who were actually killed at the face, while engaging the enemy at a depth which varied from 20 to 80 feet below the surface. There, 16 were not only killed on the spot, but completely annihilated during the encounter. Only their names are on the brass plate in front of the cross.

2. Five officers and scores of NCOs, Sappers and infantrymen were attached, who were killed while engaging the enemy underground,

but who were fortunate enough to be buried under their own individual crosses in graveyards behind the line.

3. The energy put into these hundreds of yards of galleries, dugouts and mine chambers in this underground world of one of the biggest mining systems on the western front.

4. The fortunate officers, NCOs, Sappers and infantry attached who were privileged to be there from start to finish, privileged to suffer the misery of wet dugouts, of narrow and low galleries to work in, where they had long hours and were always wet and half suffocated by lack of air, or fumes of gas, but, nevertheless, who, by their attention to duty accomplished the complete defeat of the Germans in their mining campaign.

These statements are hereby verified as correct.

A.E.Dalgas, Captain.

Late officer i/c Railway Wood mining system."[1]

His letters, coupled with the efforts of former members of 177 Tunnelling Company and a Mrs Alice Gordon who had lost her son Lt Alexander Maurice Gordon, 1st Bn, Royal Fusiliers in action near the ruins of Bellewaerde Farm on 20th January 1916, were successful. In February 1922 the Imperial War Graves Commission agreed to treat the site as a multiple grave and erect a permanent memorial to the men buried under the sector. The wooden memorial was removed and replaced with

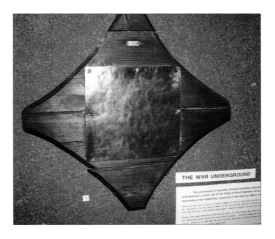

The only piece of the original memorial still surviving. The board and brass plaque, upon which is inscribed those names that the memorial commemorates, is now displayed in the Royal Engineers Museum in Chatham. (Author's collection)

the permanent one which stands today. Agner Dalgas moved to Nelson, BC after becoming a member of The Association of Professional Engineers of the Province of British Columbia and continued his practice as a civil engineer. In 1936 the 111th Battery, Royal Canadian Artillery was formed and he took command. When the Second World War broke out he was deemed too old to serve. Not to be outdone, this old soldier resigned his commission and rejoined the Canadian Army as an enlisted man lying about his age. He was commissioned again and in 1945 during the liberation of Western Europe he was serving with the General List. He was killed on 29th April 1945 just

Identity bracelets belonging to Lt F.V. Alexander who served with 1 Section. 177 Tunnelling Company until September 1918 when he transferred to the Royal Air Force. (Author's collection)

227

Sapper Alfred Parton, one of the first men to serve with 177 Tunnelling Company. He was gassed and medically discharged in January 1918. He died of stomach cancer in 1921. All applications for a war pension were rejected having far-reaching consequences for his family. (Photo courtesy Jayne Cheslin)

Far right: Sapper James Swain. Served with 177 Tunnelling Company from November 1915 until the end of the war. He returned to coalmining after the war and was a strict teetoller until 11th November when he would drink to the memory of his lost comrades and was often carried home by the village policeman. (Photo courtesy of Gary Woolaston)

nine days before VE day. It is believed that whilst driving a jeep he drove over a mine. He was 57 years old. He is buried in Plot 12, Row B, Grave 3 of Holten Canadian War Cemetery in the north east of Holland.

Many of the other ranks who had returned home after the war now began the long struggle to claim war pensions for injuries sustained during the war. The land they returned to may have been home, but it certainly was not the land fit for heroes as described by Prime Minister, David Lloyd George. The war may have been over but many continued fighting the war, some until the day they died. Some, after facing months and years of terror and hardship at the front, now faced rack and ruin. The times could be very cruel indeed as was the case of Sapper Alfred George Parton. He was one of the very first batches of men to be posted into the newly formed 177 Tunnelling Company in June 1915 and served with 177 until he was

medically discharged in January 1918 and returned home to Pensnett, Staffordshire. He had been gassed during the war and had stomach problems pre-war which led to his medical discharge. Rightly believing that the stomach cancer that he had now been diagnosed with had been attributable to or aggravated by his service in the army, Alfred made his claim for a war pension. He passed away on 3rd May 1921, the claim for a pension continued by his widow Sarah. The claim was eventually rejected having far reaching implications on her family. Left with four children to bring up, Sarah took up washing and as soon as her children were old enough they went into service. Alfred's Victory medal was returned to the medal office in 1924.

The fact that the memories of what these men went through stayed with them is also reflected in the story of Sapper James Swain, a 28-year-old coalminer from Bedworth, Warwickshire, who joined the

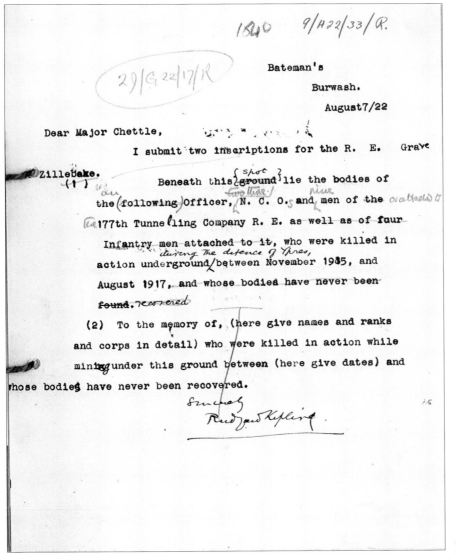

1840   9/H22/33/R.

29/G 22/17/R

Bateman's

Burwash.

August 7/22

Dear Major Chettle,

I submit two inscriptions for the R. E.   Grave

Zillebeke.

(1)   Beneath this {spot} ground lie the bodies of

the (following) Officer, N. C. O.s and men of the

177th Tunnelling Company R. E. as well as of four

Infantry men attached to it, who were killed in

action underground between November 1915, and

August 1917, and whose bodies have never been

found. recovered

(2) To the memory of, (here give names and ranks

and corps in detail) who were killed in action while

mining under this ground between (here give dates) and

whose bodies have never been recovered.

Sincerely

Rudyard Kipling.

Letter from Rudyard Kipling showing his choice of words to be inscribed onto the Cross of sacrifice at RE Grave Cemetery.
(TNA. WO32-5892)

army not long after the death of his first born daughter aged just three days. James returned home in 1919 and went back to work in the coalmines. He was a teetotal 364 days per year that is until 11th November every year when he would go out and get blindingly drunk on rum in memory of his colleagues, being carried home by the local policeman. The family story was that he hated the taste of rum but would drink it in large quantities on 11th November to remember his comrades.

The current memorial to the men of or attached to 177 Tunnelling Company which stands next to Railway Wood was finished by Autumn 1923. There is no record as to whether there was an unveiling ceremony or not. The wording on the memorial was chosen by Rudyard Kipling. Just behind the memorial, now full of water, is crater

Oblique aerial photograph taken in the 1960s of Railway Wood. The Ypres to Roulers railway is no longer in use and has yet to be converted to a road. Craters X and Y can still be seen. (Author's collection)

Aerial photograph of Railway Wood taken in the early 1980s. The crater below Railway Wood in the photo was filled in during the late 1980s. (Author's collection)

Aerial photograph taken in the early 1980s of Railway Wood looking northwards along the old front line. (Author's collection)

number 2 with the edge of number 2a still visible to the right of crater number 2. The small wood just behind the memorial is still full of mine craters, the result of deadly blows by 177 and their German opponents. This piece of land once pock-marked by shellfire, devoid of all greenery and resembling a lunar landscape, is now thriving with plants and wildlife. The wood is private property but a polite request to the farmer at Bellewaerde Farm normally results in kind permission to explore. It is also rumoured that for the approaching centenary years that the Ypres authorities may open and interpret the land. Still visible, although for most of the year overgrown, is Momber Crater, 177's largest mine fired in the war. Also visible is the crater formed by the final mine fired by 177 in the war, its objective to destroy German mine workings emanating from James Crater, the remnants of which are still visible. The wood is a fitting visible memorial to the brutal underground war that existed here almost

a hundred years ago. RE Grave is visited regulary by groups and individuals visiting the battlefields. In recent years, Clayesmore School has conducted an annual pilgrimage to the memorial in special remembrance of one of their old boys, Geoffrey Boothby. Just north of RE Grave is Railway Wood now dotted with a number of houses; one wonders if the current owners realise what is under their feet. The author was informed by a reliable local source that many years ago one of the residents living in the wood would open part of the Railway Wood dugout for a fee of five Belgian Francs. He would only allow visitors a short way into it as parts of the dugout had been stripped of wood probably after the war by the returning locals. A number of years ago the author had the pleasure of meeting the late Eugeen Vanoudendycke who owned a

piece of land at Railway Wood. On his land still remains one of the original inclined stairways and vertical shafts that descend into the Cambridge Road dugouts system under Railway Wood. The stairway and shaft are now full of water as would be the rest of the dugout and mine workings leading off under the sector. A few years ago local historian, tunneller and co-author of *Beneath Flanders Fields*, Johan Vandewalle, attempted to explore the system from the existing stairway but came upon a collapse which blocked his route. Both the 177 and the German mine workings under the Railway Wood sector will all be now full of water. Starved of its oxygen content the water will have acted as a great preservative slowing the decay of the wood lining the various galleries and preserving items relative to the lives of the tunnellers left behind when they moved away in September 1917. If we were ever able to enter them in the future

Left: Pupils from Clayesmore School remember Lt Boothby on their annual pilgrimage to the RE Grave Memorial in 2010. (Author's collection)

Johan Vandewalle in Ravine Wood dugout in 1993. (Photo courtesy of Johan Vandewalle)

Looking up one of the inclined stairways of the Ravine Wood dugout during a project in 1993 led by Johan Vandewalle. (Photo courtesy of Johan Vandewalle)

In 2011, with permission, a small hole was made in the bricked up entrance to the Ramparts Dugout North by the Works Department of Ypres. The old dugout has been backfilled with the debris of war, but the entrance was still clearly visible. (Author's collection)

it would be comparable to exploring a submerged shipwreck. Parts of the workings have shown signs of collapse. About twenty years ago a major sinkhole appeared on the ground above the old number 16 workings possibly warning of a collapse deep underground. The fields around Railway Wood, once a belt of mine craters, are now once again worked by farming. Little trace remains of the craters in the fields apart from a crater on the north-eastern edge of Railway Wood. The current farmer filled in a few of the craters in the 1980s but traces of their existence can still be seen. The Ypres to Roulers railway, after which Railway Wood was named, now no longer exists. It is now a long, busy road linking Ypres to Zonnebeke and the A19 motorway.

Whilst carrying out the research that has led to the book, the author was always intrigued as to what became of the Ramparts North dugout in Ypres. From the plans it is easy to see that one of the entrances of the dugout was made in the wall of one of the older tunnels that ran through Ypres old ramparts. In 2009 this old tunnel was located at the rear of a council property and upon exploration by the author and Johan Vandewalle it was found that the entrance to the dugout was still very visible in the wall of the older tunnel. The WWI dugout, 177's first dugout, had been bricked up. With help from local friends, the author wrote to Mr Frans Lignel, the deputy Mayor of Ypres, and made a case to him asking what the possibilities would be to have a few of the old bricks removed and to see if it were possible to look into the old dugout. With kind consideration, in March 2011 some of the bricks were removed and for the first time in about ninety years we peered into

A view over the double bunks in Ravine Wood dugout 1993. (Photo courtesy Johan Vandewalle)

A view down the access route to the bunks in the Ravine Wood dugout 1993. (Photo courtesy Johan Vandewalle)

Major Edward Marie Felix Momber who died of wounds on 20th June 1916. 177's second Officer Commanding and the only tunnelling officer on the Western Front to have two craters named after him. (Author's collection)

the Ramparts North dugout. Not far to be exact, as it appeared to be filled with the rubble of the town of Ypres destroyed during the war. The wood used in the construction of the dugout, a valuable resource to those citizens trying to rebuild their town and lives after the war, had been stripped from

Pre-war photo of Maurice Wilkinson who commanded the Company following the death of Major Momber and was himself killed in action on 31st July 1917. (Author's collection)

the dugout expediting its collapse. The sight that greeted them was a huge steel girder, no doubt used in the construction of the dugout, now lying across the entrance and surrounded by brick-filled earth. The floor of the dugout was still visible for the first few feet. It sadly became apparent very quickly that it would require a lot of time, effort and money in trying to clear out a dugout of this size, and so it was left.

What of 177's workings elsewhere on the Western Front? After their long tenure at the Railway Wood sector the company was employed in the Messines area on dugout construction. Once again, these systems, similar to the condition of the Railway Wood sector mine workings will be filled with water, probably in an amazing state of preservation. One of 177's dugouts in the Messines/Wijtschaete area has been recently explored. A group led by Johan Vandewalle, entered the Ravine Wood dugout to carry out a survey and explore the dugout. It was in an amazing state of preservation and testament to the work of 177 Tunnelling Company.

Further south, on the southeast edge of Plugstreet Wood, the four mines which were laid under the Birdcage, as part of the Messines offensive scheme, and then not used, remained intact and in place long after 177's short tenure of custodianship. This mine system remained unchanged until July 1955. During a thunder storm one of the mines exploded, luckily not killing or injuring anyone. It was a rude awakening to those now living in the area as to what they potentially had under their feet.

The further south 177 travelled, as the war progressed, the nature of the geology changed. For many years they had worked in the Flanders clay, now they were working in chalk. The many dugouts and caves to be utilised as troop accommodation still survive underground. Most French villages in this region have underground catacombs below them. Many were started as far back as Roman times in order to quarry out the chalk and were used in times of strife by the local inhabitants. 177 and many other tunnelling companies worked and extended these systems which still sit, largely unexplored under the villages.

As the company advanced east in 1918, supporting the Canadian Corps it was heavily involved in clearing booby traps, especially during the entry of the British Army to the city of Cambrai. The Railway bridges that 177 searched and discovered German chargesm still remain intact. Most of them still, on closer inspection, display the scars of war.

177 Tunnelling Company was just one of 32 Tunnelling Companies in existence in the British Army during the Great War. Its roll of honour of the men who paid the supreme sacrifice may not compare to that of a front line infantry unit but this was a company that for the first years of its existence joined the few other soldiers that were closer to the German lines than any soldier holding a position on the surface. They protected the very apex of the old Ypres Salient from German underground strikes building up a reputation in and under the front that was second to none. Nowhere else in my First World War studies have I ever found a unit who spent longer both in and under the front than the officers, NCOs and men of 177 Tunnelling Company. The men both in 177 and other tunnelling companies were for the most part a civilian force of workers thrown into the army under the cap badge of the Royal Engineers and set about working on and under the Western Front. How many of them could have ever wondered that they would be taken away from their mining villages and towns at home and their skills used to combat and defeat a threat of mining from another nation?

As we approach the hundredth anniversary year of the Great War none of the men are with us anymore. All of them have now joined their comrades they lost during the war. On the memorials and headstones that dot the old front line their names and memory lives on as it also does with the many descendants of the men still living today. In 1921 when describing the work of the Tunneller in the Great War, Sir John Norton Griffiths stated:

> "….no record in the world ever touched the footage, yield per ounce of pluck, endurance and devotion to duty, and no forces endured more."

Let their memory and hard work be never forgotten. UBIQUE!

---

1 Captain Dalgas's letter is contained in file WO32 – 5892 at The National Archives which contains the exchange of letters between relevant parties that led to the erection of the permanent memorial at Railway Wood.

ROLL OF HONOUR
177 TUNNELLING COMPANY RE

IN DATE ORDER

1915

102296	Spr	Pattison	E	DoW	11/07/15
102951	Spr	Onions	R	KIA	02/09/15
102429	Spr	Newby	HE	KIA	22/09/15
102713	Spr	Thomas	A	KIA	22/09/15
132737	Spr	Bennett	W	KIA	30/11/15
102449	Spr	Chatt	GA	KIA	14/12/15

1916

86953	LCpl	Hayward	JA	DoW	08/01/16
102418	Spr	Cockburn	WC	DaH	10/02/16
	2Lt	MacFarlane	RG	DoW	06/03/16
102689	Spr	Simpson	T	D	11/03/16
102256	Spr	Milburn	JT	D	31/03/16
96988	Spr	Wade	J	DoW	12/04/16
	2Lt	Boothby	CG	KIA	28/04/16
147525	Cpl	Brindley	R	KIA	28/04/16
112505	Spr	Spooner	W	KIA	28/04/16
102953	Cpl	Whitehouse	SR	DaH	29/04/16
91979	LCpl	Parker	F	DoW	03/05/16
	2Lt	Earnshaw	O	KIA	02/06/16
96902	Spr	Jones	EH	KIA	02/06/16
132897	Spr	Cheeseman	F	KIA	12/06/16
132856	Spr	Carter	M	KIA	13/06/16
102406	Spr	Dawson	TS	DoW	13/06/16
	Lt	Holms	AS	KIA	01/07/16
132805	Spr	Dennis	JE	KIA	22/10/16

1917

121983	Spr	Nettell	A	DoW	09/01/17	MM	
102808	Spr	Bird	T	DoW	04/02/17		
132967	Spr	Firth	S	KIA	09/03/17		
132729	Spr	Cadman	JJ	KIA	03/06/17		
102450	Spr	Creegan	P	KIA	03/06/17		
102425	Spr	Hull	E	KIA	03/06/17		
	Maj	Momber	EMF	DoW	20/06/17	DSO, MC	
102368	Spr	Mosbey	R	DoW	20/06/17		
157781	Spr	Bagley	WH	KIA	04/07/17		
155828	Spr	Cotterill	JH	KIA	22/07/17		
86601	Spr	Woolley	GA	KIA	22/07/17		
102957	Spr	Judson	S	KIA	31/07/17		
	Maj	Wilkinson	MH	KIA	31/07/17	MC	
112753	Spr	Nancarrow	W	KIA	22/08/17		

1918

132933	Spr	Hayton	W	DoW	01/04/18		
102015	Spr	Fellows	B	D	15/05/18		
102818	Sgt	Ball	GH	DoW	19/09/18	MM	
79886	Spr	Howells	JT	KIA	04/10/18	DCM	
147848	Spr	Muirhead	G	KIA	04/10/18		
155837	LCpl	Neville	E	KIA	01/11/18		

List of Resources Used in the Compiling of this Book

BOOKS

Beneath Flanders Fields, Peter Barton, Peter Doyle and Johan Vandewalle, Spellmount Publishers 2004.

War Underground, Alexander Barrie, Spellmount Publishers, 1999.

Underground Warfare 1914 to 1918, Simon Jones, Pen and Sword, 2010.

Tunnellers, W. Grant Grieve and Bernard Newman, Naval and Military Press, 2001.

30 Odd Feet Below Belgium, Arthur Stockwin, Parapress Ltd, 2005.

Tunnel Master and Arsonist: The Norton-Griffiths Story, Tony Bridgland, Pen and Sword, 2003

Military Operations in France and Belgium 1917 Volume 2, Brigadier J. Edmonds, IWM 1992.

Military Operations in France and Belgium 1918 Volume 4, Brigadier J. Edmonds, IWM 1992

Military Operations in France and Belgium 1918 Volume 5, Lt Col Maxwell-Hyslop, IWM 1992

1918 A Very British Victory, Peter Hart, Phoenix, 2002.

WAR DIARIES AND DOCUMENTS AT THE NATIONAL ARCHIVES, LONDON

Tunnelling

WO95/404, 177 Tunnelling Company RE
WO95/404, 175 Tunnelling Company RE
WO95/551, 250 Tunnelling Company RE

Army

WO95/268 to WO95/358, Second Army
WO95/359 to WO95/430, Third Army
WO95/518 to WO95/571, Fifth Army

Corps

WO95/629 to WO95/667, II Corps
WO95/767 to WO95/703, VI Corps
WO95/804 to WO95/819, VII Corps
WO95/820 to WO95/834, VIII Corps
WO95/910 to WO95/920, XIV Corps
WO95/934 to WO95/950, XVII Corps
WO95/1045 to WO95/1087, Canadian Corps

Infantry Divisions and their relevant units

WO95/1864 to WO95/1910, 14th (Light) Division

WO95/1581 to WO95/1626, 6th Division

WO95/1190 to WO95/1226, Guards Division

WO95/2280 to WO95/2309, 29th Division

WO95/2899 to WO95/2930, 55th (West Lancashire) Division

WO95/1671 to WO95/1732, 8th Division

WO95/3155 to WO95/3253, 1st Australian Division

WO95/3837 to WO95/3879, 3rd Canadian Division

WO95/3526 to WO95/3657, 5th Australian Division

WO95/1733 to WO95/1786, 9th (Scottish) Division

WO95/1955 to WO95/1970, 16th (Irish) Division

WO95/2491 to WO95/2511, 36th (Ulster) Division

WO95/2889 to WO95/2898, 52nd (Lowland) Division

WO95/2931 to WO95/2963, 56th (London) Division

WO95/3010 to WO95/3025, 59th (North Midland) Division

WO95/3093 to WO95/3119, 63rd (Royal Navy) Division

Misc

WO32/5892, Permanent Memorial to 177 Tunnelling Company RE

WO158/134, AEMMBC weekly reports.

WO158/158, Summary of work of Tunnelling Companies during 1918

WO161/86, Mine Rescue on the Western Front by Lt Col Dale Logan

Royal Engineers Library and Museum, Chatham.

Copy of 174 Tunnelling Company war diary

Copy of 175 Tunnelling Company war diary

Copy of 177 Tunnelling Company war diary

Barrie Papers

Railway Wood Sector 177 Tunnelling Company large tunnelling plans.

War diary of Major SH Cowan, 175 Tunnelling Company.

Mining Notes

Tunnelling old Comrades Association Bulletins

GHQ Mining notes by Army and Company. January 1917 to March 1919.

The Work of the Miner on the Western Front 1915 to 1918. H. Standish Ball 1919.

INDEX